BROKERAGE
FRAUD

BROKERAGE FRAUD

What Wall Street Doesn't Want You to Know

Tracy Pride Stoneman
Douglas J. Schulz

Dearborn™
Trade Publishing
A **Kaplan Professional** Company

This publication is designed to provide accurate and authoritative information in regard to the subject matter covered. It is sold with the understanding that the publisher is not engaged in rendering legal, accounting, or other professional service. If legal advice or other expert assistance is required, the services of a competent professional person should be sought.

Vice President and Publisher: Cynthia A. Zigmund
Editorial Director: Donald J. Hull
Senior Managing Editor: Jack Kiburz
Interior Design: Lucy Jenkins
Cover Design: DePinto Studios
Typesetting: the dotted i

Published by Dearborn Trade Publishing, a Kaplan Professional Company

Printed in the United States of America

02 03 04   10 9 8 7 6 5 4 3 2 1

Library of Congress Cataloging-in-Publication Data

Stoneman, Tracy Pride.
    Brokerage fraud : what Wall Street doesn't want you to know / Tracy
Pride Stoneman and Douglas J. Schulz.
        p.   cm.
    ISBN 0-7931-4555-4
    1. Stockbrokers—United States. 2. Stockbrokers—Corrupt practices—
United States. 3. Investments—United States. I. Schulz, Douglas J.
(Douglas Jerome) II. Title.
HG4928.5 .S77 2002
364.16′3—dc21

2001003600

DEDICATION

This book is dedicated to the millions of Americans who have worked hard to save their money, only to have lost some or all of it at the sometimes unscrupulous hands of the securities industry. We hope that this book will put a dent in those numbers for future investors.

Contents

Foreword

When I was young, Wall Street seemed like a place of honor and mystery. People—usually men—joined a brokerage firm and then helped to build vast industries and guide individuals toward the means to meet their dreams. It seemed almost no profession could hold a more solemn duty, and I was awed by those with the ability and courage to take on such responsibility.

Then I grew up and learned the truth. All I had seen was the good side, the portion that Wall Street wanted me—and others just learning about the concepts of money—to see. Sure, there are noble financial advisors, just as there are lawyers who fight for justice, doctors who are dedicated to the needs of their patients, and journalists who are only interested in ferreting out truth. Unfortunately, all too often they seem to be in the minority, overshadowed by the vast hordes seeking a buck.

As I began writing about the investment world in the late 1980s, I was perplexed as the financial world's conflicts emerged so starkly. I listened incredulous as an investment banker danced around the obvious flaws in a multi-billion-dollar takeover deal that doomed the companies to bankruptcy. I held back tears as families told me of trusting their life savings to some investment advisor, only to see it all disappear. I seethed as a senior lawyer with the Securities and

Exchange Commission laid out his opinion that most brokers were not qualified to sell shoes, much less financial plans.

As the giddy 1990s rolled into the gloomy new millennium, falling markets threw a splash of cold water on investors everywhere. Those brokerage firms with the fancy marketing campaigns featuring swelling music and smiling senior citizens are more interested in some dot-com's investment banking fees than in your financial future. And the same goes for hoity-toity research analysts, whose financial prognostications can move markets and industries. Almost everyone—from brokers to managers, from analysts to traders—is playing some inside game that most of us don't get the chance to see, playing on our foolishness to enrich themselves and their friends. And if we don't get to come along for the ride, well—they tell us—markets fluctuate.

How could something with so noble a purpose go so far astray? Douglas Schulz and Tracy Pride Stoneman may know the answer. Schulz, a former stockbroker, and Stoneman, an arbitration lawyer, are guides into an investment world that will never be featured in a marketing campaign. In this book, they peel back the curtain that hides what happens in the brokerage firm office and, later, in the arbitration hearing room—events that have left countless investors ruing the day they met their former broker.

There will be plenty in these pages that will get noses out of joint on Wall Street—in particular, the impression that brokerage firms are really out for themselves and not for their customers. But Wall Street itself is the author of that unfortunate tale.

Some of the most interesting details laid out by Schulz and Stoneman are the compensation systems that brokerage houses put together for their investment advisors. Through them, brokers get paid more for selling you a particular product on a particular day, or qualify for free trips and rewards.

What does that have to do with your financial needs? Nothing. In fact, as everyone on Wall Street knows (but will never say in public), compensation systems are effectively designed to induce brokers to *ignore* your financial situation. If the Bucket Shop Global Growth Fund was the right investment for you, with a strong history and promising future, then there would be no need for the added inducement.

Of course, Wall Streeters argue that the additional money is just designed to get these products noticed in the maze of investment choices. For that to be true, these folks would have to believe that no one would ever compromise their clients for cash. And, given the piles of arbitration claims that arrive each day at the legal departments of the nation's brokerage houses, only a fool or a fraud could support that argument.

This may be harsh, and it certainly runs counter to the image Wall Street wants to project. However, the executives of modern brokerage firms did not build our capital markets; they are simply the lucky inheritors of a marvelous system constructed from the blood, sweat, and intellectual firepower of countless generations. These markets are a treasure, which should be cultivated and preserved. But, with each deceived investor, with each financial recommendation pushed on individuals because of secret financial inducements, the market's credibility—the foundation of Wall Street that allows billions of dollars to trade each day—is chipped away a little bit more.

Honor could return to Wall Street, but only if brokerage firms attack the ethical shortcomings of the current system that is laid bare by Schulz and Stoneman. Brokerage firms have demonstrated an inability to handle the conflicts of interest in the system. The fact that Wall Street analysts so rarely issue a "sell" recommendation on the companies they cover is proof of that. So perhaps it's time that investment firms line up their compensation to coincide with their advertising. If they want to claim they are here to help individuals save for their financial future, then give them a share of the profits and nothing else. Don't pay brokers for trading—just for making money. Or, as some firms have begun to do, put everything on a flat annual fee, with no secret compensation. Then, brokers only make money by holding on to clients.

Some on Wall Street would call this unrealistic, as if saying that success-based compensation was some sort of radical concept. And maybe it is. But, as this book makes clear, the present system is not putting brokers on the same side of the table as their client. Until that happens, investors need to know about the conflicts faced by their brokers—and then keep a close eye on them.

—Kurt Eichenwald
   Senior Writer, *The New York Times*, and
   Author, *The Informant: A True Story* and *Serpent on the Rock*

Preface

The investing public has been bombarded with the benefits of investing, from the warm and fuzzy advertisements to the deluge of books on investing tips, how to get rich, how to day trade, and the like. Yet very few books, if any, address what goes on behind the scenes of a brokerage firm, events that very much impact investors. *Brokerage Fraud* is the first book to unveil what your brokerage firm, stockbroker, and financial advisor fail to tell you about their business, about your investments, and about your account. These secrets allow brokerage firms, stockbrokers, and other investment advisors to defraud millions of Americans every year. Yet only a fraction of those deceived ever realize it, much less do something about it.

The authors of *Brokerage Fraud* offer a unique combination of expertise. Tracy is a lawyer who represents aggrieved investors in claims against brokerage firms and stockbrokers. Douglas is a former stockbroker, a current Registered Investment Advisor, and a nationally recognized securities fraud expert witness and author. On a daily basis, Tracy and Douglas deal with individuals all over the country who have been harmed by their stockbrokers and brokerage firms. Between the two of them, they have been involved in thousands of customer complaints and securities violations. Drawing on their combined 30 years of experience in securities litigation and the securities industry, they share their experience in business as well as what they have learned from the testimony of stockbrokers, brokerage firm owners, branch managers, and compliance personnel behind the closed doors of securities arbitrations.

Though their perspective is unique, it is not necessarily a narrow one. There are over 650,000 licensed stockbrokers in the country, each one of whom may have hundreds of clients. Though the majority of brokers and advisors are honest, hardworking, and ethical, even a small percentage of erring stockbrokers can inflict widespread damage.

The vast majority of investors do not appreciate that the securities business is the most regulated industry in the country and that there are hundreds of laws, rules, regulations, and guidelines at the federal, state, and industry level specifically designed to protect their rights. *Brokerage Fraud* simplifies the morass of regulation and demonstrates that when brokers run afoul of the rules and regulations, it doesn't necessarily mean that they are scam artists, evil people, or criminals (though those do exist). Rather, the vast majority of erring stockbrokers simply succumb to the pressures brought to bear upon them by their brokerage firms. The industry employs practices that tempt stockbrokers to bend and break the rules to the detriment of investors. The book describes the major abuses seen in brokerage accounts and how a firm caught with its hand in the cookie jar employs specialized tricks and defenses designed to immobilize the investor.

The book explores the myriad of conflicts of interest that abound in the industry and how the securities industry motivates stockbrokers to work against your interest. A special section on online trading exposes the unique conflicts within the online firms. Our goal is that *Brokerage Fraud* will be required reading for a growing population of investors nationwide.

Whether an investor relies on the advice of a stockbroker or investment advisor or makes independent investment decisions, investors who read the book will be better equipped to not only understand how the rules apply to their particular situation but will be able to monitor their trades and portfolios to detect any misdeeds. Also, *Brokerage Fraud* provides investors with yardsticks they can use when selecting brokers and advisors. And it will empower investors to evaluate their current stockbroker or brokerage firm to determine if changes need to be made. Though the book is not a "how to" book in the traditional sense, the authors do provide some sound advice, which will help investors monitor and manage their investments or advisors. Finally, the book offers investors who have been wronged a guideline of steps that they can take to recoup their losses.

A WORD TO THOSE
WHO OFFER FINANCIAL ADVICE

We would be remiss if we did not say something to those who offer financial advice and were brave enough to buy our book. Though we appreciate your purchase, we would prefer that your clients gave you this book in a gesture of mutual understanding. When you have completed the book, we hope you will realize two important factors. First, chances are you are not one of the erring brokers or advisors that so much of this book is about. Second, you will realize that as good as you are, that you can always improve on your relationships and business dealings with your clients.

Every year that Tracy and Douglas continue in their line of work, they learn something new, and they are always thankful to those who share good ideas with them. We hope that you, the securities professional, will take this book for what it is: our attempt to help individual investors get the most for their hard-earned money. Don't be too much on the defensive from our criticism; it is most likely not directed at you. If you work in one of the better branch offices, you may not be familiar with the travesties that we see on a daily basis—wrongdoing that others rarely see. Our views and insights might be very different from yours.

And before you accuse us of being unfair in our criticism of some of the faults within the brokerage industry, remember you work in the most regulated industry in this country. If you were selling used cars, where Buyer Beware is the accepted motto, we would find no fault. But before most of us were born, the United States legislature enacted securities laws in 1933 and 1934. In so doing, Congress proclaimed that protecting and properly informing the investing public, along with maintaining its faith in the American securities markets, were paramount national goals. And with more people in the securities markets than ever in this country's history, the goals seem more vital now than ever before. Our book is only an attempt to further Congress's goals.

CHAPTER 1

The Brokerage Industry
More Secretive Than You Know

We recognize that there are not many books like this one on the market. In fact, it's part of the reason we were motivated to write one. The brokerage industry has done a very good job of shielding the investing public from the underbelly of the brokerage world. In this chapter, we highlight a few aspects of the industry that you just may not know about.

BROKERS MAKE MILLIONS—WITHOUT BEING ON A STUPID GAME SHOW

Sorry if we misled you. It is not you who stands to make the million bucks. It is your broker or advisor who works in the securities industry. And he can do it right there in his day-to-day job without being on a stupid game show.

When you research the highest paid professions in the United States, you will find that after professional athletes, rock stars, and movie stars, the upper end of the list is composed primarily of people whose profession is centered in the securities and financial industry. Investment bankers, senior officers and directors of brokerage firms, portfolio managers, research analysts, and stockbrokers rank very, very high. The average doctor or lawyer should do so well. Not only do brokerage industry employees get paid handsomely, but the firms themselves also profit very nicely.

The year 2000 was a landmark one for performance in the securities industry. Pretax profits for U.S. firms were up 29 percent over 1999 and up a whopping 89 percent over 1998.[1] That's a significant jump. *Registered Representative* magazine's survey published in its November 2000 issue stated that a broker's average income was $180,300, and the broker's average household net worth was $1,072,000. That's a rather nauseating thought when you consider that many investors lost a lot of money in 2000.

WHAT'S GLOSSY ON THE OUTSIDE AND TARNISHED ON THE INSIDE?

Come on America; don't get caught up in the investment hype. One online firm ran a special that if you opened an account, you would get the first 25 trades free and 2 free airline tickets. Such incentives might be reasons to buy a refrigerator, but they are not good reasons to risk your children's college education fund.

What's the message here? Investing is not a game. Or perhaps that is the problem: the two of us are just not hip. We are sure there will be much criticism of our book by many in the securities industry. And maybe they are right and we are wrong: perhaps you *should* open an account at a brokerage firm based on the freebie promotions or the really cool ads the firm runs. And your stockbroker should make recommendations to you based on the latest sales contest in his office. And who cares if you have to work until you are 75 years old because your investments did not turn out as well as the brokerage ads and come-ons told you they would?

But we do care, and because you were smart enough to not only buy this book but to read it completely, we know you care too. Despite the impending criticism, we know that we are right and that bombarding you with the negatives only serves to slightly compensate for the media hype that assaults you daily.

You live in a country where marketing rules. Advertising confronts you almost everywhere you look and in every format imaginable (the back of bathroom stalls is one of our favorites). We are waiting for high-end ads on the bottom of men's shoes so that when men cross their legs, the ad is seen. The brokerage industry in particular has done an amazing job of permeating just about everything we touch, see, and hear. Don't fall for the hype. Do you really think PaineWebber does business "one investor at a time" and DeanWitter does "business the old-fashioned way"? We think not. They all do it the same.

The vast majority of this book deals with issues affecting individual investors like you. We think it's important for you to appreciate that the brokerage industry has had more than its fair share of serious scandals and improprieties. And we don't mean just brokerage firms. The Nasdaq stock market was sanctioned and fined by the Securities and Exchange Commission (SEC) for myriad infractions by its members. Later in this book, we encourage investors to adhere to the general principle that when choosing a brokerage firm, bigger is better. Don't forget, though, that the big boys have suffered from significant problems themselves. Kidder Peabody is no longer with us today because a fixed-income trader cost the firm roughly $350 million dollars in his fixed-income trading activity. Later investigations found that Kidder failed to properly supervise this individual trader, presumably because he was making so much money for the firm. Another firm that has gone by the wayside as a result of improprieties and securities violations is Drexel Burnham Lambert. In the 1990s, Prudential Securities, Inc. (Prudential), found itself assessed with one of the largest fines in SEC history. The incident that brought about the demise of Salomon Brothers, Inc., was a violation of regulations covering bids on U.S. Treasury securities by one of its managing directors who was also head of Salomon's government trading desk. And remember that old marketing campaign, "When E. F. Hutton talks, people listen"? The firm was embroiled in a check-kiting scandal years ago, so E. F. Hutton isn't talking anymore. Though many of the criticisms we levy are really focused on a minority of brokers and firms, remember that the minority doesn't necessarily mean that scandal and improprieties are relegated to lowly, little-heard-of brokerage firms. Like certain diseases, scandal and wrongdoing are unaffected by demographics, size, or anything else.

When contemplating the title for this book, we thought long and hard. After a few cocktails and four minutes of deep concentration, we decided on the title *Screwed Again*. We liked it, but the thought that neither of our parents would approve nagged at us, so in their honor we tried to think of a different title for what the securities industry has done to millions of investors. We thought of the word *hosed*, but that's a youthful term describing what your girl-friend or boyfriend does to you. *Bilked* was out, because that's what banks do. *Abuses.* Now that was a great term, except someone told us that certain kinky people like to be abused. With our religious upbringing, the "F" word was out. We thought of *Swindle*, but that sounded too much like a current dance craze. *Rip-off* sounded too much like a drug deal. We were about to use *Fleece* but were told that people would confuse the book with an L.L. Bean product. And anyway, isn't fleece the subject of a mythical tale involving Jason and the Argonauts?

During one of our regular Saturday night reading sessions of a Webster's dictionary and old Zap comic books, we stumbled on the following definition of the word *screw:* "to extort or practice extor-tion on; as, he screwed me out of money."[2] Sure sounded like *Screwed Again* was going to be the title, but then our publisher thought it might be mistaken for a sexual manual of some kind.[3] We think that after you read the book, the title *Brokerage Fraud: What Wall Street Doesn't Want You to Know* fits perfectly. *Fraud* is a broad word that encompasses everything you aren't told but should have been told and everything that you are told that is wrong or misleading. That pretty much sums up our book. If, after reading the book, you think the title should have been *Screwed Again,* please send us a letter and we will gladly refund your money. Please do not forget to include a check for $100 to cover shipping and handling costs. And upon re-ceipt, we will know that you have been screwed again.

All kidding aside, it doesn't matter if the stock market is going up, going down, or just hanging there in neutral, stockbrokers will be recommending that you buy, and online firms will be clamoring for your investment dollars. Either way, you have to be careful. Doing business with traditional or online firms without being informed of critical aspects of their industry is like accidentally washing your clothes without detergent. You may not realize it at first because you may wear the clothes and not realize that anything is wrong. But once you realize the clothes were washed without detergent, every-thing seems grimy.

Until late 2000, the U.S. stock markets have basically been in an 18-year bull market. Though this bull market has been an incred-ible benefit for investors, putting trillions of dollars into many pock-ets, this bull market has masked and, to some degree, accentuated some negatives in the securities industry. As the downturn in the market carried over from 2000 to 2001, the press started acknowledging a number of conflicts within the industry that had been somewhat ignored until the downturn. As we discuss in Chapter 2, brokerage analysts are now being exposed for their serious conflicts. The downturn also exposed wrongdoing in the initial public offering (IPO) market. Investors realized, as their life savings were wiped out, that their accounts had been mismanaged for years, but this only came to light with the market downturn. The point is that the regulators, the brokerage industry, and to some degree investors themselves were either ignorant of, or turned their heads away from, wrongdoing because the bull market shrouded the problems.

The subject of stockbrokers was injected into Douglas's life at an early age. Lying was not tolerated in his house, and his parents practiced what they preached—except when a phone call came from their stockbroker. Many times, Douglas would answer the phone and yell at his mom or dad, "Carl, your broker from Bache is on the phone." His parents would invariably respond with, "Tell him we are not here." This experience was troubling for Douglas because he felt like an accomplice of sorts. It was not until 20 years later that he found out why his parents were hiding from their stockbroker. But in a flat or down market, there's nowhere to hide.

A PEEK INTO THIS HIGHLY GUARDED AND HIGHLY REGULATED INDUSTRY

If someone is hit by a car and then experiences throbbing neck pain, he or she might immediately think, "Maybe I should call a lawyer." Why? Because you can hardly pass a billboard or open the yellow pages without seeing a full-page ad in English and Spanish that says "Auto accident? I can help you. Call 1-800-GET-EVEN."

The opposite scenario plays itself out in the securities industry. Every day hundreds of investors are defrauded of millions of dollars. Yet the vast majority does not pursue a remedy. Why not? America is a litigious society and increasingly so. The public is bombarded with news about lawsuits—from the woman who sued McDonald's for serving her too-hot coffee to the company that sued another for stealing its domain name. Come to think of it, we bet you can't recall any press coverage about an individual investor who sued his or her brokerage firm, can you? There's a reason for that.

The brokerage industry has guarded itself in a number of ways, all with a view to protecting itself from investor lawsuits. One of the biggest shields that the industry has erected is the arbitration clause, the provision that requires investors to pursue their claims through arbitration as opposed to court. Arbitrations are private. The press, the media, and the public do not have access to them. News reporters routinely comb daily court filings in order to give an account of titillating lawsuits that might grab the public's interest. Yet reporters will never stumble on a lawsuit by an investor against a brokerage firm at the courthouse. You have read much about class action lawsuits; however, these suits typically are not against brokerage firms or stockbrokers but against the stock company itself. And you can read about class actions because class actions do not have to go to arbitration.

You can see that people may be prone to call a lawyer when they are hurt, because they have been conditioned through the media that that's the thing to do or is at least an available option. They've read about or known others who have won personal injury claims in similar circumstances. Given the absence of media coverage of investor claims and remedies, media conditioning has not occurred with the investing public. Private arbitrations virtually eliminate media coverage, which in turn perpetuate an ignorant public. If you happen to see a news story about an investor who won a case against a brokerage firm, the investor's lawyer likely submitted the story to the press. That's about the only way that the media would find out about it.

The brokerage industry depends on, thrives on, and, as you will see, sometimes encourages the human traits that tend to immobilize the investing public from asserting their rights. Those who realize that they may have a claim often talk themselves out of it. They may reason that they were to blame for being duped and could have prevented it if only they had done X. It is quite common for many rich or successful people to be embarrassed to admit that a broker conned them or that they lost significant sums. In Mexico, the wealthy are extremely private about their finances. We have had experiences with some who would rather take their losses, large though they may be, and go on rather than risk the potential exposure in disclosing their finances. Finally, there are those who think that taking on a large brokerage firm would be too monumental and too costly a task.

The brokerage industry is not only highly guarded; it is highly regulated. We are not talking about the qualifications required to become a stockbroker (discussed in Chapter 3) but rather the bulk of rules and regulations that dictate the conduct of stockbrokers and brokerage firms around the country. As early as 1911, it was thought that brokers peddled their securities in such a tantalizing way that it seemed to investors as if they were buying "a piece of blue sky." That is the origin of blue-sky laws, each state's securities act that governs the registration of investments and the brokers who sell securities to their residents and that explicitly prohibits deceptive conduct involving securities transactions. Many states also have deceptive trade practice statutes that address a much broader array of wrongdoing and also encompass stock transactions. In addition, every state has a state securities board or commission, whose primary mission is to protect investors in the state. The Texas State Securities Board's Web site, for example, prominently displays its mission "to protect Texas investors." South Dakota's mission is "to ensure that investments sold in South Dakota meet standards of fairness and disclosure."

At the federal level are the grandfathers of all securities statutes: the Securities Act of 1933 and the Securities and Exchange Act of 1934, both of which were enacted on the heels of America's depression. We think that the members of our U.S. Supreme Court summed up these two statutes well when they opined in 1987: "Both the Securities Act of 1933 and the Securities Exchange Act of 1934 were enacted to protect investors from predatory behavior of securities industry personnel."[4] The word *predatory* was a rather omniscient word to use in 1987. The 1933 and 1934 acts have spawned a menagerie of rules enacted over the years. For all of their minutia, the provision cited most often from these massive statutes and their attendant rules is the language that prevents brokers and brokerage firms from engaging "in any act, practice, or course of business which operates or would operate as a fraud or deceit upon any person, in connection with the purchase or sale of any security." Fraud and deceit are pretty broad words that encompass a whole host of behaviors. And that is precisely what was intended.

The National Association of Securities Dealers (NASD) and the New York Stock Exchange (NYSE) have also enacted their own sets of rules to govern the conduct of brokers and brokerage firms. Each of these organizations has several thick manuals bulging with rules. In addition, the NASD faces the challenge of dealing with a rapidly changing financial sector with what is called its Notice to Members. These documents, anywhere from several paragraphs to several pages long, keep brokers and firms apprised of rules and regulations that may impact them. The NASD issues about 100 Notice to Members each year, with a slight increase in the last several years most likely resulting from new issues raised by online trading.

If that's not enough, all brokerage firms are required to have their own set of written rules and procedures. These usually take the form of a Compliance Manual and a Supervisory Manual—one governing brokers and one governing supervisors. There may also be an Operations and Procedures manual that governs the more technical aspects of the firm's operation. If a brokerage firm is found to have violated *any* of the rules put in place by these various sources, it could spell financial trouble for the firm and possibly financial havoc for the wronged investor.

The effect of all of these regulations is that one single wrongful act by a stockbroker may violate a multitude of rules and regulations, which makes for some very long and cumbersome claims filed in arbitration! In Tracy's closing arguments in securities arbitrations, she may summarize all of these rules as follows:

> Remember, panel members, that in order to establish liability, we need only establish that Barry Broker's conduct violated but one rule or regulation. However, Barry Broker did more than violate his own firm's compliance manual; he violated the state securities act, the state consumer protection act, NASD regulations, and the federal securities laws. This abundance of rules and regulations that were violated more than amply put Barry Broker and his firm on notice that what he did was wrong.

The point that the securities industry is so highly regulated is a very significant one. As mentioned earlier, this book would not be so useful if we were writing about the new or used car industry. That and other less regulated industries are "buyer beware" markets. The securities industry is not. This book is filled with not only many of the industry's rules and guidelines that you should know but also numerous examples of how these rules are broken or skirted. If the industry would do a better job of self-policing and enforcing the rules that are in place, this book would not be necessary.

CRIME PAYS—THEM

One of the older and more accepted premises of criminology that Douglas learned in college was that deterring crimes is only effective when (1) the likelihood of being caught is high, (2) the punishment is timely, and (3) the punishment fits the crime. In the securities industry, these three factors play a small role in deterring improper behavior.

Let's take them one at a time. The first factor—the likelihood that brokers and firms are caught—is, well, amusing. Generally speaking, the SEC and other regulators pose little threat because they are so overworked and understaffed. The NASD's membership is composed of more than 5,500 securities firms that operate in excess of 82,000 branch offices across the United States and employ more than one-half a million registered securities professionals. That's a lot of folks to oversee. The bigger problem is that the NASD and the NYSE are a bit like the fox watching the henhouse. Brokerage firms are dues-paying members of the NASD and/or the NYSE. As "self-regulators" of their own members, these organizations have inherent conflicts of interest. It's not wise to bite the hand that feeds you. For the same reasons, brokerage firms do a poor job of policing their own stockbrokers.

Brokerage firm supervisors are often paid a percentage of the gross commissions generated by the brokers they supervise. So if a manager oversees a broker who is churning his customers' accounts and generating a lot of commissions for the firm—as well as for the manager—you can see how it might be easier for the manager to turn his head and look the other way. If the manager tells the broker to cool it, the broker's commissions will go down and thus reduce the amount going into the manager's pocket. Similarly, if a brokerage firm's compliance officer, responsible for supervising branch offices, discovers that a branch is consistently filling out order tickets improperly, it is arguably better to ignore the problem. If the officer documents it, he may bring the problem to the attention of the regulators who otherwise might never discover it. Then someone higher up could blame him for allowing the situation to occur in the first place.

These conflicts of interest exert a tremendous disincentive on all of those responsible for supervising to put the skids on questionable conduct. For stockbrokers, this means that the risk of getting "caught" is very, very low and therefore serves as little deterrent to improper behavior.

And additionally, the likelihood of being caught is low because it is *a numbers game*. Every year, brokerage firms abuse the accounts of millions of customers, causing those customers financial losses. Yet only a few thousand customers ever realize that the broker or firm bears some culpability. Still fewer complain. And even fewer take legal action; and of those who do, only a small percentage actually proceed to arbitration. Most cases settle for amounts far less than would be sought at arbitration.

The second factor—the punishment is timely—has little effect on the conduct of brokers and brokerage firms. In the mid-1990s, folks were bringing arbitration claims in waves against Prudential Securities for its sale of billions of dollars of limited partnerships to about 400,000 investors in the 1980s. In 1994, the SEC stepped up to the plate and sanctioned the firm for its improper sale of these investments;[5] however, the principals and executives of Prudential were left unscathed. The slow pace at which the SEC investigated the Prudential executives involved came back to bite the SEC when a 1996 federal court decision held that the SEC could not bring actions against people more than five years after the conduct in question took place.[6] Out the window went years of investigation, because many of the SEC's potential claims were time barred.

The third requirement is that the punishment must fit the crime. This simply means that the envisioned punishment must be just bad enough that it causes the actor to make a causal connection between the two and possibly not perform the crime for fear of receiving the punishment.

Punishment of brokers and firms can emanate from one of three sources: the criminal justice system, the regulators, or claims brought by investors. Very few brokers or firms are accused of criminal wrongdoing, although the government prosecutes the same type of misconduct as investors sue for—insider trading, fraud, churning, and stock manipulation. Remember Michael Milken? He was convicted of stock manipulation of junk bonds. Milken's fine was $1.1

billion, and he spent 22 months in a minimum-security facility. And he was required to do some public service work.[7] Again in 2000, Milken made the *Forbes* list of the 400 richest Americans. Do you need help with the math? There was a joke among people in the securities industry about Milken: "Where do I get in line for that deal?" His punishment did not fit his crime.

Nor does the punishment levied by regulators usually fit the wrongdoing committed by brokers and firms. The regulators have the power to levy hefty fines on stockbrokers and firms as well as suspend them or kick them out of the business. Very rarely do the regulators use that most powerful of sanctions, suspension or bar from the industry. If you read Section B of the *Wall Street Journal*, you will occasionally see what the NASD, NYSE, or SEC does when disciplining brokers and firms. Note how small the fines are and how little else is done. The fine is rarely relative to the amount the brokers and firms collect in revenues.

As an example, the SEC fined Ernie Olde, the founder of Olde Discount Corporation, $1 million individually in 1998.[8] In 1999, Ernie renounced his U.S. citizenship and moved to the Caribbean to an island where residents pay no income tax, and subsequently that same year, sold the firm to H&R Block for a cool $850 million in cash. That sure makes Ernie's fine seem like a pittance.

Similarly, in July 2001, the NASD sanctioned E*Trade for false and misleading advertising in connection with two direct mail campaigns that targeted almost 10 million potential investors and with respect to a mutual fund that E*Trade represented as being ranked by Morningstar, when it was not ranked at all. The NASD's fine was $90,000, a meager amount when compared to the $45 million that E*Trade expended just two months earlier to purchase another online brokerage firm.[9]

The third source of punishment for a brokerage firm is the customer arbitration claim. Now you would think, and in an ideal world would expect, that concern over customer claims or disputes would certainly be enough incentive to deter wrongdoing. But because arbitrations are so few and far between in relation to the wrongdoing, no one feels much of a threat. If the industry kicked out all the bad apples and put more pressure on marginal brokers to follow the letter of the law, the industry would lose millions in commissions. When it compares all the money it pays annually in arbitration awards and settlements with what it would lose in commissions, the decision is a simple business one. Arbitrations are a cost of being in the securities business—not much of a cost when compared with the very lucrative business that it is.

And to make matters worse, rarely does anything happen to the broker. A customer complaint may soil the broker's public record, but that is about the extent of punishment for the broker. His firm will probably not discipline him for receiving a customer complaint or being named in an arbitration claim, because the firm will reason that it's just the cost of doing business. Even if the customer wins an arbitration case and there is an award against the broker and the firm, the firm will usually pay it for the broker. And the firm will not subsequently discipline the broker in any way. So assuming that a broker sees increasing his own income as the objective of his job, and consequently cares little about a somewhat tarnished record, no deterrence exists to persuade the broker to follow the straight and narrow path.

Economically speaking, it's the time value of money that firms can count on to justify defending customer complaints and arbitrations. Under the trickle-down theory, brokerage firms have to pay on only a small percentage of claims, whether through settlement or arbitration award. The payout occurs anywhere from a year and a half to six years down the road from when the wrongdoing occurred. Although arbitration is a lot faster and has a lot more finality than a court case, it can still take a year or more to conclude. Assuming that the firm ultimately pays something, the firm has had the use of ill-gotten money for quite some time. Crime pays very well in the securities industry.

WHY FIRMS DON'T CLEAN UP THEIR ACTS— THE JUST-SAY-NO SYNDROME

Simply put, brokerage firms don't clean up their act because they don't have to. It is so easy and profitable for firms to continue to bend the rules despite the financial havoc it wreaks on investors. Tracy was taught at a very early age that when you are caught with your hand in the cookie jar, you had better fess up. Yet you can catch a broker with his hand in the cookie jar, and he will not only deny that he likes cookies but he and his firm will try to convince you that you are responsible for the broker's being in the kitchen in the first place.

Brokers, securities analysts, brokerage compliance departments, and brokerage firm managers all seem to never admit they are wrong. This is known as the just-say-no tactic. However, we must first address another, rarer tactic employed by brokerage firms whereby they simply do not respond to customer complaints in the hope that the customer will go away. Unfortunately, some firms employ this tactic because it works! A substantial percentage of investors who get no response to their complaint simply shrug their shoulders, eat their loss, and go on with life. Tracy had a case against one brokerage firm in which her client first wrote a complaint letter to the head of the firm's compliance department. After receiving no response, he wrote another complaint letter to the president of the firm. He never received a response to either letter! Where Tracy's client took action, however, many others in a similar situation might have given up.

More commonly, brokerage firms employ the just-say-no tactic in their customer response letters and in the formal answers they file in arbitration. Because wronged investors are often inclined to think that what happened was partially their fault, it only takes a few harsh words in a "get lost" letter from the firm to reinforce that line of thinking. In Chapter 11, we alert you to when you should and when you should not write a complaint letter to the firm.

We had some fun with this issue in a series of cases against the same stockbroker and a major brokerage firm. The first of these cases proceeded to arbitration but settled in the middle of the arbitration on extremely favorable terms for Tracy and her client. Despite the favorable settlement, the firm had vehemently denied everything in its arbitration answer, just as it had in our other cases that were extremely similar factually. For the second case, we prepared a five-by-five-foot exhibit on posterboard on which we highlighted the firm's harsh denials in its answer in the first case compared with the amount of money paid to settle that first case and then showed that the exact same harsh denial language was used in the second case. We actually had these large exhibits shipped to the firm's in-house counsel. We would have loved to have been flies on the wall when the higher-ups there reviewed them. The second case settled shortly thereafter—also on favorable terms for Tracy and her client.

Though a firm's harsh denial language can sometimes come back to bite it, more often than not it serves to dissuade the customer from taking further action. We hope that we can instill in you the lesson that if your brokerage firm confronts you with the just-say-no tactic, the most appropriate response just might be no right back.

SIPC—A RARELY USEFUL BANDAGE

SECURITIES INVESTOR PROTECTION CORPORATION

You may have noticed the above symbol on your brokerage account statements and may have also seen nearby the phrase "Securities in your account protected up to $500,000." What does this mean and how can it help you?

SIPC stands for the Securities Investor Protection Corporation, a nonprofit organization whose members are brokerage firms and individuals who are members of a national securities exchange. SIPC originated in 1970 in the aftermath of hundreds of brokerage firms going out of business as a result of high trading volume followed by a severe decline in stock prices. SIPC's goal is to return funds and securities to customers if the broker-dealer holding those assets becomes insolvent.

SIPC comes into play in very rare circumstances when your brokerage firm goes out of business. For the vast majority of wrongdoing that causes losses to investors, SIPC offers no protection. It does not come into play in cases alleging fraud, suitability, or churning. On June 25, 2001, the General Accounting Office (GAO) released a report that was critical of SIPC for not making better disclosure to clients that market losses are not covered by SIPC and that SIPC coverage is not the same as FDIC coverage.[10] SIPC protection would apply in the following situation.

Let's say that the day after you sold $20,000 worth of securities, you learned your broker-dealer went out of business, and you did not get your cash. Because your loss was attributable to the financial failure of the firm, your claim for $20,000 in cash would be covered by SIPC. Let's say that at the time of the firm's failure, $420,000 of your securities and $100,000 in cash are held by the firm. SIPC would attempt to return your securities to you. If that is not possible, SIPC would attempt to purchase your securities for you on the open market. When missing securities cannot be replaced, SIPC will pay the value of the securities on the date that you began your SIPC proceeding. In this scenario, all but $20,000 of the claim would be paid.

Membership in SIPC is not voluntary; it is required if a firm is registered under the 1934 securities act. Although more than 7,000 broker-dealers are members of SIPC, however, many are not. Some broker-dealers are excluded from SIPC membership because of the nature of their business; for example, protection if the firm's principal place of business is outside the United States or if the firm deals exclusively in variable annuities or insurance. Also, beware of the situation in which SIPC members use affiliated or related companies whose names are similar to the name of the SIPC member or that operate from the same offices or with the same employees, but the affiliate is *not* a member of SIPC.

We hope that we have caught your interest by showing you how, in many respects, the securities industry is not what it pretends to be. The next two chapters delve in more detail into why you need to be circumspect when dealing with the securities and investment industry and its agents.

CHAPTER 2

Conflicts of Interest
Which Side Are Firms Really On?

The reality of life is that much of what you do every day involves conflicts of interest. When you're at home cutting up a steak for family members, you're experiencing a built-in conflict of interest. You know which parts are more tender and thus possibly benefiting you because you are in charge of distributing the pieces. You have a built-in conflict of interest when you and your spouse are discussing the movie you are going to see, and one wants to see the war epic and the other wants to see the love story. This conflict may taint the truthfulness of your opinions as you debate why you should see one movie over the other. Newspaper and magazine articles you read may be shaped by the conflicts of interest of the author or the publisher, either of whom may have predetermined opinions about the subject. Some reporters may mask their conflicts of interest because they can simply interview only those people whom they know will give them the slant they are seeking.

IDENTIFYING THE CONFLICTS—
WE SAID CONFLICTS, NOT CONVICTS

Conflicts of interest among professionals abound as well. Doctors, lawyers, and accountants, just like stockbrokers, must obtain licenses before they can perform their services for the public. One famous gangster characterized such a license in the following way: "I learned too late that you need just as good a brain to make a crooked million as an honest million. These days, you apply for a license to steal from the public. . . . If I had my time again, I'd make sure I got that license first."[1] But the license is no safeguard against conflicts of interest. For professionals, the conflict always revolves around the almighty dollar. The conflict for lawyers and accountants who work on an hourly basis is to try to generate more work to bill more hours. For stockbrokers, as we highlight, the conflict is over commissions. For doctors, it's over additional services or operations; operations are to doctors what trades are to stockbrokers. For many individuals in both professions, the enticement of that extra dollar is too overwhelming to resist.

This is not to say that we all succumb like limp rag dolls to whatever conflict faces us. No. Many individuals and professionals never sense conflicts for one reason or another. They may not be driven by money, the primary conflict creator, or they may live on a higher moral ground or they may simply fear getting caught.

Over the years, Douglas has given a lot of investment advice and charged a fee for it. However, he readily dispenses one piece of advice at no charge: *identify the conflicts*. Remember watching *Perry Mason, Columbo,* or *Murder, She Wrote* while you sat on the edge of your seat trying to guess who did it? The key to solving any mystery is to pinpoint the person who has the strongest motivation. If you could pinpoint the person with the strongest motivation to kill someone, you could usually identify the murderer.

In the brokerage industry, you need not think so long and hard about motivation; it's the commissions. Commissions are the ultimate motivator within the brokerage industry.

COMMISSIONS, MARKUPS, AND FEES— CAKE WITH LOTS OF ICING

Most people's financial goal in life is to work hard, save some money, and invest their money properly. In turn, your money should start to work for you so you won't have to work as hard. Of course, if you inherited or married money (in which case you need this book as much as the person with just a little to invest), you may not have to work so hard in your job or career.

Those in the brokerage industry want to get a piece of your wealth. Their starting point is to convince you to open an account and deposit some money; hence, all the advertising and cold calls directed toward that one objective. It's what happens next that matters, though. The brokerage industry reasons: "Convince the public to deposit their savings with us and then we'll figure out how to get a chunk of it in fees, commissions, and other costs."

Not to be simplistic, but the more money you spend in commissions, front-end loads, margin interest, markups, and fees, the less money you have to invest. This is called "impairment of capital" and, by its very definition, impairment is a negative. Clearly, costs, fees, commissions, and the like create a conflict of interest in certain professions. But rarely do such sums rise to the level of impairment of capital, as they do so often within the brokerage industry.

At a 1991 securities conference, one of Merrill Lynch's top in-house attorneys said that as long as the brokerage industry maintains its commission structure with its built-in conflict of interest, the industry would have ongoing compliance and customer complaint problems. That lawyer was one of the few people in the securities industry who would admit what was so blatantly obvious—at least to those familiar with the industry.

Exactly one decade later, Arthur Levitt, the former SEC chairman, made these departing remarks: "Let's begin with the first step for a lot of investors: selecting a broker. The very first question that a person should ask his or her broker is, How do you get paid?"[2]

Brokers are compensated based on commissions beginning with their entrée into a brokerage firm throughout their entire career as a stockbroker at that or any other firm. Nothing alters this foundation of a system. Some firms pay a measly base salary plus a commission. In the 1990s, Olde Discount paid its brokers a monthly salary of $1,200.[3] That's a yearly salary of only $14,400. Commissions made up the rest. So it is at virtually every brokerage firm: brokers feed their family on their commissions.

Commissions are a benefit only to the brokers and their firm. Conversely, commissions are a detriment only to you, the investor. They are a direct cost, one that must be overcome if you hope to make money on any given investment.

It's bad enough that brokers are compensated based on commissions, but the firms have created a commission structure that only aggravates a broker's conflicts of interest. When owners of grocery stores or food outlets want to move older, and thus riskier, food off the shelves, they slash prices. Brokerage firms sometimes buy securities in bulk and then sell the stock out of their own inventory. Unlike stores, however, they don't have a sale to move the product off the shelf. Rather, a brokerage firm will turn up the pressure on its sales force to increase sales of the securities in its inventory. It does this by increasing the commission your broker can generate, which simultaneously increases your cost. The higher the commission, the higher your cost, because the commission comes out of your pocket. This is displayed in Figure 2.1, which shows a greed pyramid and gives the varying commission ranges for different types of investments.

The greed pyramid illustrates that the riskier the investment, the higher the broker's commission. Rarely, if ever, are investors made aware of these commission schedules and hence the conflicts.

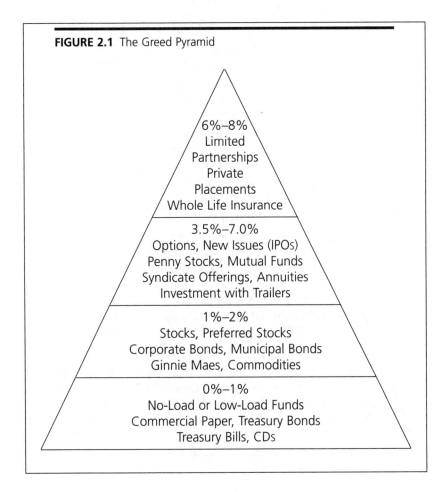

FIGURE 2.1 The Greed Pyramid

6%–8%
Limited
Partnerships
Private
Placements
Whole Life Insurance

3.5%–7.0%
Options, New Issues (IPOs)
Penny Stocks, Mutual Funds
Syndicate Offerings, Annuities
Investment with Trailers

1%–2%
Stocks, Preferred Stocks
Corporate Bonds, Municipal Bonds
Ginnie Maes, Commodities

0%–1%
No-Load or Low-Load Funds
Commercial Paper, Treasury Bonds
Treasury Bills, CDs

You may be successful in obtaining your firm's commission schedule simply by asking for a copy.[4]

You may be familiar with something called the investment pyramid (see Figure 2.2). The concept behind this pyramid is quite simple. The risks of an investment become greater as you go toward the top of the pyramid, where the pyramid is narrower than it is at the bottom, which illustrates the need for investors to have a smaller

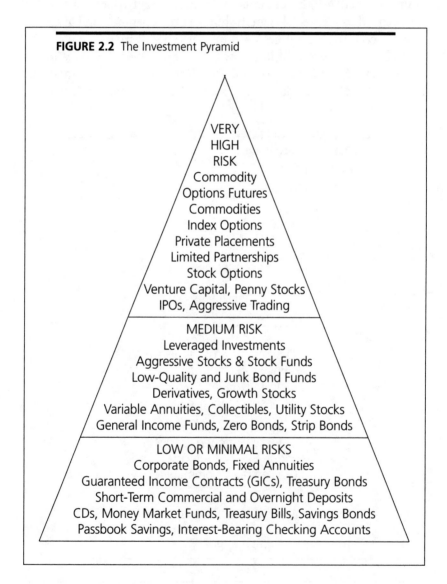

FIGURE 2.2 The Investment Pyramid

VERY
HIGH
RISK
Commodity
Options Futures
Commodities
Index Options
Private Placements
Limited Partnerships
Stock Options
Venture Capital, Penny Stocks
IPOs, Aggressive Trading

MEDIUM RISK
Leveraged Investments
Aggressive Stocks & Stock Funds
Low-Quality and Junk Bond Funds
Derivatives, Growth Stocks
Variable Annuities, Collectibles, Utility Stocks
General Income Funds, Zero Bonds, Strip Bonds

LOW OR MINIMAL RISKS
Corporate Bonds, Fixed Annuities
Guaranteed Income Contracts (GICs), Treasury Bonds
Short-Term Commercial and Overnight Deposits
CDs, Money Market Funds, Treasury Bills, Savings Bonds
Passbook Savings, Interest-Bearing Checking Accounts

portion of their money in riskier investments. Within each section of the pyramid, the investments are shown in order of their risks.

The investment pyramid moves from low risk/low reward up to high risk/high reward. Together, Figures 2.1 and 2.2 confirm that investments with the highest risk bring in the highest commissions. Brokerage firms uniformly set higher commissions on riskier investments because ideally, assuming a broker discloses all of the risks, riskier investments are harder to sell. Higher commissions serve as the carrot for the broker to steer customers toward riskier investments. The same rationale applies to some longer-term investments. Long-term investments also have higher commissions because holding an investment for the long term effectively limits your broker's ability to generate commissions on those funds. Those funds are stuck in that investment when otherwise your broker would be able to sell it and buy something else. Higher commissions always act as an incentive for your broker to push a particular product.

The manipulation of commissions takes place even on what might be considered more conservative investments. When Douglas worked at Merrill Lynch in the 1980s, the firm usually inventoried bonds, as do many firms today. If a client was interested in bonds, Douglas would pull up a computer screen to see what bonds were in inventory. In addition to all of the typical information about the bond, the screen would tell the brokers what the commissions were for selling each bond to a client. The commissions were listed in points; one point was 1 percent, which was always calculated on a face value of $1,000, or $10. Douglas learned very quickly that he needn't look at the rating of the bond or do much research to find out which bonds were riskier. If Merrill was offering its brokers $30 to $40 per bond, he could bet it was a riskier investment.

In 1998, the AARP (formerly the American Association of Retired Persons) surveyed 827 investors aged 50 and over on the issue of broker compensation. Because those surveyed were at or nearing retirement and had longer time within which to invest, you might expect them to have a fair amount of knowledge about investment firm practices. Yet a whopping 64 percent of those surveyed did not know that riskier investments often carry higher commissions. Laura Polacheck, the AARP's legislative representative, said, "It would not be intuitive for investors to think, 'This broker is recommending this to me because they'll be compensated more than for some other product.'"[5]

Many investors rarely know or appreciate the commissions they are paying on many of these products, much less the correlation between commission and risk. Take initial public offerings (IPOs)/new issues. There, the commission is hidden in the price, and you may never know what it is. But commissions on IPOs are some of the highest. Likewise, other securities, such as some over-the-counter stocks, limited partnerships, annuities, and mutual funds, can sock you with exorbitant commissions. But unless you read the prospectus in detail, you'll never know it. For still other investments, the broker may receive, in addition to the commission, a residual payment in the form of a percentage of the assets as long as you own the investment. You've probably never heard of that. In Chapter 14, we discuss why the commissions of particular investments are key.

As you can see from the greed pyramid, the commissions for various products are displayed in percentages, which is typical of full-service brokerage firms. You have probably been inundated with online brokerage firm ads that tout a flat-rate commission. Some online firms actually play up the fixed commission itself as a way to convince customers to shift to the online scene. One firm with the transparent name of Flat Fee Discount Stockbrokers states outright on its Web site:

> FLAT FEE DISCOUNT STOCKBROKERS' goal is to provide a fair and equal opportunity for all clients (large and small) to buy and sell securities on a level playing field with NO conflicts of interest between the client and firm. We have no "hidden costs" and you know exactly what the commission will be before you trade.

Some groups, including the Consumer Federation of America and the fee-only National Association of Personal Financial Advisors, say the only way to avoid conflicts of interest is for advisors to be paid by fee—the same fee—no matter what they recommend. Even online firms use fixed commissions, such as $7.95 and $8.00 per trade, as bait to lure their customers. Be sure and read Chapter 9 on other ways online firms make their money.

You should know what the total costs are for every investment you make. Costs include not only commissions but also every other item that is part and parcel of the investment, such as markups or markdowns, spreads, margin interest, and front-end or back-end loads. The cost of an investment is a determinable number. Find out what that number is and also what that number is as a percentage of the investment. If the number or the percentage seems high to you, it probably is. Realize that to profit from that investment, you have to make *more* than the total cost amount. If your costs make up 10 percent of the investment, then your investment should have a better than 10 percent return. Here are some guidelines for determining what costs are "too high":

- The shorter the term of the investment, the lower the commissions/fees should be.
- The lower the potential returns, the lower the commissions/fees should be.
- The commissions/fees should relate to how much valuable work has been done by the firm/individual collecting the fees.
- The commissions/fees should be competitive not only with industry standards but also with similar investments.

You should know what your yearly costs are. You should also know what your rate of return is after all costs are deducted. Whip off a letter to your broker asking for a breakdown of this information to learn where you stand in comparison with other types of investments, which may well lead you to conclude that your rate of return is too low.

Markups and Markdowns

Markups and markdowns are just like commissions—compensation to your broker and your firm—except that they take place when your brokerage firm acts as a principal, as opposed to an agent, on your trade. They are also a cost of the investment. It used to be that a markup or markdown was routinely built into the price so that a naïve investor, on viewing the confirmation for the trade, might think, It's free! I didn't pay anything extra to the broker. Now these costs show up on your confirmations as markups (if you are buying) or markdowns (if you are selling), and the commission field will be left blank.

Just like commissions, markups and markdowns create conflicts of interest. The SEC acknowledged this in 1992: "Markups and markdowns are direct profits for the firm and its salespeople, so you should be aware of such amounts to assess the overall value of the trade.[6] And to assess the conflicts of interest. When you are figuring out conflicts and commissions generated by your broker, be sure to take into consideration markups and markdowns.

THE SPREADS—THE HIDDEN PROFIT CENTER BUT NOT FOR YOU

The issue of spreads is unusually tangled with conflicts of interest. Again, like commissions and markups and markdowns, the spread is, as the SEC has stated, "another source of profit for the brokerage firm and compensates the firm for the risk of owning the stock." A brokerage firm has risk if it is a market maker in a particular security. If your firm makes a market in a stock, that means your firm is trading for its own accounts while also handling orders for you and other customers. The bid is what that firm is willing to pay for that security and the ask is what that firm is willing to sell that security for. The spread is the difference between the bid and the ask. The market maker profits by buying on the bid and selling at the ask and thereby capturing the spread between the two. The market maker will also sell at the ask and then try to replace the stock sold by buying it on the bid.

Spreads and their attendant conflicts of interest have become a hot issue in just the last few years. In the past, if the broker-dealer was not the market maker on a security, it would not share in any profits from the spread. But now, under a practice called "payment for order flow," market makers are paying part of the profit they make from the spread to the broker-dealer in exchange for the broker-dealer's directing trades to the market maker. This in and of itself poses a direct conflict of interest. In the past, broker-dealers were supposed to check with at least three different market makers and direct your order to the market maker that offered the best price. Now, firms are bypassing this process and are directing your order to a market maker regardless of its current bid or offer. Although the requirement to give you the best bid and offer cannot be bypassed, too often it is.

An additional conflict occurs when it comes to spreads. Not all securities trade with the same amount of spread. Generally, spreads are larger on more thinly traded stocks, even with the move from fractional to decimal pricing. The spread on IBM may be as little as a few cents, whereas the spread on a thinly traded over-the-counter stock may be as much as 50 cents. Are you beginning to see the pattern? Brokerage firms make more money on investments that are not in your best interest. Clearly, a broker has more incentive to steer you into a stock in which his firm makes a market and in which there is additional profit in the spread over and above the commissions or markup. To boot, the spread is a direct cost to you, one that you must factor in along with commissions or markups and markdowns. Be mindful of the spreads in the stocks in which your firm makes a market.

MARGIN—THE COSTLY DOUBLE-EDGED SWORD

With the advent of online trading coupled with the prolonged bull market, millions of Americans were flocking to the Internet to not only trade but to buy on margin. Most of the margin buying appears to be in the stock market, as opposed to the bond market. No one ever accused brokerage firms of being benevolent, but at least their advertising made you feel they cared. The online firms do care, but it is only about their bottom line.

Credit issued to you by your brokerage firm does not come free; you pay interest on it. Rest assured that brokerage firms borrow the money they loan to you for less than the amount they charge you in margin interest. More commonly, brokerage firms simply lend out cash sitting in customers' accounts, an extremely cheap source of funds. Margin loans are nothing but profit—icing on the cake—for brokerage firms. Firms are secretive about exactly how much money they make as a result of margin interest. At Ameritrade and E*Trade, the difference between what the firms pay for funds versus what they charge customers for loans is about 18 percent of revenue—a pretty significant percentage.[7] And the firms make additional money in the form of commissions when you margin your account. Margin increases your buying power and your ability to buy more stocks. The more stocks you buy, the more commissions you generate for the firm or broker. Margin is simply a tool for generating commissions.

Are there conflicts of interest when brokerage firms lend you money in the form of margin? You bet—severe conflicts. The NASD summarized them well when it made the following comments in connection with the then proposed day trading rules:

We believe that there is an inherent conflict of interest when members facilitate or participate in lending activities with or between their customers. These lending activities often allow customers to continue to trade when they would not otherwise be in a financial position to do so, thereby generating more commission income to the member. These same conflicts of interest arise when principals, registered representatives, and significant shareholders of members lend funds to customers. Such conflicts of interests can arise in a variety of situations, certainly not limited to day-trading activities.[8]

The margin interest that brokerage firms collect is a humongous profit center for brokerage firms; and for online firms, it is often the most profitable revenue stream. Brokerage firms may make as much in margin interest as they do in commissions. Although margin use significantly increases your risk, it poses very little risk for firms. The firms have eliminated their risk and protected their downside through provisions in the margin agreement (see Chapter 5 for a more detailed discussion of margin use). What all of this means is that brokerage firms have a strong financial interest in increasing the margin loans they provide to customers. Keep this in mind the next time your stockbroker suggests that you make a purchase on margin.

BROKER COMPENSATION AND PERKS— YOU PAID FOR THAT BENZ

Now, if it was not bad enough that the industry creates incentives for brokers to sell higher-risk and more unsuitable investments by enticing them with higher commissions on those products, the industry takes it one step further. The industry uses a formula to calculate what to pay the broker, again based on criteria that are not in the investors' best interest. What you are about to read is one of the bigger secrets within the brokerage industry.

The commission on an investment product does not go into the pocket of your broker. Nor is that commission split between your broker and the firm. Well, it's split in a manner of speaking after several complicated machinations. Here's how it works at most firms. Every commission that a broker generates goes toward something called "gross production." The firm then pays the broker a percentage of his or her gross production number (called a "payout"), and the firm keeps the rest. The complicated part is how the percentage is calculated. Some firms have a grid that lists the varying percentages brokers will be paid based on the type of investment they sell. These grids as well as charts showing what different firms pay for different types of investments (e.g., mutual funds and annuities) are routinely published by such industry magazines as *Registered Representative* and *On Wall Street*.

What brokerage firms strive to keep secret, though, are breakdowns within the breakdowns, of which the industry should not be so proud and which they do not publicize. For example, a firm might credit a broker a few extra basis points based on the level of margin balances the broker's customers have: the higher the margin balances, the closer the broker inches toward that next higher payout level. More commonly, proprietary investments, such as stocks that a firm makes a market in or mutual funds that the firm creates and manages, often net brokers points toward a higher percentage payout. The firm, as well as the broker, makes extra money on these proprietary investments. As you now know, if the firm makes a market in the stock, the firm may also make money on the trade through the spread in addition to making a markup or markdown on the trade. If the investment is an in-house mutual fund, the firm will charge you management fees in addition to the commission or sales load. Proprietary investments are moneymakers for both the broker and the firm, and that's why the firm dangles the incentive of a higher percentage payout before its brokers.

In 1995, the SEC issued a report on the compensation practices of brokerage firms because of what it called "persistent conflicts of interest within the industry." Specifically, the report identified "incentives to encourage the sale of proprietary investment products" as being one of the primary culprits in causing conflicts of interest. The SEC stated: "That some products provide significantly higher payouts than others—even within the same product category—is often pointed to as a practice that jeopardizes the provision of unbiased investment advice." The report pointed out that some firms were employing what the SEC called "best practices," that is, the payment of identical commissions to stockbrokers for proprietary and nonproprietary products within the same product family and for principal and agency transactions to ensure that stockbrokers are indifferent to incentives when making recommendations—at least with respect to products in the same category. This is the ideal to which all brokerage firms should strive.

A. G. Edwards deserves high marks for staying away from proprietary products. In the 1980s, when many firms were selling such proprietary products as limited partnerships and private placements, A. G. Edwards avoided this practice. Even today, A. G. Edwards does not believe in selling proprietary products and is one of the few powerhouses on Wall Street that does not offer its own mutual funds.

Other than asking your stockbroker whether he or she is receiving a higher payout on a recommended security, as opposed to others in the same class, there is no clear way for you to learn whether your firm provides its brokers a higher payout for proprietary products. The firm may do it for some products but not for others. It may do it for one month but not the next. Or it may not do it all. One thing is clear, though: there is no rule or regulation to prevent the conduct.

Let's look further into brokers' gross production levels and the evils that attend firms employing those levels. At certain yearly levels of gross production, an incentive is built in to entice your broker to reach the next level. For example, a stockbroker's payout schedule might look like this:

1st $100,000 Gross production	30% Payout to broker
2nd $100,000 Gross production	33% Payout to broker
3rd $100,000 Gross production	36% Payout to broker
> $300,000 Gross production	40% Payout to broker

A formula like the one above exerts constant pressure on brokers to generate more and more commissions. Brokerage firms also set quotas for not only higher payouts but also for minimum payouts, for penalties if the broker misses them, and for kickers if they make them. For example, if a broker reaches $300,000 in gross production, the broker might get a retroactive payout and the entire $300,000 paid at a 33 percent payout. In 2001, one brokerage firm paid kickers from 2 to 6 percent to brokers bringing in monthly commissions between $18,000 to $57,500 but socked brokers with a 10 to 14 percent penalty for bringing in less than $15,500 a month in commissions!⁹ In the mind of a broker laboring under these production quotas, you can see how the mantra might be "trade my clients' accounts, trade my clients' accounts." You may think your broker is working in your best interest to recommend the XYZ Company to you. Little do you know that your broker may really just be focused on trying to get over a breakpoint in his percentage payout.

Brokers not only get special financial incentives for gross production levels over a certain amount, but they are often rated and scored based on their annual gross production levels. Certain production levels may gain a broker entry into special elite clubs within the brokerage firm with such impressive-sounding titles as The President's Club or The Chairman's Council. Stockbrokers then use these titles to garner more clients. Usually, once a broker starts producing above $400,000 in gross production in a major wire house, he acquires such additional perks as a nicer office, a full-time sales assistant, and expense allowances.

The establishment of incentive production levels leads to something we call "The Year-End Push," which explains why you must be very careful about not only *what* is being sold to you but *when*. Naturally, brokers are apt to concentrate on their yearly production level at, you guessed it, year-end. December may be a broker's last stab at being a big shot. So be careful when your broker seems a bit too enthusiastic at year-end. He may be struggling to increase his numbers in December just to hang onto his job or to catapult himself into a higher production category and a bonus. Either way, quotas and production levels motivate your broker to work for other than your interests. Commonly, brokers mask their less-than-noble motives by characterizing the push to sell stocks as a year-end tax strategy. Be wary. It is a broker's own taxes that will actually be affected.

Do you ever wonder why so many brokers work for smaller regional brokerage firms instead of for the big boys? Why would any self-respecting broker work at Acme Financial Services when he can work for A. G. Edwards, Merrill Lynch, or Goldman Sachs? These large firms offer name recognition around the country, prestige, marketing clout, fancy advertisements to lure in numerous clients, and analysts who are quoted in the *Wall Street Journal*. Why on earth would a broker do anything but vie for a job at one of these big firms? The answer: higher payout.

The average payout at the larger firms (Merrill Lynch, Salomon Smith Barney, Morgan Stanley, Prudential, PaineWebber, and A. G. Edwards) ranges from 30 to 45 percent depending on products and gross production levels.[10] The payout range at smaller firms is typically from 50 to 95 percent, and quite a few offer payouts at the upper end of that range. In trade magazines, brokers are lured away from larger firms to smaller ones with ads like these:

- "It's not what you make . . . It's what you keep that counts! With Financial West Group, your payout is 80–90% versus your current 25–42%."
- "There were wire houses that offered me bigger payouts. But my instincts led me to a bigger payoff." Nathan & Lewis Securities, Inc.
- Football star John Elway appeared in an ad in both *Registered Representative* magazine and *On Wall Street* for JWGenesis Financial Services that said, "You're about to score. The last thing you need is for someone to drop the ball. JWGenesis offers you the support you need plus up to 95% payout."

Should this concern you? Great question, yet one with no clear-cut answer. The thought process you should go through may be just as helpful as an answer though. Large brokerage firms, just like large law firms and large CPA firms, would have you believe that bigger is better. In the brokerage industry, there is some truth to this axiom, as there is little to no advantage for you, the investor, to have your account at a small firm. Of course, there are always exceptions. For example, if you like to buy stocks in locally based firms, then a regional brokerage firm that specializes in local companies is just the thing for you.

But generally speaking, the small firm's services, products, and access to knowledgeable people will be fewer and farther between at a smaller firm. If you are paying the same commission at the small firm, your benefits look even worse. So the fact that your broker has moved his business to a smaller firm that pays him twice the commission payout may very well be only in his best interest, not yours. See Chapter 10 for a discussion of the disadvantages of small firms to investors.

CONTESTS—YOU'RE IN SPRINGFIELD; YOUR BROKER'S IN MAUI

Sales contests are another incentive that brokerage firms have used extensively to motivate their sales force. Contests are an American way of life. One meaning for the word *contest* in a Webster's dictionary is "any race, game, debate, etc., in which there is a struggle to be a winner." Businesses have used contests widely as a means to get people to do things that, without the incentive of a contest, they might not otherwise do.

Would people really go through all that junk mail if they didn't think they may win the Publishers Clearing House Sweepstakes? Procter & Gamble used sales contests very effectively to motivate its sales force. When Douglas worked there, the company held contests to motivate salespeople to push as much product as possible before temporary plant closings to minimize the loss of business during the closing. But should sales contests be used to encourage brokers to sell certain investments? The answer is *no!* The problem is that there is no rule against it. Brokerage firms do a fine enough job of breaking the rules; you surely can't expect them to always do the right thing when there is no rule forbidding it.

Let's take a look at a sample contest. Your brokerage firm announces a new in-house mutual fund. Of course, it comes with a tasty front-end commission (tasty to the broker and the firm, not you). Unknown to you, the firm does make known to your broker that his payout will be 70 percent on the first three months' sales, when ordinarily the payout would be 30 percent. As an extra incentive, the firm tells your broker that the top 50 brokers in the country who sell the most of this new in-house mutual fund will each partake in a luxurious, all-expense-paid trip to Cancun, Mexico.

No doubt your broker may sell this mutual fund to many clients for whom it is perfectly suitable. You may even be one of them. But far, far too often, the conflicts created by the contest and the incentives encourage brokers to sell the product to customers for whom the investment is not suitable. A common occurrence is a broker flipping a client out of one load fund into the new load fund. Or the new fund may be too risky for a certain client or may pay tax-free income to a client who doesn't need it. Or, still worse, because the contest rewards how much of the mutual fund is sold, not how many times it is sold, a broker may sell much more of the mutual fund than he should to a particular client. When the contest is over, the broker's enthusiasm for the new mutual fund will wane.

Consumer groups and many industry personnel object to product-specific sales contests as undue temptations for brokers to place their own interests ahead of their customers' interests. The SEC faced problems with brokerage firms' use of single-product contests and stated the following in its 1995 report:

> Some firms use single product contests to encourage sales. For example, a firm might devise a four-week contest to encourage its representatives to sell a newly offered stock mutual fund. These contests, often sponsored by third-party vendors, offer resort vacations, VCRs, television sets, and other inducements to [brokers] who reach specified sales levels of a particular mutual fund, limited partnerships, or other financial products.

Other firms sponsor contests that are non–product-specific. They reward the number of new accounts opened, the total sale of all categories of fixed-income securities, new client assets brought into the firm, and so forth. As for these types of contests, the SEC rightfully recognized though that these broader measures "do not in themselves eliminate the potential for conflicts of interest between [broker] and client." The conflicts remain.

Douglas must confess that not only did he participate in a sales contest at Merrill Lynch but he was one of the winners. It was 1982 and Merrill had recently introduced the CMA (Cash Managed Accounts) program, which allowed people to earn interest at higher money market rates in one account that contained the investor's stocks and cash balances on which the investor could write checks and use a credit card. The contest involved how many accounts brokers could open, with a minimum number required to qualify. In 1982 Americans were earning low, single-digit interest rates on their bank accounts, savings accounts, and most brokerage accounts. On the other hand, interest rates on the CMA money market account were in the double digits. Douglas had no problem opening a substantial number of accounts.

So is Douglas a hypocrite? Not in the least. He was doing his CMA customers a great service. They were not required to buy a single investment from him, yet he doubled the interest rate they were earning on their money. No conflict of interest reared its ugly head in that scenario. As a matter of fact, Douglas openly told potential clients that he was going to win a contest if he opened a certain number of accounts.

Has your broker ever told you about a contest, trip, or prize he stood to win if he sold a certain investment to just one more customer? We bet not. The SEC found that among the 26 broker-dealers that provided input to the committee through panel discussions, interviews, and field research, no firm provided disclosure of such items. The SEC report described "disclosure" as an "antidote to client/firm conflicts of interest" as well as "a time-tested approach to protecting the interests of investors." Yet it found no firm that disclosed the extra compensation brokers receive for the sale of particular products and no disclosure of special incentives beyond the normal commission to sell a particular product.

Hoards of unsuitable transactions will be thwarted if, at a minimum, the regulators required disclosure of contests and incentives to be made to the investing public. An even greater number will be thwarted if contests are eliminated, as they have no place in an industry that deals with people's life savings.

One other aspect of a stockbroker's compensation should be explored. In the securities industry, the word *trailers* represents the additional commissions a broker may receive after a client's initial purchase of an investment. It is somewhat akin to insurance salespeople getting commissions each year when you pay your premium, the main difference being that the investor is not committing any more money. Well, not exactly. The two products in which trailers are most prevalent are limited partnerships and mutual funds. Some of these investments have annual fees that are charged against the investor's money. In mutual funds these are the 12b-1 fees, which usually go straight into the pocket of the brokerage firm and are sometimes distributed to the brokers.

In some ways, trailers are more deceiving than the initial commissions charged. Sure, some disclosure in fine print may be tucked away in the prospectus. But rarely is it made clear to you that this fee is going to go to the broker who sold you the product. Stay away from brokers who sell products with trailers; they may be more worried about their own future than yours.

Brokers may also be paid on the basis of the assets in your account, although this rarely takes place unless you are being charged some fee based on assets under management. (We discuss this under the topic of wrap fees.) Don't think that just because you aren't trading, your broker is not making money in these kinds of accounts.

We have rarely seen a broker dissuade an investor from a product because the commission was too high or because the client's capital would be impaired. If your broker consistently does such dissuading, hold onto him or her; you have a gem of a broker. There are such brokers out there.

ANALYST RESEARCH REPORTS— TAROT CARD READERS SCOFF

There are about 2,500 research analysts in the country. You've seen them and heard them. They appear often on television cloaked in an aura of objective wisdom explaining why a particular company's earnings are on the upswing or how bad news in a sector will not affect a company. They work in the investment banking departments of such large firms as Merrill Lynch, Prudential, and Bear Stearns; and less powerful analysts work for smaller firms. The produce of their trade is a research report that discusses a security and culminates in a recommendation regarding the stock. Recommendations come in varying shades of black, white, and gray, such as "buy, attractive, hold, long-term accumulate, neutral, or, less commonly, sell."

For many years, analysts culled their information from private, invitation-only conference calls and meetings with upper-level management of the company at issue. You may have read about conferences at luxury resorts for company representatives that are hosted by brokerages or investment banking firms and their analysts. Because a firm foots the bill for the company representatives, such a conference was a gigantic carrot for company reps to let analysts in on the scoop regarding company prospects and business plans. In both conference calls and personal meetings between research analysts and company representatives, analysts were often provided material, nonpublic information about the companies. The analysts then used that information in their research reports to prop up their recommendations on the stock.

In the year 2000, the SEC became increasingly concerned about what came to be known as "selective disclosure," the practice of stock issuers releasing important nonpublic information to research analysts before the general public got wind of the news. The SEC had noticed that sometimes a sharp spike in stock trading just happened to coincide with research analyst conference calls or those luxury resort conferences we spoke of earlier. To you, the investor, who sees this dramatic price change and only later receives the news that prompted it, well, you can rightly question whether you are trading on a level playing field. As a result, the SEC adopted a regulation that became effective on October 23, 2000.

The rule (Rule 100 of Regulation FD, available at <www.sec.gov>) requires that when an issuer intentionally discloses material, nonpublic information to certain people, including research analysts, the issuer must make public disclosure of that same information simultaneously to the public. This rule is certainly a step in the right direction, as it should lessen the pressure analysts feel if they report negatively on a stock. No longer will companies be able to retaliate by excluding the analyst from future information. Of course, the analyst may still be terminated or otherwise penalized by the analyst's employer. Rule 100 does nothing to influence or alleviate the pressures resulting from the business relationship between the stock issuer and the analyst's employer.

To stockbrokers, research reports are security blankets, much like a firm's recommended list of securities. Brokers rely on the recommendations and then trumpet them to customers. Even online firms cite the recommendations of research analysts. Your broker might, in an effort to get you to buy a stock, tout the research capabilities of the research analyst, saying such things as, "Our analyst has been following this stock on a daily basis for eight months now. He talks with upper-level management in the company regularly and is in the know." That would probably impress you as a customer. You might reason, How can I go wrong? If the analyst is so attuned to this company, which is his job, certainly I will be advised if something bad is about to happen. I will be told when to sell to avert a decline in price." Right?

Wrong. Research analysts rarely issue sell recommendations. The SEC reported that in the year 2000, less than 1 percent of brokerage house analysts' recommendations were to sell.[11] The reason is simple: it's called backlash. It used to be that if an analyst recommended selling a stock, the representatives at the company whose stock they have recommended to sell would be so mad that they would exclude this analyst from any future conference calls and essentially cut off his access to information.

In addition, and in spite of the new regulation, there are many stories of analysts issuing a sell recommendation and then losing their job or being demoted or having their bonuses dramatically cut. Such punishments can be explained by the fact that the analyst's employer typically has a business relationship with the stock issuer that could be directly affected by the analyst's commentary. The firm that is paying an analyst to talk about a particular company may be the same firm that was paid to handle the issuance of that company's stock. In fact, that is usually the case. In April 1999, Chairman Arthur Levitt of the SEC gave a speech in which he said, "The vast majority of analysts speaking to the public today work for firms that have business relationships with the companies the analysts follow."[12] These professional and financial pressures faced by analysts prompt analysts to dispense recommendations that are more in their employer's interest than in the public's interest. And that means buy, buy, buy. Chairman Levitt in his speech put it well when he said that many analysts are "just a bit too eager to report that what looks like a frog is really a prince . . . sometimes, a frog is just a frog."[13]

In an arbitration several years ago, Tracy cross-examined a Bear Stearns (BS) analyst about these inherent conflicts. In that case, Tracy's clients, on the recommendations of their Bear Sterns broker, had purchased the stock of Cityscape Financial Corporation (CTYS), a company that serviced home mortgage loans primarily in the United Kingdom. As it turned out, Bear Sterns had an ongoing relationship with CTYS that could have influenced the stockbroker's decision to continue to recommend the stock, even as negative news reports about the company were being issued. In Figure 2.3 are excerpts from the exhibit Tracy introduced to demonstrate the inherent conflicts.

Throughout the above timeline, the stock price of CTYS steadily declined. And throughout it all the stockbroker involved in Tracy's case continued to recommend CTYS stock to some of his clients without advising them of the negative news reports. Rather, he held up those Bear Stearns research reports like beacons in a dark, dark night in a raging storm.[14]

When Douglas first started at Merrill, each morning began with a conference call with Merrill's analyst department. This con-

FIGURE 2.3 Comparing Pubic Information about CTYS with
Purchase Recommendations

Date	Bear Stearns's (BS) Relationship with CTYS	What Bear Stearns's Analyst Was Saying	Negative, Public Reports about CTYS
04/26/96	BS co-manages issuance by CTYS of $143,750,000 of debt.		
05/13/96			*Barron's* reports "increased regulation in Britain could seriously hurt Cityscape."
05/21/96		BS analyst initiates coverage of CTYS with an "attractive rating;" 12-month price target of 27.	
05/28/96		BS analyst issues follow-up on CTYS—27 target "could prove conservative."	
08/14/96			CTYS 10Q reports company has negative cash flow.
09/30/96			*Barron's* reports CTYS heavily condemned by British press for its "mortgages from hell." "All in all, not a cheery outlook."

(continued)

FIGURE 2.3 Comparing Public Information . . . , *continued*

Date	Bear Stearns's (BS) Relation- ship with CTYS	What Bear Stearns's Analyst Was Saying	Negative, Public Reports about CTYS
11/26/96		BS analyst reiterates "attractive" rating on CTYS, raises 97 est. and calls CTYS "a major buying opportunity" that has dominant position in UK market.	
12/96			*Worth* magazine identifies CTYS as one of 10 stocks to avoid
02/02/97			CTYS to be investigated for possible extortionate interest rates by British Office of Fair Trade
03/07/97		BS analyst reiterates "attractive rating" on CTYS; no change in estimated E/S for 1997.	
04/21/97			Moody's lowers CTYS debt rating, citing increasing level of delinquent loans, negative cash flow, and significant competition

FIGURE 2.3 Comparing Public Information . . . , *continued*

Date	Bear Stearns's (BS) Relationship with CTYS	What Bear Stearns's Analyst Was Saying	Negative, Public Reports about CTYS
06/05/97		BS analyst reiterates "attractive rating" on CTYS; no change in estimated E/S for 1997.	
06/10/97	BS co-manages CTYS offering of home loan asset-backed notes		
08/04/97			Moody's again downgrades CTYS debt; says "outlook on CTYS is negative" because of UK regulatory changes.
08/06/97		BS analyst states, "We still regard the company's US & UK prospects as bright"; as for UK negative press, "the perception is worse than the reality"; "we are reiterating our Attractive Rating." CTYS stock price should rise over next two quarters.	
08/22/97			S&P revises outlook on CTYS from "stable" to

(continued)

FIGURE 2.3 Comparing Public Information . . . , *continued*

Date	Bear Stearns's (BS) Relationship with CTYS	What Bear Stearns's Analyst Was Saying	Negative, Public Reports about CTYS
			"negative," citing among other factors margin compression in the UK and potential asset quality problems.
09/04/97	BS and CTYS enter into a $300,000,000 Master Financing Agreement.		
09/16/97	BS co-manages sale by CTYS of 198,000,000 of home loan asset-backed notes.		
10/06/97			Class action lawsuit filed against CTYS
10/10/97			Moody's for 3rd time lowers rates on CTYS debt.
10/21/97	CTYS hires BS "to explore strategic alternatives"; BS receives cash fee of $200,000.		
12/15/97			*Barron's* reports CTYS in "precarious financial position."
01/28/98			CTYS is delisted from Nasdaq
10/06/98			CTYS files for bankruptcy.

ference was referred to as the "squawk box" call because it came across speakers on the brokers' desks, whose quality was so bad that everything sounded like a squawk.[15] Douglas recalls hanging on to every word of those revered analysts. It was exciting for him, as a young broker, to hear specific advice on the picks of the day and how he could make money for his customers. Though he was still in training and had no customers, he reasoned that what would be good for Merrill's customers would surely be just as good for him. So he religiously followed the advice of the Merill analyst in those morning conferences.

Douglas remembers vividly to this day that for several weeks he bought put options on McDonald's and call options on Delta Airlines. That's what the analyst had said to do. Yet things didn't work out as the analyst had explained. But Douglas kept the faith, reasoning that this was Merrill Lynch and these analysts have fancy degrees, titles, and connections. He kept the faith as he proceeded to lose all of his savings. Almost everything the analyst said to do, Douglas did and lost money. In several of the morning calls, Douglas tried to question the analyst about the idea earlier in the week that was not working. The analyst did not want to talk about that.

As a general rule, research analysts have no accountability. As long as they are reporting favorably on a company, they operate in a bubble of impunity. As with meteorologists, no one really rags on them for being wrong. Analysts hold no brokerage licenses. Therefore, no securities rule or regulation applies to them. Where a stockbroker must have a "reasonable basis" to recommend a stock to a customer, no rules or regulations dictate what an analyst says or what must be in a research report. An analyst's job is to talk up a stock, get it sold, and then go on to the next stock. Did you have any idea that when it comes to stock analysts, it is buyer beware?

The market crash in late 2000 and early 2001 exposed many of the conflicts of brokerage firm stock analysts and raised serious concerns about their reliability. There were horror stories of how a large percentage of stock analysts not only missed warning investors in time from crashing but continued to recommend stocks as they declined further and further.

What's worse, on August 15, 2001, the *Wall Street Journal* reported on a study that disclosed that analysts' picks over the past three years reveal that stocks the analysts rated as strong buys or buys had far more risk than the average stock in the market and only marginally higher returns.[16] The study looked at nearly 89,000 stock recommendations from seven big Wall Street firms going back to 1989.[17] A principal at one of these firms indicated that many firms require their analysts to focus on companies with potential upsides of 20 percent or more for strong buy ratings.[18] Naturally, this means that analysts gravitated toward more risky stocks. And where there is a potential for a big upside, there is certainly that same potential for a big drop, which is precisely what happened.

Whether an investment or a business opportunity, it is always good advice to find out the hidden conflicts of interest. You can always decide to ignore them. Our advice, when the conflicts appear large, is to tread lightly. Even the past chairman of the SEC recognized the problems caused by hidden conflicts within the securities industry:

> Both in the private sector and during my time at the commission, I've come across a number of instances that, quite frankly, do not honor an investor's rights. Instances where conflicts of interest cast doubt on the motivation of a broker, analyst, or corporate manager; where hidden costs hurt an investment's bottom line; where "spin" and "hype" mask the true performance of a mutual fund; and where accounting tricks and sleight of hand dress up a company's financial results.[19]

Stockbrokers and other financial service personnel routinely succumb to the conflicts that lurk everywhere. In a speech to members in November 2000, the president of the NASD said, "I believe that the overwhelming majority of members of the NASD are honest. When they trip up, it is most often inadvertent, much like a foot fault in tennis."[20] We do not agree with this analogy. In tennis, if you footfault on your first serve, you lose that ball and go on to your second serve. This is nothing but a disadvantage. On the other hand, when a broker "trips up," odds are he is going to benefit in some way—usually financially. A foot fault in tennis is not motivated by a system that rewards foot faults.

CHAPTER 3

Stockbrokers Are Salespeople

Let's face it. Stockbrokers are salespeople. Instead of selling shoes or tires, they are selling investments, intangibles, and dreams. Even the editor in chief of *Registered Representative* magazine wrote in a column to his stockbroker readers: "But let's face it: You were hired, trained, and are paid as a salesperson, not a business owner."[1] Now, there is nothing at all wrong with being a salesperson. Hundreds of thousands of individuals in this country make their living as salespeople. Tracy sold encyclopedias door-to-door one summer in Dallas, Texas (during the worst heat wave of the century). Her father was a salesman for Nabisco and later an olive distributor's sales representative. Douglas spent a few early years selling soap for Procter & Gamble, after which he moved up to sales management. Historically, many CEOs of the country's largest corporations came from sales divisions. And in a sense we are all selling something.

The reason for devoting an entire chapter, and a long one at that, to the topic of stockbrokers as salespeople is that brokers, with the support of their employers, go to such great lengths to make the investing public think they are everything *but* salespeople. They dress up in expensive suits with suspenders, slick their hair, and are given highfalutin, misleading titles. Through brochures and print and television ads, stockbrokers are portrayed as well-trained, educated fountains of knowledge about the world of investments. Stockbrokers are depicted as financial planners, investment advisors, money managers, and engineers of your financial success. The image projected by the firms belies the reality behind the scenes of Wall Street.

BROKER QUALIFICATIONS—
DID YOUR BROKER GO TO COLLEGE?

Brokers, like other professionals such as doctors, certified public accountants (CPAs), and lawyers, are required to have licenses to conduct their jobs. The qualifications required to obtain a broker's license, though, are significantly fewer than in other professions.

Being a medical doctor requires a person to concentrate his undergraduate years in the sciences followed by many years of more specialized and expensive schooling. After schooling comes the residency program that culminates in a rigorous licensing agenda.

Becoming a lawyer requires three years of law school. Law school is neither easy to get into nor cheap to attend. Then there is the dreaded and grueling bar exam, which may have to be passed in more than one state, depending on where the lawyer intends to practice.

For CPAs, almost all states require a college degree plus a number of years of experience depending on whether the degree was in accounting. And, of course, state licensing is also demanding.

In Chapter 13, we discuss what traits and business practices make a good stockbroker from the customer's point of view. But for now, let's discuss what qualifications are needed to become a stockbroker.

Unlike doctors, lawyers, and CPAs, stockbrokers need have no special schooling or training to be hired by a brokerage firm, other than acquiring the NASD Series 7 license. Being a stockbroker requires no formal education at all. A high school dropout could be a stockbroker! Seriously, you would probably be surprised at how many stockbrokers have never attended college. In addition, an NASD rule prohibits persons convicted of financial-related crimes from being stockbrokers, but only if the conviction occurred within the last ten years.[2] There is no special area of expertise that brokers are required to have other than being a good salesperson.

The following is a list of qualifications that brokerage firms look for when hiring someone who has not previously worked as a stockbroker:

- The ability to sell
- The ability to sell
- The ability to sell

To a brokerage firm branch manager or sales manager, who many times conducts the initial interview, the ability to sell is the primary qualification. Although some firms have much stricter standards than others when it comes to new hires, virtually every trait or attribute that is examined by the brokerage firm relates back to the question, Will this attribute enable the applicant to sell? With that in mind, we finish the list of qualifications firms seek:

- A proven track record of selling (not necessary but a big plus)
- A great communicator, which means the ability to talk on the phone
- Confident, slick, vocal, gutsy—call it what you will. It is the ability to call a total stranger in the middle of her dinner and convince her to invest thousands of dollars in a company she has never heard of.

It was 1980 and as the rest of Dallas settled in for their favorite television show on a Tuesday night, Douglas sat in a brightly lit office with a handful of applicants in a closed and darkened Merrill Lynch office in north Dallas. He and the others had made it through the initial interview process at Merrill and now were being put through "the sales test" to become a Merrill Lynch stockbroker. Each applicant was given a desk, an investment to peddle, and a card that contained a limited amount of information on the prospects they were about to call. Merrill was measuring Douglas's ability to sell intangibles to strangers. It's funny to think that not much has changed over time. Twenty years later, the identical sales process was depicted in the movie *Boiler Room*. That criticism aside, Merrill Lynch has an excellent training system in place.

What qualifications or traits are *not* important to the brokerage industry when reviewing stockbroker applicants? They are:

- Appearance (The majority of stockbrokers never see their customers.)
- Intelligence (The major wirehouses create and promote the products and investments they want their brokers to sell; thinking and researching only limits the time the broker could be selling.)
- Knowledge of finance or investments (Likewise, brokerage firms provide this information to the broker, figuring that if the broker can pass his Series 7 exam, that's good enough.)
- Level of education or education emphasis
- Previous employment unless sales related

The qualifications change dramatically if a broker is going from one brokerage firm to another. Then the following list of qualifications would be important:

- Total number of accounts
- Total assets in dollars in those accounts
- Record of opening new accounts
- Total commissions generated in the previous year
- Ability to promise the world to his new manager
- Ability to sell

You may note one critically important item missing from this last list: how much money the broker made for his customers. This computation is not performed when brokerage firms evaluate stockbrokers. Behind the walls of Wall Street, in fact, this calculation is rarely, if ever, performed.

What we have illustrated is that there is little in the hiring practices of brokerage firms or in the desired qualifications for stockbrokers that relates to the best interest of investors.

BROKER RANKING—NUMBER ONE BECAUSE OF YOU!

The fact that stockbrokers are ranked at all may surprise you. It's one thing to have a competition for the car salesperson who sells the most cars for the month or the clothing salesperson who sells the most clothes. There is little danger there, because buying a car or buying clothes involves personal style and taste that are quite subjective. And unlike stockbrokers, those salespeople don't hold licenses. The aura of a licensed professional naturally dispels any notion of a performance-ranking system. What if you walked into your doctor's office and saw a sign that said "Congratulations to Dr. Sperry—Most Operations for the Month of February"? Make you feel a bit queasy about your upcoming operation with Dr. Sperry? Well, that's how stockbrokers are ranked.

The vast majority of stockbrokers are ranked primarily on a single computation: the amount of commissions brokers produce for their firm. Because every transaction in a customer's account results in a commission, part of which goes to the broker and part to the firm, you can see that a performance-ranking system based on commissions is the same criterion as the number of operations a doctor performs in a month. Such a compensation system is the biggest "rub" in the securities industry, as discussed in more detail in Chapters 2 and 5.

At least every month, brokerage firms generate branch office printouts showing exactly what each broker produced that month and for the year in total or gross commissions. The printouts are broken down by broker, by product, and by customer and reflect how much commission goes to each broker and how much to the firm. It may also give averages for commissions by product type. It might report the number of trades and the average commission per trade. It might reflect such things as how many new accounts a broker has opened, the total amount of money a broker's customers have deposited into their accounts, the number of sales contests a broker has won, or the number of proprietary firm products a broker has sold. The industry goes to great lengths to analyze a broker's commission business and how it is growing or changing. One thing is certain: each factor that goes into a broker's ranking revolves around the ability to sell.

We suggest the following hypothetical ranking system for brokers that would revolutionize the industry:

- The annualized return of customers' portfolios
- The annualized return of customers' portfolios outperforming certain indices or benchmarks
- Reduction of taxes, fees, and the hassles of financial planning for customers

- Customer satisfaction
- Customer education
- Low account and customer turnover for a broker

A broker's ranking might also be based on the attainment of certain levels of advanced education or specialized training and licensing, but these are lofty goals not embraced by the brokerage industry. Commissions are the industry's lifeblood.

At Merrill, in addition to a report that ranked how Douglas was doing in competition with his fellow brokers in the office, Douglas was also ranked nationally. This is done at many of the major brokerage firms. Douglas competed against Merrill brokers who were in his original training class in New York and then scattered to work at Merrill offices all over the country. These statistics were published in Merrill's ranking reports at the time. After his first year in production, Merrill ranked Douglas sixth in the nation out of one of the larger graduating classes ever, a class of 180. Like many brokers in the throes of competition and personal recognition, Douglas's pride may have been misplaced. In the brokerage industry, the ability to reap financial rewards personally and for one's firm should take a backseat to doing what's in the best interest of the firm's customers.

All the trips, gifts, awards, staff support, computers, titles, and accommodations a broker receives are based on the commissions the broker generates. Now you might be thinking, I don't care how my broker is ranked or rated because that's an internal function and doesn't affect me. You might be wrong. The following are some of the perks that brokers receive as a result of a high ranking in gross commissions and how they might affect a customer:

- Broker says, "Call my assistant and she will help you with those forms."
  Customer thinks, Hmmm . . . my broker must be doing well to have an assistant.
- Broker sends something to the customer that says at the top, "Chairman's Council—Only for the Elite."
  Customer thinks, Hmmm . . . my broker is good! He's going to do good for me!

There are many other rewards flowing to your broker as a result of rankings that you may never know about, such as bigger private offices, special computers, expense allowances, bonuses, or trips to exotic places. But just as important is the impact of perks like these on the brokers who are constantly striving to obtain them but never do. A ranking or reward system based on sales provides an incentive for every single broker in the firm to try and make a sale that may not be in the best interest of the customer. And that could be you. If you have previously been impressed by any of these perks your broker may have bragged about, recognize them for what they really are.

BROKER TITLES—A DIME A DOZEN

"We can't afford to give them a raise, so give them a new title!" The brokerage industry copied the banking industry in the seventies and eighties and started giving stockbrokers fancy titles. Did you ever meet anyone at a major bank who was not a vice president? It's the same at brokerages: Everyone is a vice president. Okay, there's the guy who cleans the ashtrays in the lobby. He's still in training—VP-in-Training. Broker titles can be misleading. Your broker might have been a high school dropout selling used tires the year before you met him. His business card will reflect a title designed to attract new customers.

Worse yet, and very confusing to the investing public, stockbrokers are no longer called stockbrokers. Instead, they are called financial advisors, account executives, financial consultants, or even certified financial managers. And brokers who generate significant commissions for their firm may become a senior portfolio manager.

The industry does not regulate titles, so it has made a mockery of them, which could be one reason many stockbrokers want to avoid management positions. Not only would they make less money, but they would also have to give up many of the fancy titles they retain as brokers.

Titles at brokerage firms can be negotiated just like the size of one's office and the quality of one's sales assistant. The negotiation is the hottest when a broker changes firms. Depending on the size of a broker's book, his customer base, and his previous year's commissions, there may be an impressive list of titles at the broker's disposal.

Titles Used by Brokers

Vice President
Vice President Investments
Vice President Trading Specialist
Vice President Portfolio Management
Senior Vice President
Senior Portfolio Manager

Our favorite misleading title is senior vice president international, which reminds us of the Amarillo International Airport in Amarillo, Texas. We joke that long ago a Mexican drug smuggler was forced to land his plane there and hence the designation "international." The stockbroker bearing the prestigious senior vice president international title is 23 years old and has been in the securities business not much longer than it has taken the ink to dry on his business cards. And "International"? Well, it turns out he had purchased a lot of stock in an Italian fast-food chain.

Of course, the industry would never think of using a title such as stockbroker. At many firms, brokers are financial consultants and registered representatives but never stockbrokers. A fancier title makes a person appear to be more important. It's like calling a résumé a curriculum vitae; it's the same document, but curriculum vitae sounds more impressive.

Many companies across various industries bestow fancy titles on employees moving up the ranks. However, the vice president in a manufacturing company is not handling the money that will be used in your retirement or will put your children through college. Our advice is to not give any weight to stockbroker titles.

BROKER TRAINING—
SELL, SELL, SELL

Regardless of stockbrokers' fancy titles, it is likely that the only training they have received is whatever sales training their first firm provided in addition to their passing the Series 7 exam. The NASD Series 7 exam is known as the General Securities Representative license. A grade is given for the exam, but the only score that matters is pass or fail. Brokers can take the exam as many times as they need to finally pass. We have seen many brokers who have taken the exam four or five times before passing. A worse practice is one allowing brokers to pay others to take the exams for them. The NASD cracked down on a group of professional exam takers who were doing just that.

We can be brief about training because you already know what few qualifications it takes to become a stockbroker. Only at the major retail wirehouses such as Merrill Lynch or Smith Barney will rookie brokers enter a formal training program. And sometimes that's not a given; Prudential announced in the summer of 2001 that it was halting its training program for new brokers until March 2002 as a result of cutbacks.[3] Training can be broken down into four basic parts: (1) learning to pass the Series 7 exam, (2) learning investment products, (3) learning how the firm operates, and (4) learning to sell. If brokers start their career at a less prominent brokerage firm, they will probably not receive any formal training other than the weekly sales meeting, where they are taught to sell, sell, sell. Although not much better than pure sales training, the major wirehouse training is better than no training at all. In addition, since 1998, brokers have been required to undergo continuing education classes at intervals. But the majority of training that brokers receive is merely basic sales training. We believe that considerably more time should be spent educating and training brokers in the areas of ethics, morals, and high standards.

Other than learning the products, most broker training is of little importance to you, the investor. Generally speaking, brokers are taught hardly anything about portfolio management, economics, modern portfolio theory, estate planning, taxes, retirement planning, finance, and accounting or how to read balance sheets, 10Ks, or other financial documents. There, of course, are exceptions. Merrill Lynch has in place a financial planning program for its brokers that includes retirement planning, allocation, and college planning for the kids and more.

If you are still not convinced that stockbrokers are more salespeople than true money managers, then you must have a relative that is a stockbroker or your current broker is one of those excellent exceptions. We are merely attempting to help you siphon out the good from the bad. Let's take one more crack at this salesperson label with cold calling.

SMILING AND DIALING—
THE ART OF COLD CALLING

If you have not been *cold called* by a stockbroker, then you must have borrowed the money to buy this book. The term refers to the practice in the industry whereby a broker calls a person on the phone, usually someone known to have some excess funds but whom the broker doesn't know. That is, the broker is calling the person "cold." Stockbroker cold calls often originate from distant locations and tout stocks typically unknown to the general public. We wonder how a person who drives across town to save $10 on a major appliance can be the same person who in the span of one telephone call will write a substantial check to a complete stranger to purchase an unknown investment. The practice of cold calling continues to this day for the simple reason that lots of people respond favorably to cold calls.

In the future, before you whip out your checkbook and excitedly write a check and send it to the stranger on the other end of the line, keep your ears open to the following ten red flags. If you hear them, think about hanging up. You may also hear these comments from your current broker, which should cause you to consider changing brokers:

1. *Yap, yap, yap.* Is the stockbroker doing all the talking? Stockbrokers are required to learn essential facts about you *before* recommending an investment. The NASD requires a stockbroker, before executing a transaction for you, to obtain information about your financial status, your tax status, and your investment objectives. If you are being pitched a low-priced security, you should be asked about your other security holdings. If the stockbroker is doing all of the talking, then he or she simply cannot know you well enough to make a recommendation.

2. *I'm buying it in my own account and in my mother's account.* It is not a per se violation for a stockbroker to make this statement. However, you should know that brokerage firm policies often discourage this type of statement. It is very persuasive for prospective customers to hear. Realize that just because the investment may be suitable for the stockbroker or his mother, that does not mean it is suitable for

you. There is also the possibility that the claim is not true, but you have no way of verifying it. Although the broker's assertion is titillating, it leaves you in the dark about how much stock was bought, what price was paid, or if the stock was subsequently sold.

3. *It's going fast—you need to "Fed-Ex" me a check*. This is usually a ploy to short-circuit your ability to ask questions, seek outside information, or receive and review written materials. Don't fall victim to the time pressure or the undertone of "Everyone else is buying it and you should too."

4. *You can't lose. It's a sure winner. I promise. I guarantee it*. If you hear these words, don't even waste your time or breath. Hang up. It is a direct violation for stockbrokers to assure customers or potential customers of the profitability of a particular investment. Words like *promise* and *guarantee* are the reddest of red flags. The above remarks also cry out that there is no risk in this investment, which is not true. All investments involve some degree of risk. And the stocks touted in cold calls are often some of the riskiest.

5. *You don't need to read the literature*. For almost every investment, some kind of literature goes with it—usually a prospectus, research or analyst report, or other documentation about the company. You may not have the time, expertise, or desire to review and understand this material, but the stockbroker should not discourage you from receiving or reviewing such information.

6. *I'm a specialist in* . . . As a rookie broker at Merrill Lynch working in a room of cubicles, Douglas could hear the pitches made by his fellow brokers. He recalls hearing one young broker tell a customer he was a specialist in municipal bonds (in 1981 and 1982 municipal bonds were paying 13 percent). A minute went by, and he overheard the broker say, "I am also a specialist in corporate bonds." The prospect must have mentioned stocks, because finally the broker said, "Oh, stocks? Sure, I am also a specialist in stocks." The irony of the broker's statements is that he literally talked himself out of being a specialist!

The majority of stockbrokers are generalists, which makes them well suited to advise all types of people because they have a broad understanding of all investments.

There are very few specialist stockbrokers and those who are typically sell to institutions, not individuals. Any other so-called specialists are specializing in either what they are interested in that day or what their firm is selling that day.

7. *I won't charge you commissions.* No stockbrokers are calling to sell you something in which they are not making some sort of commission or fee. You'll end up paying it one way or another. If it's not on the front end, it's on the back end. And if it's not a commission, it's another form of payment to the broker disguised as another word. (For more details, see Chapter 2.)

8. *I only make money if you make money.* Wrong. It would seem to make far more sense for stockbrokers to be compensated based on the success of their customers' portfolios—but that's not the system. Stockbrokers make commissions no matter how poorly your investments do. In fact, they stand to make *more* money if your investment does poorly, because the next phone call you get may be urging you to sell and buy something else. The broker will make a commission on the purchase of the new stock and may even make a commission on the sale of the old stock. A double whammy.

9. *You should buy 10,000 shares.* Assume this means a large dollar value purchase as compared with a high-tech new issue trading at $.02 a share for a $200 purchase price. A large share purchase might be okay if you have told the stockbroker that you buy in large quantities and that you have ample, excess funds. But if you haven't *or* if the broker has failed to inquire about the money you have available for investment, recognize this red flag. It says you have a broker more concerned about the size of an order (that is, the commission) than what is suitable for you.

10. *Don't worry about it. Trust me.* If a stockbroker says this to you, do worry and don't trust. The primary way evildoers take advantage of their victims is by dismissing their concerns.

The NASD and NYSE have specific rules designed to rein in a stockbroker's communication with the public during a cold call. For example, a proper cold call should take place only between the hours of 8:00 AM and 9:00 PM local time, and the caller must identify himself or herself and provide you with the telephone number or address at which the caller may be contacted. Also, you must be told that the purpose of the call is to solicit the purchase of securities or related services.

The NASD also has rules that permit you to advise the broker that you wish to be placed on the firm's centralized do-not-call list of persons who do not wish to receive telephone solicitations from the firm or its brokers. Make a personal note that you have done this, and if you continue to get phone calls from that firm, advise your local NASD office. You can also protect yourself by keeping your ears open for the above telltale signs of trouble.

The major wire houses would like you to believe that cold calling is a practice engaged in only by the lowly bucket shop brokerage firms (see Chapter 10). But the reality is that the PaineWebbers, Morgan Stanleys, and Bear Stearnses of the world have their stockbrokers cold call just like all the other brokers. Douglas worked for Bear Stearns in the 1980s and witnessed the initialization and phenomenal growth of a cold-calling department in one of the branch offices. Sometimes, Douglas would call a buddy of his at another brokerage firm to come over during the lunch hour, and the two of them would watch the antics of a number of the brokers in the cold-calling department. One of the more entertaining stunts of these high-pressure brokers occurred when they would finally get a potential investor on the phone. They would jump up and stand on their desks, which encouraged the other brokers to egg them on. Another antic was the brokers' holding the phone at arms length while talking to a customer to display to their fellow brokers that it was unimportant that they listen to what their clients had to say.

Brokerage firms hire thousands of young men and women who show up wide-eyed with little knowledge and fewer customers. Cold calling is a necessity so the firm can garner clients in the numbers necessary to generate commissions. Other ways that brokers can prospect for new customers include seminars, mass mailings, and, of course, hounding family members and college buddies, but cold calling remains a part of the life of many brokers' in the securities business. If good brokers service their customers well and stay in the business for a number of years, they hope that eventually a large percentage of their new customers will come from referrals.

Positive cold calls would consist of statements grounded in fact, a discussion of the risk or downside of the investment, and little or no pressure to buy. Still, cold calling, or what is often referred to as "smiling and dialing," permeates the brokerage industry. Whether the broker is simply trying to get a person to open an account and deposit funds or convincing a person to buy an investment, the broker is selling. The broker, after all, is a salesperson.

There was a horrible saying that Douglas learned early in his brokerage career that deserves repeating. It goes like this: A customer calls a broker on the phone and asks him, "What do you think of IBM stock?" The broker responds, "It depends. Are you buying or selling?" That is the quintessence of the salesperson's mentality in the brokerage industry.

SALES SCRIPTS—"IT'S GOING FAST!"

Do you ever get a sales call—the long-distance phone companies come to mind—and in the middle of the spiel you ask an offbeat question, and it completely throws the caller off? The caller doesn't know how to respond because you've caused a diversion from the script. Sales scripts such as these are also used by the brokerage industry.

The better firms don't provide scripts to their brokers. Douglas received in-depth sales training three times in his life, and two of those times were from two of the better firms in the business of selling: Procter & Gamble (P&G) and Merrill Lynch. Neither firm ever gave him a preprinted sales script to use with his prospects or customers. P&G taught Douglas the importance of understanding the needs of his prospects and customers, which dispensed with the need for any sales script. Merrill provided Douglas suggestive phrases on opening new accounts and some memorable one-liners to sell particular products, but no sales scripts. Douglas's personal experience was a good one, but far too many who enter the brokerage industry don't get the understanding-the-needs-of-the-customers training first. These are the brokers who end up being pure sales brokers and are the ones you have to watch out for.

Can you imagine your doctor having his diagnosis for your illness on a preprinted form? Preprinted sales scripts have no place in the brokerage industry. Though the regulators don't ban them or even discourage them, they have been critical of them on many occasions. The reasons are many, but first let's address where sales scripts are most often used.

There is the hard sell and the soft sell. The soft sale entails brokers just trying to get a person to open an account by making a deposit and then trying to convince the person to make an investment or implement an investment program. On the other hand, the hard sell refers to brokers calling a prospect with one objective: to make a trade.

The soft sell might entail the use of a sales script on how to open accounts. You may wonder how sales scripts to open an account can do any harm when there can't be anything unsuitable about the mere opening of an account. Opening-account sales scripts can do damage, however, if the script misleads the prospect about the credentials or past successes of the brokerage firm or the broker. Some opening-account scripts concentrate too much on the broker's selling effort and not enough on the broker gathering the required information from the prospect.

The hard-sell sales script is much more egregious. Examples abound of the NASD and the SEC coming down on firms for using scripts. We have seen sales scripts authored by large, well-known firms that would make even a used car salesman blush.

A classic example is Hibbard Brown.[4] In a November 9, 1999, decision, NASD detailed the evidence introduced in a proceeding brought before the District Business Conduct Committee that Hibbard's stockbrokers were trained in aggressive, high-pressure telemarketing sales techniques, which included a three-call system.[5] After placing initial calls to prospective customers, Hibbard brokers would follow up by making a second series of calls (also known as "touch base" or "sizzle" calls) to interested prospects. Hibbard furnished its brokers with aggressive scripts to assist them in making these calls. During this second call, the brokers would tout an unspecified company with allegedly exciting corporate developments.

The third series of sales calls took place during the week following a firmwide telephonic sales conference call conducted from New York by Hibbard's senior management.[6] Although other products were discussed, the focus of the conference calls was the Hibbard house stocks for the month, generally low-priced, speculative, over-the-counter stocks of developmental or untested companies.

The notice stated: "On the morning of the conference call, the brokers were given an internal summary description that had been prepared by Hibbard's research director about the Hibbard house stock being discussed. The internal summaries contained bullet points for the brokers to use in closing sales with customers. The summaries contained only positive information about the stocks and omitted material negative information."[7]

In addition to the internal summaries, the brokers were also given scripts to use for closing sales during "sell week." The notice stated: "The sales scripts contained highly aggressive purchase recommendations, baseless price predictions, and material misrepresentations and omissions about the Hibbard house stocks. They contained no negative information about the stocks, no discussion of risk factors, and little or no financial information about the companies whose stock was being touted by the Hibbard brokers. The Hibbard brokers were also given generic scripts that contained standard responses to common customer objections."[8]

Olde Discount Corporation (Olde) mastered the art of dealing with common objections raised by reluctant customers. On September 10, 1998, the SEC sanctioned Olde for, among other things, sales practice violations; the following information was disclosed in that publicly available document. During the period in question that occurred from the fall of 1992 through at least August 1995, Olde distributed to new stockbrokers scripts of suggested responses to these objections:

- Customer objection: "I have no money."
- Broker script: "Let me explain how margin can work."

- Customer objection: "I never heard of the company."
- Broker script: "The company makes money, is a market leader, and the stock is going higher."

- Customer objection: "I have to check with my wife."
- Broker script: "What if she says 'NO'?—I'm telling you this idea because I'm an expert. I'm not the final authority, but I make a living doing this. I hope the person you check with cares as much about your financial success as I do."

- Customer objection: "I don't take recommendations."
- Broker script: "I spend 60 to 80 hours a week analyzing and researching investments. We are highly qualified to give recommendations."

- Customer objection: "I'll watch it."

- Broker script: "You'll only watch it go up. Stop watching and buy the stock; it is going higher" or "I've been watching this stock for two years. This is the time to buy 1,000 shares."

Given the high turnover at Olde during the relevant period, the majority of its brokers had not been in the securities industry for two years, much less followed a particular stock for two years. And former Olde employees testified that, in their experience, the only analyzing brokers did was reading Olde's research reports to extract "bullets" for their sales pitches.

The SEC found that from the fall of 1992 through at least August 1995, Olde had taught its stockbrokers a technique known among the firm brokers as "three bullets and a close." The technique required brokers to pick out three positive facts from Olde's special venture research reports and to "create a sense of urgency" by delivering those facts to the customer in rapid succession, followed immediately by a statement designed to prompt the customer to make a decision from a script of closings the firm handed out in training. If the customer did not agree to buy after the first three bullets and a close, the broker was required to pitch three more bullets and another close and to repeat the pattern until the customer bought.[9]

Nothing about sales scripts smells right. They are extremely problematic for the following reasons:

- They tend to be written by people whose job it is to elevate sales.
- They typically contain only positive information, and many people don't think to ask about the negatives or downsides of the investment.
- They tend to limit the free flow of information.
- They assume that all investors are alike, and consequently investors agree to buy investments that are not suitable for themselves.
- They tend to contain too much hype and inflammatory language, which may incite people to take actions that aren't in their best interest.

When scripts come from management, brokers rarely question their use. Printed scripts tend to get passed around, which legitimizes and promulgates their use. However, a preprinted sales script is no more a violation than if brokers speak the same words without a script. So claims of inappropriate selling techniques are often met with denials by brokers and firms with a resultant swearing match between the two. A script is written proof of a violation.

NASD rules require that scripts be approved, filed, and maintained by a firm as "sales literature." The files are then subject to "a routine spot-check procedure" by the regulators. If material is found to be misleading or unsuitable for the investing public, there is recourse for investors and considerable exposure for the firm—that is, if the firm properly files the offending material.

BROKER BOOK TURNOVER— NOT A BREAKFAST TREAT

The term *turnover* has two meanings in the securities industry and neither has anything to do with a tasty breakfast treat. You will learn about one type of turnover—churning—in Chapter 5, how a broker turns over or churns your investments to generate commissions. The other type of turnover refers to how often a broker turns over his book. The broker's book goes back to the old three-ring binders in which brokers used to keep their customer account documents. Today, computers have all but replaced the physical book. As a broker loses customers and they are replaced, his book of customers changes. Depending on many factors, it is not uncommon for a broker to turn over his customer base every three years, not necessarily intentionally, but customers just move on to other brokerage firms.

Sometimes brokers' customers must meet certain qualifications to stay with the same broker. For example, the SEC found that from fall 1992 through at least August 1995, Olde employed a practice whereby if the customer didn't purchase one of Olde's house stocks or "special venture" stocks within a six-month period, then that customer could be reclassified as a "house account," which meant that he or she could be solicited by any of its brokers and reassigned. In other firms, big-producing stockbrokers may lose customers to other brokers simply because those customers haven't met certain spending guidelines. You may have awakened one morning or will one day to find yourself reassigned to a baby broker, with a song and dance about a better fit. Don't be fooled. You were switched for reasons you may never learn and, if you did, you may well not like them. It's no wonder that so many brokers are forced to continually solicit new accounts. This is an important point because it explains why many brokers remain salespeople and never advance to portfolio or money manager status.

Do you think those millions of dollars of advertising are spent to attract brand-new investors to the firm? Most brokers and firms would prefer not to attract customers who have no experience in stocks and bonds. New investors are usually small investors who require an enormous amount of handholding. Most of the time, brokerage firms and brokers are trying to steal customers from other brokerage firms; customer stealing, of course, is not a prevalent practice among other licensed professionals like doctors, lawyers, and CPAs.

Investors don't change brokers and brokerage firms as often as they do because of advertising but for other reasons. They may realize that their costs are encroaching on their returns. They may be dissatisfied with the service they are receiving from their broker. Or they may have been the victims of unscrupulous behavior. Any one of these reasons can make investors ripe for a switch, so when the next cold call comes, they jump.

Broker book turnover forces brokers to remain salespeople for a large percentage of their career. If brokers are going to turn over their books every three years, then they have to be constantly prospecting and opening new accounts. Everyone loses in this vicious cycle. Many brokers have little loyalty to their firm, and firms return the favor. As for customers, if brokers spent more time learning to be portfolio managers and servicing customers instead of prospecting, selling products, and worrying about commissions, the massive turnover would stop.

BROKER HOPSCOTCH— ALL THE WAY TO THE BANK

In our businesses, we review the work histories of hundreds and hundreds of brokers. It is not unusual to see brokers hopscotching from one firm to another—sometimes working at as many as 10 to 12 firms within a ten-year period for less-than-appropriate reasons. Brokers who switch brokerage firms may hop, skip, and jump to the bank with huge up-front bonuses. Let's say that a major firm wants to open a new office in Albany, New York. It may send a few headhunters there to scout the competition and offer attractive incentives to brokers for leaving their current firm to work for it. The perks usually include a nicer office, a fancy title, a private sales assistant, a certain amount of expense money, and the most important of all: the up-front bonus and accelerated payout. Many brokerage firms, including the major ones, pay up-front bonuses to new-hire brokers.

The up-front bonus usually consists of the broker's last 12 months of gross commissions at his old firm or a significant percentage of it. Sometimes up-front bonuses can be so large that even the brokers at the firm paying the bonuses are critical: "It's the craziest thing," says a Prudential rep on the West Coast. "They'll pay 150 percent of gross [in an up-front bonus], and they won't spend a dime to retain."[10] These bonuses can be significant, such as the $750,000 a broker received in a case in which Douglas was the expert witness. Think of what this means. Brokers considering changing employers have huge incentives to trade, trade, trade in order to run up their commissions and thus the potential bonus from the new firm. The up-front bonus comes in the form of a several-year loan from the firm to the broker, who earns the bonus after the fact by either staying at the firm a minimum number of years or producing a certain level of commissions. As long as the terms of the agreement are met, the broker never pays back the loan.

If you think paying huge bonuses to attract brokers is questionable, another practice may be equally so. With the recent merging of brokerage firms, it is common practice for the firms to offer hefty pay packages to retain not only the stockbrokers but other employees, such as analysts and traders. These retention packages often rival those incredible multiyear salary packages you read about for professional athletes. One 40-member team got a package of about $300 million over three years to stay at its firm.[11]

In addition to an up-front bonus, a broker may also receive an accelerated payout in commissions for a 3-month to 12-month period. Let's say a broker at a major wire house customarily receives 30 to 40 percent of the gross commission. The accelerated payout could be from 50 to 70 percent of the gross commission.

While Douglas was working at Merrill Lynch in the early 1980s, the headhunters started to call. Sensing the difficulty in prospecting in a city with seven Merrill offices, he first interviewed with Prudential that, at the time, was opening a brand new office in the area. The push was on; Prudential offered the biggest corner office, numerous perks, and flew Douglas to New York to meet personally with George Ball, the chief executive officer of Prudential. And—you guessed it—Douglas was offered $100,000 in cash. He had been in business just over two years and was at a time in his life when he really could have used that cash.

But there was something that just didn't seem right about Prudential and its offer. Douglas questioned whether $100,000 was too much money. Also, Merrill had just let go two brokers who Douglas didn't admire and they went to work for this Prudential office. The manager of the Prudential office seemed too green to Douglas, so Douglas elected to go to Bear Stearns, a firm that offered no cash and little in the way of perks. For years, he wished he had that $100,000, but then things started to unravel at Prudential because of the limited partnership debacle. Douglas realized he had made the right decision. Brokers are enticed many times to move to the wrong firms for the wrong reasons.

Why should investors be concerned about the up-front loans/bonuses and accelerated payouts that brokers routinely receive? Your broker may be trying to generate excessive commissions in anticipation of a switch in firms to increase her bonus. Or she may seek to generate excessive commissions after moving to a new firm because, for a limited number of months, she will make double her normal commission payout. If you have had brokerage accounts for years, you probably have experienced that exuberant phone call from your broker in which she informs you that she is changing firms for *your* benefit. She tells you all of the reasons the current firm is not adequate to fulfill your needs and how the new firm will have much better information and better fills, among other things. Of course, she won't mention her bonus or accelerated payout.

The reality is that there is probably not much of a benefit for you in the move, firm-wise, assuming the broker is moving within the same tier of firms. For example, not a great deal of difference exists between Merrill Lynch, Morgan Stanley, PaineWebber, or Smith Barney in terms of products, information, opinions, or order execution.

Before you decide whether to move with your broker when she hopscotches to another firm, let's consider other reasons why she could be making the move. She may not get along with current management and may have some compliance or supervisory problems with her current firm. None of these are positives from your perspective.

You should also know what happens if you decide to move with your broker. At many firms, the manager divides the accounts of the departing broker among the remaining brokers that he favors, who may be offered a several-month accelerated payout on those accounts they are able to keep. Are you starting to get the feeling that something is terribly wrong with this scenario? One firm pays a broker accelerated commissions on your account if you move, and the other firm offers accelerated commissions on your account if you stay. And you thought all that extra trading in your account was just your broker's attempt to make more money for you! Wrong.

So if your broker announces plans to depart her current employer, should you stay or should you leave? Consider it an excellent opportunity to ask a lot of questions, some of which you probably should have asked much earlier. Totally reevaluate your situation. People get divorced at the tip of a hat, but for some reason they stay with a broker they should have never been with while the broker jumps from firm to firm. This book will give you the ammunition you need to ask the right questions for determining what is best for you. Here is a list of questions you should explore with your broker if your broker is changing firms:

- Did your broker voluntarily resign, was she permitted to resign, or was she terminated?
- What was wrong with the current firm?
- What specifically is better at the new firm?
- What at the new firm will lower your costs?
- What products and/or services are better at the new firm?
- What are the drawbacks for you as a result of the switch?
- Is your broker getting a signing bonus that is based, in part, on gross commissions for a certain period of time? As a predicate to this question, first ask when your broker began thinking about making a move. You want an honest answer to this question before asking about a signing bonus.

- Will your broker be getting an accelerated payout at the new firm?
- What will be your broker's new payout on commissions compared with the payout at the old firm?
- How much more or better staffing will the new firm provide your broker?
- Are the monthly and yearly reports you receive better at the new firm?
- What other benefits are there for you as a result of a move?

Your broker and her old firm are required to report on what's called a U-5 form whether the broker's termination was voluntary, permitted, or requested. Although the U-5 form is not public, it must be filed with the NASD, so your broker's answer to the first question in the list above should not be willy-nilly. If your broker replies that she will receive a bonus based, in part, on gross commissions, examine your portfolio for disproportionate trading volume from the point when she began thinking about the move. It would be during this time that the incentive to trade would be greatest. For every buy and every sell in your account, your broker credited herself a higher gross commission figure. If within this time, you find a distinct increase in activity in your account, you can rightly question whether your broker was acting in her best interest or yours by recommending those trades.

If you elect to move with your broker to a new firm and you learn that your broker will receive an accelerated payout for a certain period, be wary of heavy trading during that period. If you have any doubts about the answers you receive, you can always ask the same set of questions to your broker's manager or supervisor. Be dutiful in making notes of the answers you receive. For example, if your broker says you will pay lower commissions at the new firm, and you make the move but subsequently discover that you are not paying lower commissions, you have a reference point to raise with your broker.

Now you have an arsenal of information about the world of stockbrokers—all of the components of the salesperson mentality that the brokerage firms try to keep secret from investors. You can see why. Brokerage firms will cringe when they learn about the knowledge imparted in this chapter. They don't want investors to know the behind-the-scenes reality about broker qualifications, broker ranking, broker titles, broker training, cold calling, sales scripts, broker book turnover, and brokers jumping from firm to firm. This knowledge, they will claim, will only serve to make investors warier of brokers' personal motivations and representations. And that is precisely the point of this chapter.

CHAPTER 4

Suitability

The Number One Abuse
in the Industry

$\mathbf{J}$ust like the Ten Commandments, rules are usually written to curb activity already taking place. The rules that govern the brokerage industry are no different; they were written, though sometimes not quite so artfully, to combat specific problems. The abuses outlined in this chapter and the next are nothing new. Brokers have been committing these violations for many, many years. Why would any broker knowingly violate a rule or regulation? You've learned by now that the answer is commissions. Just like doctors who sometimes succumb to the lure of bigger dollars when they recommend an operation that may not be necessary, it's simple math.

We discuss in Chapters 4 and 5 how brokers and brokerage firms perpetrate the number one abuse in the industry, as well as a host of others, and how they get away with it. We explain the rules and then show you how brokers work around them to your detriment. We expose some of the standard defenses brokerage firms use in responding to claims about these abuses. And finally we describe how you can take preventative measures and monitor your account so that you can detect, and thereby prevent, these abuses from occurring in your account.

We do not attempt to outline every single rule that may govern these abuses. As you have learned, many of the multitude of rules may come into play from one specific act. Plenty of books have been written on the subject. Better yet, you can obtain many of the rules yourself by contacting the NASD and the NYSE and asking for them or by logging on to their respective Web sites (<www.nasdr.com> and <www.nyse.com>).

After reading Chapters 4 and 5, you will be in an excellent position to supervise and monitor your brokerage accounts. Be sure to put this newly acquired knowledge to use by reviewing your monthly statements and confirmations and conversing with your broker on a regular basis.

Suitability is a term that is not limited to the brokerage industry. One dictionary defines the word *suitable* as "fitting, appropriate, and agreeable." Just as a doctor must prescribe medicine tailored to a patient's sickness, so a broker must make suggestions to an investor that are appropriate based on the investor's needs and desires. Suitability is a somewhat catchall term because, arguably, every shade of improper activity is, by definition, not suitable for an investor.

The classic unsuitable investment is made when a broker buys or recommends a risky, speculative security for a customer who can not afford to take undue risks with his or her money. However, losses in and of themselves are not always indicative of wrongful conduct. Naturally, though, it is the losses that cause investors to note the problem and complain. When Douglas was a broker, he used to think that to be a successful broker you had to be part duck. Customers' concerns about losing money would need to just roll off your back like water on a duck. Douglas was always amazed at how unemotional his fellow brokers were when their clients lost large sums of money, a situation that caused Douglas many a sleepless night.

When an investor claims that the broker violated "the suitability rule," the industry has a specific interpretation of a specific rule. The NASD and the NYSE each articulates its suitability rule in its respective rule book. This is the NASD rule:

> *Recommendations to Customers, NASD Rule 2310*
> In recommending to a customer the purchase, sale or exchange of any security, a member shall have reasonable grounds for believing that the recommendation is suitable for such customer upon the basis of the facts, if any, disclosed by such customer as to his other security holdings and as to his financial situation and needs.

Because every brokerage firm is a member of the NASD, Rule 2310 applies to every firm and every broker working within that firm. But a broker needs facts to formulate reasonable grounds, and the rule goes on to provide what facts must be acquired from the customer:

> Prior to the execution of a transaction recommended to a non-institutional customer, other than transactions with customers where investments are limited to money market mutual funds, a member shall make reasonable efforts to obtain information concerning:
> 1. the customer's financial status;
> 2. the customer's tax status;
> 3. the customer's investment objectives; and
> 4. such other information used or considered to be reasonable by such member or registered representative in making recommendations to the customer.

Now you may be thinking to yourself, Wait a minute, I have gotten phone calls from brokers who immediately began trying to pitch me a stock, and those brokers didn't ask me any of the above questions. They violated the suitability rule. The sad fact is that for too many brokers, the suitability test is the ability to pay.

Other exchanges have similar language, but instead of reasonable grounds, they call for due diligence, and instead of itemizing the data that must be acquired, they require the gathering of essential facts, a broad, sweeping phrase.

The NYSE rule is Rule 405, also known as the "Know Your Customer" rule. It states:

> Use due diligence to learn the essential facts relative to every customer, every order, every cash or margin account accepted or carried by such organization and every person holding power of attorney over any account accepted or carried by such organization.

The NYSE rule requires the gathering of facts not only about the customer, but also about the order, that is, the investment itself. See Chapter 8 for a discussion of whether the NASD and the NYSE rules apply to online brokerage firms where the traditional broker is removed.

THE ABCs OF SUITABILITY ANALYSIS

The suitability determination is supposed to be an A, B, and C process, so let's go through these three steps in detail.

Step A is the broker's assessment of her customer's investment objectives based not only on what the customer says they are, but also on an assimilation of all the information culled by the broker in the initial question and answer session. When brokers are sizing up a client for suitability, they must take into account all that is known about the customer and specifically how the customer responds to questions about investment experience, level of knowledge, and understanding of investments; age, job stability, and income; dependents; spending needs; retirement goals; other investments; ability to deal with risks or losses; and education level, among other items. The new account form provides a place for brokers to record some of this information about each customer (see Chapter 7 for a more detailed discussion of what appears on the forms). Only after this detailed question and answer session is complete can the broker or advisor properly evaluate your situation. The broker should be able to make some initial conclusions about your investment objectives based on this data-gathering session alone.

The second part of the interview is determining how you articulate your investment goals. Brokers should be mindful that customers often don't know how to articulate their goals. Tracy has had many conservative clients who, when asked about their investment objectives, responded, "To make money!" Tracy's clients, like many individuals, didn't appreciate that in the industry making money means taking risks that might cause a loss of capital. In the minds of many investors, and understandably so, making money means *keeping* what you have and making it grow. It is your broker's responsibility to siphon through any misunderstandings based on terminology and come up with what you truly want to accomplish with your money. Brokers are not allowed to make assumptions.

Another common problem in this area is the lack of incentive brokers have to truly discern just how much customers want their money to grow. Most new account forms have as a choice for invest-ment objective the word *growth*. It has always amazed us that this objective is often not further defined, such as conservative growth, moderate growth, or aggressive growth. Tracy had a case against a major firm involving a couple's retirement money that had been placed in high-risk, speculative investments, leaving the account decimated. Growth was the investment objective recorded on the new account form. The firm's compliance manager attempted to de-fend the trading activity by claiming that the investments fit the ob-jective of growth—they just happened to be on the more speculative, aggressive side of growth. This testimony was apparently so alarm-ing to one of the arbitrators that the arbitrator finally queried the manager, "Mr. Doe, would you have bought these investments for your mother?" Even more incredible was the manager's stoic, emotionless response: "Yes, I would have." The arbitration panel found against the firm in that case and awarded the claimants their damages.

Your question may be, Why do brokers and advisors try to change or not follow their customers' investment goals? The simple reason is that the more conservative an investor's goals, the fewer commissions a broker will make. Conservative investments and conservative investment strategies tend to generate the least amount of commissions. So unscrupulous brokers take various steps to push an investor's goals into the more aggressive range. This point is il-lustrated in Chapter 2, where the greed and risk pyramids show that the greater the risks in the investment, the higher the commissions.

The customers' stated investment objectives should rule the day when the customers have a basic understanding of the securi-ties markets and a good grasp of their own financial situation. A com-mon scenario is a very wealthy person stating conservative goals, but the broker viewing the customer's wealth as a license to trade aggressively. The broker reasons that the customer can afford it, and the broker will make more money by doing it.

Many wealthy people don't want to take risks with their money. They don't need to. Or they may divide up their money and allow some brokerage accounts to take a certain amount of risk and other accounts minimal risk. Then Governor George W. Bush invested more than $6 million of his own assets in Treasury bills. So it is with many wealthy individuals. In the 1980s, it was rumored that Ross Perot kept a large portion of his capital in U.S. Treasury bills and bonds; at the time, Perot was one of the richest men in America. Being that wealthy, he could take lots of risks and lose millions of dollars, but it wouldn't dent his net worth or lifestyle. But Perot chose not to take those risks. His investment goals for the money he placed in Treasuries were for conservation and safety of principal. So what if some broker told Perot that he had some Ginnie Mae bonds that were just as safe as the Treasuries and convinced Perot to invest in them; and subsequently Perot lost millions of dollars on those bonds. Could he sue and claim a violation of the suitability rule? You bet.

Don't be dissuaded from feeling you've been wronged just because you're wealthy. Douglas was the expert witness for one of the wealthiest families in the world, and the family recovered unprecedented millions of dollars for the wrongdoing done to it. And certainly don't be dissuaded by the brokerage firm's response to your complaint letter that may contain some of the defenses pointed out in the next section.

What about customers who have a limited net worth and income but insist on a speculative trading strategy, like options, with a significant percentage of their funds? We said that the customer's investment objective was paramount, but should it be relied on to the exclusion of other red flags in an account, like losses that are disproportionate to stated net worth and income? A number of arbitration panels have said no in this situation because the suitability obligation is ongoing, and, in essence, the brokerage firm has an obligation to protect customers from themselves. Although it may be acceptable for an individual to plop his or her entire net worth on black at the roulette table in a Las Vegas casino, that same individual should not be permitted to commit financial suicide while in the custody, if you will, of a licensed broker and brokerage firm. In the mid-1990s, Smith Barney ran an ad that said, "Sometimes, no is the most positive advice we can give." Though many brokers may never recommend an unsuitable investment, the problem is that far too many brokers will not turn down an unsolicited order from their clients that they know is unsuitable.

The industry has created a horrible double standard in the way that it responds to these types of claims. If customers with few assets and little experience want to take certain risks that are out of line with their finances, firms will claim the investments were suitable because the customers wanted to take the risks. As in the case described earlier, firms attempt to ignore the financial data evidencing that the customer could not afford to take such risks. On the flip side, if customers say they don't want to take any risks, but it turns out they are rich, sophisticated investors, brokerage firms will ignore the customers' stated investment objectives and will instead focus solely on the financial data and claim that the customers could afford to take the risks. This is referred to as the "rich man defense."

The industry also tries to pull a sneaky little trick when it comes to trades initiated by customers (unsolicited trades) versus solicited trades (when it's the broker's idea). You might have noticed that the NASD rule uses the phrase "in recommending to a customer. . . ." Well, some firms argue that when customers call up with an investment idea, there is no suitability obligation under NASD rules because the broker did not recommend it. Our response is twofold. First, the NYSE rule does not use the term *recommending,* and it would make no sense for firms governed by the NYSE rules to comply with such a vastly different standard in such a basic area. Second, the NASD is already on record stating that firms should give "a careful review of the appropriateness of transactions in low-priced, speculative securities, *whether solicited or unsolicited*"[1] (emphasis added). This issue is even hotter now than ever because of the advent of online trading, where almost all of the trading is directed and controlled by investors (see Chapter 8).

Step B is the broker's and firm's obligation to know the investment being recommended. Brokers are required under the rules cited above to know the product. The term *due diligence* is used to define the extent of effort brokers and their firm must employ to satisfy this prong of suitability. Common sense dictates that brokers must fully understand all of the essential and important facts regarding the investment they are recommending, including the risks, the potential return, the tax ramifications, the costs, and so on. You would expect that in the same way you expect your doctor to understand the medicines she is prescribing, and your CPA to understand recent changes in tax law.

Let's say that a broker sells you stock in a company that tanks, and later he tells you that he didn't know the company was about to file for bankruptcy when he sold you the stock. He would be at fault if the mere reading of the company's 10-K or other available information on the company had alerted him to the potential of a bankruptcy. You are not at fault for not discovering this same publicly available information. It's the broker's obligation to do the due diligence, not yours. Now if you did, in fact, know about the potential bankruptcy and went ahead and agreed to the investment anyway, you would have no right to complain that your broker didn't tell you about it.

There is an ongoing problem relating to brokers knowing their investments. First, many brokerage firms never give brokers the full set of facts on each investment. We don't know which is worse: firms that never do their proper due diligence on a particular investment or firms that do but don't pass on to the brokers all they have learned. In the 1980s, when brokerage firms were pushing the sale of limited partnerships, firms were famous for providing their brokers with scripts about the limited partnerships that touted only the positives and none of the negatives. If brokers veered from the scripts, they were seen as renegades and nonloyal employees, who were sometimes terminated or otherwise penalized. In those situations, and in many others described in this book, it's not the broker's fault but the firm's fault for creating an environment fraught with the potential for wrongdoing.

Today, a more subtle form of pressure is exerted on brokers in the form of the analyst report. Brokers are taught to parrot the firm analyst's opinion about a stock and to not look beyond it. If the analyst says, "Buy," the broker says, "Buy." As you learned in Chapter 2, the investment banking department of brokerage firms is a profit center with a tremendous incentive for its analysts to skip over negatives to get a stock sold. And as we pointed out in Chapter 2, analysts are free to cater to the hand that feeds them, as the securities rules and regulations that govern brokers don't govern analysts.

This feeding of information by brokerage firms to brokers gives rise to the question of whether brokers can rely solely on the information their firms tell them about a particular investment or whether they are under a duty to conduct their own due diligence? It is our firm belief that brokers, as separately licensed individuals, are required to fulfill a personal obligation of due diligence. Both brokerage firms and brokers are licensed, so a dual duty pertains to suitability. Brokers are required to make sure all their recommendations are suitable, and the firms are required to make sure that all investments recommended by their brokers are suitable. Neither group can shift the duty to the other.

Step C, the last part of the process, is when a broker determines if the investment the broker got to know in Step B is compatible with the investment objectives of the customer he got to know in Step A. If compatibility is absent, the broker should not even mention the investment to the customer.

COMMON BROKERAGE FIRM DEFENSES

You may hear some of the varied defenses that brokerage firms use to deny suitability claims if you call your broker or manager to complain or if you write a complaint letter. You are assured of seeing these defenses if you file an arbitration claim. We hope we can alter your perspective on the viability of these defenses.

One of our favorite defenses used by the brokerage industry is the "sophisticated investor defense," which is seen when a customer complains about almost any securities abuse. The first words you will hear or see from the brokerage firms are, "You are a sophisticated investor" and words to the effect that you should have known better. The term *sophisticated* derives from the SEC regulations pertaining to Regulation (Reg) D offerings. Certain investments are exempt from SEC registration when they meet specific criteria. One of the criteria is that the investor to whom the prospective investment will be shown must have a level of income and/or net worth beyond certain thresholds. If the potential investor exceeds those monetary thresholds, the individual is referred to as a sophisticated investor.

The brokerage industry regularly and indiscriminately uses this phrase to defend against almost every claim of wrongdoing. Its premise is that if an investor is sophisticated, the brokerage firm can do no wrong. Together, we have seen just about every type of individual that you can think of being called a sophisticated investor—an elevator operator, a janitor, a college student, and a housewife. Our favorite was a young female truck driver with about a sixth-grade education. The industry also tries to trick the investing public by making the claim of sophistication about individuals who may very well be sophisticated in their business but not in investments. We have represented MBAs who didn't have a clue about the investment markets. Douglas recently completed the NASD's Wharton School of Business course for Certified Regulatory and Compliance Professionals (CRCPs). At one of the classes, he heard one of the other attendees opine that the industry rules are written to protect the average investor and that those truly ignorant, inexperienced, naïve, and gullible investors may not be protected by securities regulations. We vehemently disagree. The ignorant people are the ones who need the most protection. Our U.S. Supreme Court put it well: "The [Exchange Act] does not speak in terms of 'sophisticated' as opposed to 'unsophisticated' people dealing in securities. The rules when the giants play are the same as when the pygmies enter the market."[2] Today, the market is saturated with pygmies.

Another classic defense used by brokerage firms when you complain that an investment is unsuitable is the "you-took-risks-elsewhere" defense. If you end up in an arbitration hearing or court hearing against a brokerage firm, one thing you can count on is that the firm will want to go through every investment you ever made in your entire life, regardless of how petty. The firm is trying to find some event, no matter how insignificant or brief, how unrelated, or how long ago, where you took risks with your money. The firm then argues that your taking risks elsewhere proves you are a risk taker and wanted to take risk in your account at the firm. Under this theory, it would be impossible for someone to have different goals for different monies or to change investment goals over time.

We often accuse brokerage firms of playing a game of hindsight and going on a fishing expedition with their inquiries. The only relevant question is whether an investment was suitable for the customer at the time of the investment. Is it really fair or relevant to dig into the customer's Las Vegas casino loss at the crap table one year before the investment when it has nothing to do with the investment at issue and the broker was not aware of it when he made the recommendation? We think not.

We mentioned earlier the rich man defense. For some reason, the industry views extremely wealthy individuals as granting it a license to conduct speculative activity in their accounts. Perhaps the industry reasons that if individuals are rich, they can afford to take large or above-average risks. This is often not the case. Douglas is involved in a securities arbitration wherein his client lost over $54 million at the hands of a brokerage firm, an American dream story. Douglas's client didn't go to college but started a small business that grew and grew. Because of the client's limited education and business acumen, the client hired professionals to help him grow the business to a multi-million-dollar operation. Through a number of mergers and acquisitions, the client acquired $54 million. As is too often the case, the vultures descended, calling the client and offering to help him manage his newfound wealth. The client had far exceeded his wildest dreams of wealth. His lifestyle was such that he would have a hard time spending the interest on the interest. He didn't need or want to take any risk.

But the broker thought differently and embarked on an incredibly speculative option-trading strategy that, with the downturn in the market in 2000, essentially wiped out the account. The client's American dream had suddenly become the American nightmare. The brokerage firm's rich man defense seems hollow. Inducing someone into losing the majority of his life savings or earnings is more than unsuitable; it is unconscionable. The fact that the loss was $54 million and not perhaps someone else's $200,000 does not change the egregiousness of the wrongdoing.

THE SOLICITED VERSUS THE UNSOLICITED TRICK

What would be a brokerage firm's strongest defense to a claim of suitability that you can imagine? It would be as follows: "Those trades were not your broker's idea; they were your idea." This brings us to the last trick or defense we must make you aware of: manipulating the determination of whose idea the investment was. After a broker gets her customer to agree to a certain investment, be it a buy or a sell, the broker fills out information about that trade on what is called an order ticket. You never see order tickets, as they are internal brokerage documents and nowadays are often memorialized on computers. You see something similar to them several days after your trade when you receive a confirmation of the trade. However, one piece of information that should be on every order ticket and every confirmation is whose idea the trade was: the broker's or the customer's. In securities vernacular, the terms *solicited* and *unsolicited* refer to whose idea the trade was.

It's easy to remember these terms if you always think of them from the stockbroker's perspective, solicited by the broker versus unsolicited by the broker. Brokers are required to designate if a trade is unsolicited at the time of an order ticket's entry. If a trade is solicited, sometimes no marking is required. Therefore, if your confirmation shows it was neither solicited nor unsolicited, it is presumed to be a solicited trade (except with some online brokerage firms).

What you need to watch out for is the word *Unsolicited* on your confirmation. That word should be a red flag to you only if that investment idea was your broker's, not yours. One major wire house does a good job of spelling out the difference between a solicited and an unsolicited trade:

> Whenever an account executive recommends a transaction to a customer and the customer follows that suggestion, the resulting order is considered to be solicited, provided that the time that has elapsed between the suggestion and the actual order is not unreasonable and there has been no material change in the recommended security. . . . An order resulting from the mailing of any research report or written communication concerning a specific security is also considered solicited.

Tracy and Douglas together are working on a case wherein the broker misled their client on what a solicited order was. Our client maintains that the broker told him that unsolicited meant "not enticed by a prospectus." Our client sustained a loss of $10 million in options trading that the broker says was completely our client's idea. Our client says it was all the broker's idea. Somebody is lying.

When a broker marks an order ticket or a series of order tickets on losing trades as unsolicited, he may say such things as, "I told the customer not to trade so much, but she insisted" and "I would never have recommended that stock to the customer." A broker's claim that the trade was the client's idea and not the broker's also helps defend against fraud claims and unauthorized trading claims. We have heard it in hundreds of hearings, read it in hundreds of answers to claims, and seen it written in numerous investigations. The problem is it's your word against your broker's, and with mismarked order tickets/confirmations, the scale is tipped slightly in favor of the brokerage industry.

Don't let that deter you, though. Arizona, as well as some other states, specifically prohibits "[e]ngaging in a pattern of marking order tickets as unsolicited when the dealer or salesman directly or indirectly recommended the transaction or introduced the customer to the security."[3] Some firms make the existence of a series of trades marked unsolicited a red flag. Think about it: why would someone who wants to make his own investment decisions sign on with a full-service, full-commission brokerage?

Many investors have no appreciation of the difference between solicited and unsolicited. It's certainly not something that brokerage firms advise their customers about when they open an account. It's surprising to hear the number of definitions given by brokers and experts of just what constitutes a solicited versus an unsolicited trade. Even most compliance manuals are devoid of explanations of the difference. The securities industry can only look inward for blame.

Fortunately, there exist other facts that may tip the scales toward the wronged investor. One investor complained that his account had been wiped out because the broker recommended that he put all of his money in one stock. The brokerage firm and the broker responded with the defense that this particular trade had been unsolicited by the broker. Obviously, someone was lying. Douglas, who worked as the expert for the investor on the case, demanded the complete commission run for the broker. A broker's commission run shows all of the trades the broker makes in all of the broker's clients' accounts. The brokerage firm fought hard to avoid producing the document. Finally the fax came. Low and behold, it showed that almost every one of the broker's clients had this same supposedly unsolicited stock in their accounts. Will the broker dare testify that, coincidentally, all of his other clients called in and wanted to buy that same stock that day? Hardly. The brokerage firm called and offered to settle at the same time it was faxing the document.

The sad moral of these stories is that brokerage firms will go to great lengths to attempt to cover up or hide the fraud and unsuitable recommendations of their stockbrokers. The firms' potential benefit is a double whammy. First, they may not have to pay out any money to settle a customer's claim, and second, they ensure the perpetuation of a broker very skilled at bringing in those coveted commissions and margin interest.

If this whole issue of solicited versus unsolicited is new to you, then it's time to do a little financial housekeeping. Flip through all of your confirmations to see if you find the word "Unsolicited" on any transactions. Make sure that the word appears only on trades that, in fact, were your idea and not brought to you by the broker. If you find any mismarked trades, you should take action, even if you have closed that account and no longer do business with the broker. In that case, write a letter to the brokerage firm management, even if the broker has since left, advising it of the specific trades that were mismarked and telling them what your review has disclosed. It will send a message that the firm's supervisors were not doing their job. Also, copy the letter to the firm where the broker is now employed to alert it that it had better watch the broker's marking of order tickets. State in the letter that you just read this book and received an education, which is what prompted you to go back and look at your confirmations. If many individuals across the country took these steps, it would go a long way toward preventing the misconduct of stockbrokers for future investors. You might be one of them.

If you discover mismarked confirmations in your current account, you can pursue several courses of action. You can call and ask your broker why the trade was marked unsolicited when it was his idea. If your broker says, "Oh, that was a mistake," then say, "Fine, please send me a revised confirmation or a letter confirming that the trade was mismarked." Tell your broker to make sure that the firm management approves the letter. This is important because otherwise you may have a broker who is trying to hide his mistakes and misdeeds from management. Again, a supervisor must approve any correspondence from your broker to you. If your broker tries to give you a different explanation of unsolicited, confirm it in writing—either ask him to write a letter or, better yet, write the letter to your broker yourself: "Dear Ms. Smith . . . This will confirm that on [today's date] you told me that the reason XYZ Corporation was marked unsolicited was because unsolicited meant that I had previously heard of the company." Or whatever other crazy definition you might have been given. That letter should spark an immediate investigation into the broker's conduct and your account. This is a good thing for you.

At some point during this analysis, you may have to make some judgment calls about whether your broker and her firm are working in your best interest. It may be based on the way your broker responds to your questions about why trades are mismarked or it may be based on the number of trades that are mismarked. If, based on your review of the confirmations, you are alarmed at how many of the trades have been mismarked, then in addition to documenting the problem and sending a letter to the firm, you need to get a new broker (see Chapter 13). You also need to switch brokers if the firm doesn't acknowledge that the trades were mismarked or if you are otherwise dissatisfied with the firm's response to the problem.

If you find that a significant percentage of the trades are marked unsolicited when they should not be, you probably have a real problem. If you don't have any significant losses in your account, write the same letter, and after you get the response, move your account and get a new stockbroker and a new firm. If you have significant losses, immediately consult a securities arbitration attorney before writing to the firm.

CHAPTER 5

Tricks of the Trade
What Wall Street *Really* Doesn't Want You to Know

This is one of the longer chapters in the book because, you guessed it, there are sooooo many ways that brokerage firms and stockbrokers can pull the wool over your eyes, so many secrets that Wall Street would just as soon you not know. So sit back, relax, and have a yellow highlighter handy.

FRAUD—THE ROOT OF ALL EVIL

Wouldn't you agree there is enough risk in the marketplace that you don't need to face the risk of fraud and deception by your stockbroker? You may be thinking, Not my stockbroker; she would never do anything to harm me; she goes to my church! Well, as in any industry or profession, there are always degrees of good and bad. The majority of stockbrokers are honest, trustworthy individuals. But with hundreds of thousands of stockbrokers, a lot of them just don't quite make it to that admirable standard. It doesn't mean that your broker is evil, a con artist, or a criminal (although a fair share of those are attracted to the brokerage industry, too). Honesty is measured in an interesting way in this country. Many who tread the line and conduct themselves in the gray area of right and wrong think of themselves as honest, forthright people for several reasons. First, many people go through a comparative analysis in their mind. Those who are 10 to 15 pounds overweight may not be too concerned about their weight because there are many more people who are significantly *more* overweight. Obese people make fat people look . . . well . . . not so fat. So it is that people who conduct themselves in a questionable manner do not question their conduct because there are so many others who do the same. When in Rome . . .

Many of the pressures that prompt stockbrokers to do the wrong thing are brought to bear by the firm, the industry, and, even broader, the system. Brokers simply succumb to the environment into which they are thrust when they join a brokerage firm, just as do all of their coworkers. This is not to say that every brokerage firm is like those depicted in the movie *Boiler Room*. But even the largest, most respectable firms do things that encourage brokers to act against your best interest. Your broker may really be trying to give you good advice and make money for you, but it's more important that *she* make a lot of money than that *you* make a lot of money. As you will see, the path to making a lot of money as a stockbroker can also be the path that harms the investor.

The vast majority of Americans are trusting people. Originally, trust was a concept we all learned to accept as a positive; it was good and virtuous to trust. Yet the realities of human nature have compelled many of us to become less trusting. We no longer leave our doors unlocked or our car keys in the car, as generations before us did. Today, we fear letting our notebook computer out of our sight to go through the x-ray machine at the airport. What signaled the demise of trust in this country? Perhaps it was that memorable line from the movie *Animal House:* "Hey, you f**ked up— you trusted me!" Also, many events of the last ten years involving major political and influential people have done much to lower our country's ethical standards.

We know you think you should be able to trust your stockbroker. We agree. Even the regulators agree. As one court poignantly put it, "Though the law of fraud does not endorse a hear-no-evil, see-no-evil approach, neither does it require that an aggrieved party . . . [proceed] from the outset as if he were dealing with thieves."[1] You should not have to question your broker's motives and his or her every recommendation. You should not have to invest the time or expense to get a second opinion. But those are all "shoulds" and ideals; not reality. Although we don't advocate viewing your broker or brokerage firm as thieves, we do encourage investors to become savvier about their brokerage accounts and the hidden motives of those handling them.

Fraud and suitability claims go hand in hand. You hardly ever see one violation without the other because fraud usually results in unsuitable investments. Unsuitable investments occur when a broker either misrepresents an investment to a customer or fails to tell the customer all of the material facts about the investment. That's fraud. People often think of fraud as a lie, but they don't realize that a lie can take two forms: misrepresentation or omission. Even in law, fraud is defined as not only material misrepresentations—for example, when someone says a car is new although it's used—but also as omissions of material fact—for example, when you buy a new car and later discover it's been in a wreck, which the salesman failed to tell you.

According to Rule 10(b)(5) of the Securities and Exchange Act of 1934, fraud is

> "(1) to employ any device, scheme or artifice to defraud, or
> (2) to make any untrue statement of material fact or to omit to state a material fact necessary in order to make the statements made, in light of the circumstances under which they were made, not misleading, or
> (3) to engage in any act, practice, or course of business which operates or would operate as a fraud or deceit upon any person . . . in connection with the purchase or sale of any security."

The fraud rules of the NASD and the NYSE follow this language closely and each state's securities act contains similar language.

What there is less agreement about are the facts that give rise to fraud. Fraud and suitability cases are almost always he said/she said. For an industry that has such a vast array of rules, the paucity of documentation of the conversations between brokers and customers is incredible. Brokers are not instructed to make notes of conversations, and they don't. Only two documents memorialize the substance of any conversation between a broker and a customer. First is the New Account form, on which the broker will check some boxes and fill in some limited blanks (see Chapter 7). But there's not even a place on the form that asks for other important information. The form is quite limited. Second is the order ticket and subsequent confirmation that purportedly reflect the conversation about each particular transaction in the account. Yet even these documents record only the most basic of information—the security, the amount, the number of shares, and the price.

Think of the complaints, problems, and claims that would be avoided if brokerage firms simply recorded all conversations between their brokers and their clients. Recording would serve a deterrent function; brokers would be less likely to omit material facts, less likely to exaggerate, less likely to misrepresent the investment if they knew they were being recorded. Brokerage firms like Schwab have been recording conversations for years, but until recently, Schwab did not make investment recommendations; the tapes served only to resolve disputes over order errors. Many online firms record conversations, but because most people using an online firm are doing so through their computer on the Internet, those recorded conversations are generally after the fact. Tracy has a case in which her client immediately complained to a major online firm about a problem on a specific day. The firm's response to the request for the recorded conversation? The firm can't find it.

Most brokerage firms do not record conversations; none of the big, old-line firms—Merrill Lynch, Smith Barney, PaineWeber, Prudential—do. Some of the smaller firms are being forced to record conversations because of a new rule we'll discuss later in the chapter. Forcing a brokerage firm to record telephone calls with its customers is a penalty, which means that it's a detriment to the brokerage firm and hence a benefit to customers. Brokerage firms realize that recorded conversations would quickly resolve most customer complaints. Firms also realize that recording all telephone calls could take a sizeable bite out of their two major sources of revenue: commissions and margin interest.

We wish there were special litmus paper that you could hold up to the phone when you suspected a broker was lying to you or not giving you the full picture. We suspect that the color it would turn to signify a problem would be green, the color of money—your broker's, not yours. Barring this yet undiscovered invention, our hope is that you will become the litmus paper. After reading this book, you'll know the questions to ask your broker that will force out the full picture and alert you to potential problems.

When dealing with a stockbroker, it is often more important to notice what your broker *isn't* telling you than what he is. Granted, you will always hear the positive aspects of the investment, but what you will find in many instances is that the broker fails to advise you of any or all of the investment's risks. An example is the broker who pushes his client to use a margin but doesn't fully explain the downside, that is, the negative spread. More common is the stock described by the broker as a solid performer or a sure thing, without any disclosure that the company was formed a year ago and has had a volatile performance.

One of the smartest things to ask when your broker is recommending an investment to you is, "How would you rank this investment on a risk scale of 1 to 10 with 10 the riskiest?" You can get even more specific: "How does the risk compare to a blue chip stock or an aggressive growth mutual fund?" Comparing the investment to other investments you have in your account or with which you are familiar is a very good way to gauge the risk level of the investment. Regardless of what number your broker assigns the investment, follow up with, "List the risks for me." It is very important that you take detailed notes of how your broker responds; and make sure to date the notes and keep them. Better yet, if on the date of your conversation, you type the notes in a document on your computer, save the document with a notation like "06-17-01 conversation with [broker's name] re XYZ stock," and never edit the document, you will have created a virtually indisputable piece of evidence of what the broker said to you on that date. This may come in handy down the line if you later discover that the investment was misrepresented to you or a material risk was omitted.

Be prepared if you suggest to your broker or firm that you were not made aware of all of the facts regarding an investment; you may get a response that makes you feel as though you're the one to blame. Brokerage firms are famous for pointing the finger back at a complaining customer, implying that if you, the customer, weren't so gullible, the misconduct wouldn't have happened. We call this the "you-should-have-caught-me" defense, but don't be deterred by it. Some courts have penned fabulous language covering the defense. In one case, the court wrote, "[D]efendant is in essence saying that 'because your negligence allowed me to defraud you or to continue to defraud you, you should not be allowed to recover from me to the extent that a reasonable person would not have allowed me to defraud him.' Such a defense is patently unfair and unjustifiable as a matter of law."[2] Another court long ago rejected a similar you-should-have-caught-me defense with the following: "We are not inclined to encourage falsehood and dishonesty by protecting one who is guilty of such fraud on the ground that his victim had faith in his word, and for that reason did not pursue inquiries that would have disclosed the falsehood."[3]

What if your stockbroker tells you that some hot initial public offering (IPO) is a sure thing and at the same time hands you a prospectus stating on page five that the investment is "high risk"? You didn't read the prospectus before investing because you flipped through it, and it appeared extremely legalistic, complicated, and over your head. Besides, you are comfortable relying on your broker's description of the investment. You believe that he would tell you if there was something important about the investment you needed to know. Perhaps your broker dismissed the prospectus as simply a required document and not something that you needed to spend much time reviewing.

The reality is that the prospectus generally speaks the full truth about an investment. The risks noted in a prospectus are real, true, potential risks that the investment faces. And when investments fail, it is invariably because one of the risks in the prospectus came to fruition. A prospectus, however, accompanies only new issues (IPOs) or secondary offerings of a new issue, a small percentage of the investments bought each year.

One of the most anti-investor decisions came from New York in 1990, where the court wrote: "Any reasonable investor knows to be somewhat wary of a selling agent's oral representations and to check them against the written materials."[4] Ouch. It hurts to type those words. It's not true. Reasonable investors do not know that they should second-guess their broker. They don't know that they should be wary. Some do, but it's a small percentage. This New York court's decision goes against the grain of the securities rules and regulations, against brokerage firm advertising, and against reality. Brokerage firms often wave this court decision around, arguing that written disclosures trump oral ones, but fortunately they seldom win with that position because it just doesn't smell right. And as Douglas always contends, it's not what some judge says that dictates the conduct of stockbrokers and brokerage firms; it's the securities rules and regulations, state laws, and the practices in the industry.

It is a sad situation that some courts have ruled that a broker can lie as long as he gives you a document that contradicts that lie. It reminds us of a great couple of lines from another court opinion:

> General risk disclosures in the face of specific known risks, which border on certainties, do not bespeak caution. The doctrine of bespeaks caution provides no protection to someone who warns his hiking companion to walk slowly because there might be a ditch ahead when he knows with near certainty that the Grand Canyon lies one foot away.[5]

Be alert. If you read something in any literature or prospectus that contradicts what your broker has told you, get to the bottom of this discrepancy as soon as possible. Don't take the broker's word that the written document is not important or should be ignored. It may come back to bite you later. Immediately seek to clarify the discrepancy in writing. If, as a result, your broker retreats from the investment, don't think you have spoiled an opportunity. Realize that you have just taken proactive steps to protect your assets.

The broker who entices you with such statements as "You can't lose," "I bought it for my entire family," "It's the hottest thing going," "It's the buy of a lifetime," or "You are going to make a ton of money" violates rules that govern brokers' communication with the public. Many brokerage firm training manuals discourage their brokers from high-pressure sales tactics, which consist of exaggerated, inflammatory, or promissory statements made to customers in order to induce a sale. Even prohibited are exaggerated statements—that is, statements that are not properly qualified and are therefore an overstated or enlarged statement of the truth. Likewise, firms discourage brokers from making inflammatory or promissory statements that incite investors to buy or sell securities on an emotional, rather than reasoned, basis.

After reading Chapter 3, we can all agree that few stockbrokers could make a living if they were not allowed to pitch sales. The industry therefore allows brokers to use puffery, although the regulations don't allow them to go beyond puffery. What is puffery? The SEC has found such statements as "This bond is cheap" and "I really like this investment" to be more in the nature of sales puffery than pressure.[6] Examples of high pressure: "You have to buy now";

"Hurry before all the stock is sold"; "If you don't buy 10,000 shares, you will regret it the rest of your life"; and "The stock is doubling; you don't have time to think about it."

Additional prohibitions on brokers' sales pitches:

- No communication can imply or guarantee a specific rate of return.
- Any communication relating to a prior track record of the company must be properly qualified and must state that the prior successful track record does not ensure future success.
- Opinions must be able to be supported with factual evidence.

Whether a stockbroker communicates with you through the telephone, a personal meeting, an e-mail, a message board, or in a chat room, all communications are subject to regulatory oversight. Stockbrokers are not allowed to e-mail you from their home or personal computers unless the firm is capable of monitoring such activity, which means firms must have established some sort of spot-checking of these e-mails. Many firms, though not required to, are prereviewing all outgoing stockbroker e-mails as a result, in part, of the ease of such review provided by computerized systems. Any hard-copy document a stockbroker provides you—a letter, sales literature, a brochure, a note—must each be reviewed and approved before being sent to you. If you receive something that you think is questionable or you simply want to confirm the veracity of a written representation, whip off a letter to your brokerage firm manager, enclose a copy of the document, and ask that the document be verified.

Remember the story of Pinocchio? Each time he lied, his nose grew larger and larger. That's because when one lies once, it's very hard to continue the lie without getting caught up in it. We close this section by sharing with you some of the more incredible stories of fraud. Double fraud, that is—fraud on the investor at the time of the investment and later fraud in the attempt to cover up the original fraud.

When a young boy was in a motorcycle accident that left him a paraplegic, he surely thought that he had experienced the single worst event of his entire life. After receiving a hefty insurance settlement, he at least had the comfort of knowing he would not want for money. He entrusted his money to two stockbrokers who, the boy said, convinced him to invest the majority of his funds in several limited partnerships. The boy saw the majority of his insurance settlement dwindle to nothing. At the arbitration hearing, the boy testified from a wheelchair that the two brokers did not tell him of any warnings or risks, but if they had, he would not have allowed them to invest his money in the limited partnerships. The two brokers testified that when they met with the boy at his house, they had a played a videotape for the boy that outlined all of the risks of the limited partnerships.

The crucial testimony was not from the boy who testified that no such tape was played but from his nursemaid, who, unbeknown to the brokers, was in an adjoining room. She testified that the TV was not turned on during that meeting. If the boy and his nursemaid were telling the truth, the brokers led this young paraplegic boy astray by encouraging him to make a highly unsuitable investment decision. Although the boy prevailed in the arbitration, he was not awarded his full damages. Shortly after the award, the boy committed suicide.

Tracy had a case in which, unbeknown to the broker/branch manager whom she was cross-examining, she had the witness's testimony from an earlier case where he had given the exact opposite testimony regarding what he had told his clients. Tracy confronted the witness with the prior testimony and then asked him, "So were you lying to the arbitration panel in that other case, or are you lying to this arbitration panel?" This is much like the When did you stop beating your wife? question. There is no good answer. Tracy's case settled shortly thereafter.

When an investor claims that a stockbroker failed to point out important material, negative facts about an investment, it's very easy for the broker to respond, "Oh, yes I did." In arbitration, Tracy first commits the broker to this response and then takes it to the extreme. She asks the broker, "Did you tell my client that she could lose all or most of her money if she agreed to this investment?" The broker responds with an affirmative and haughty, "Yes, I did." The follow-up question proves the lie: "Well then, tell us, how did my client respond when you told her that this investment could wipe out her savings and retirement?" The resulting strained silence speaks volumes.

The point of these war stories is that efforts to deceive by those who have done wrong often have no limits. For this reason, you must be vigilant. You should be able to rely on your stockbroker for the full story. To ensure that you get it, ask questions and probe into the downside of every investment. Make and retain notes of conversations with your broker. By asking your broker to list the risks of every investment he brings you, you will send a message that you are risk conscious and perhaps risk adverse. In turn, your broker will be more mindful of recommending to you only the most suitable investments and giving you the full and complete story sans omissions.

UNAUTHORIZED TRADING—A DEADLY VIOLATION THAT FEW UNDERSTAND

No rules of the securities industry are more sacrosanct than those governing unauthorized trading. Even people not versed in securities can imagine the abuses that might result if a stockbroker were able to buy and sell securities in a customer's account with little or no discussion between the broker and customer beforehand.

The securities rules on unauthorized trading can be broken down into two sets. The first set dictates that the brokerage firm must have a client's prior, *written* permission before the broker can make a trade without first discussing it with the client. The second set concerns what the broker must say to the customer to produce a valid order. A related set of rules, which we touch on in this chapter, govern a broker's communication with an investor when soliciting an order. A violation of these rules, however, does not necessarily constitute grounds for an unauthorized trading claim.

Many people confuse *unauthorized trading* with *discretionary trading* because each of these phrases describes a situation in which the broker makes trades in your account without first discussing them with you. If you have *not* granted your broker the authority to conduct such trades in writing, then the trades are unauthorized, and something is horribly amiss. If you *have* signed the brokerage firm's unique document that grants your broker the ability to make trades without first discussing them with you, then the groundwork is laid for proper discretionary trading and everything is copasetic. The rules of both the NASD (Rule 2510) and the NYSE (Rule 408) require that *the authority to make discretionary trades must be in writing and signed by the client* prior to any discretionary trading.

Investors often approach us and tell stories about how they orally agreed with their broker that the broker would make all the decisions with no involvement from them. These situations occur where the client is naïve, is related to the broker, or simply places unqualified trust in and reliance on the broker. Many customers have said to their brokers, "I don't understand and I don't want to understand," which is why they may have hired a stockbroker rather than direct the trading themselves. When their broker calls and begins a litany of disclosures, these customers cut off the broker and say, "Okay, just do what you think is best." Sometimes, brokerage firms have defended unauthorized trading claims by stating that the customer was fully aware the broker was making decisions in the account and granted the broker the authority to do so. These situations may be termed a "de facto discretionary account." Again, without the customer's written authority in place prior to the trades, the broker and the brokerage firm are in violation of both the NASD and the NYSE rules.

An unauthorized trading claim is a type of wrongdoing that gives rise to a number of legal claims, such as breach of contract, fraud, and negligence. The nice thing about unauthorized trading claims, from the investor's perspective, is that the remedy is clean, simple, and uniform (regardless of where you live). All unauthorized trades should be rescinded or reversed, putting you in the position you were in before the unauthorized trades. If you had authorized trades that were winners, those gains should not be offset against the unauthorized trades. This is a most beneficial remedy where the unauthorized trades were losers. Remember that there is a higher probability unauthorized trades will be losers because the trades your broker would have an incentive to make without first discussing them with you, as required, would be higher-risk investments, which pay the broker more (see Chapter 2).

Information Brokers Are Required to Provide Clients

Brokers must communicate certain information to clients in soliciting an order for a particular investment. And customers must give their approval of the orders before they are entered. Your broker cannot leave a message for you on your answering machine about his suggestion, though he can leave a message about the execution of a previously discussed order. Nor are brokers allowed the luxury of placing orders based on general conversations with investors concerning an investment; conversations about a particular investment must be specific. The order-taking process may occur in a single phone call or a series of phone calls regarding the same order. At a minimum, brokers must discuss with a client the information they must then specify on an order ticket, such as the following items:

- The type of trade, such as a buy, sell, sell short, and so on
- The specific security to be purchased or sold
- Exactly how many shares/units to be purchased
- The exact price at which the order is to be entered (unless it is a market order)
- The current price at which the security is trading
- Any special instructions

But there's more. Much more. Having participated in hundreds of arbitrations, we have heard stockbrokers and brokerage managers spout all kinds of opinions about what the necessary communications must be between brokers and their customers according to the regulations and norms of the securities industry when brokers are placing an order. In July 1994, Douglas wrote an article that was published in the Practicing Law Institute's Securities Arbitration manual entitled "When Is an Order an Order?" To prepare, Douglas conducted a survey of brokers, brokerage managers, and compliance and supervisory personnel for their opinions on when an order is really an order. In addition, he spoke with regulators concerning their interpretation of the rules and regulations governing proper order entry and communications between a stockbroker and a customer.

Inasmuch as the authority to make a particular trade is typically given by the customer in a telephone conversation with the stockbroker, the potential for abuse—and hence the necessity for proper communication—is great. Probably the most abused aspect of these conversations between brokers and their customers is the omission of a discussion of the risk or downside of the investment (see the discussion of fraud in this chapter). Material facts must be disclosed to clients under NASD Rule 2210 (d)(1)(A) and NYSE Rule 472.30. However, a host of other material facts that should be disclosed include the following:

- The total approximate dollars (including commissions) the trade will involve

- The total approximate commissions the trade will generate
- Whether the broker is trading the security personally or in other accounts
- Significant recent news concerning the investment in question
- The nature and rationale of the trading strategy, including its expected tax consequences
- The anticipated volume and frequency of trading
- The potential net profit considering market risks, tax consequences, and commission costs
- A two-step process if the trade is an initial public offering (IPO), whereby the broker obtains from the client an indication of interest and subsequently confirms the availability of the shares with the client
- Advising the client of sales charges, letters of intention (LOI), and rights of accumulation (ROA) if the trade is a mutual fund order
- A verbal explanation of the computation if margin is to be utilized in the transaction and the terms of the margin interest charges
- The brokerage firm makes a market in the security or is acting as a principal in the transaction
- The firm was a manager or comanager of any IPO in the past three years of any securities of the issuer
- The brokerage firm has an employee that is a director of the security issuer
- The customer's understanding of these factors

Investors can only consent or authorize a trade if they understand what the broker is saying when the broker calls to suggest or solicit a trade. It is the stockbroker's responsibility to determine a customer's level of understanding of the securities markets and adjust the specificity of the conversations accordingly. The broker's fulfillment of the Know Your Customer rule (see the suitability discussion in this chapter) provides the foundation for obtaining a properly authorized order.

Although brokerage firms don't declare in writing that if the items listed above are not communicated to the client, then the trade is unauthorized, an argument can certainly be made that if knowledge of the above items would have influenced the investor to not make the transaction, then the trade may well be unauthorized. Such facts would also give rise to a fraud claim.

You might think that given the detailed information required to be conveyed on every single transaction, brokerage firms would sign up discretionary accounts in droves to avoid making so many disclosures. It's actually quite the opposite because discretionary accounts require significantly more supervision than do standard brokerage accounts. Both the NASD Rule 2510 and the NYSE Rule 408 covering discretionary trading specifically state that supervisors must monitor discretionary trades to detect and prevent transactions that are excessive in size or frequency in view of the client's financial resources and the character of the account. Arguably, this monitoring should be performed in nondiscretionary accounts as well, but no NASD or NYSE rule spells it out so clearly.

Accordingly, many firms discourage discretionary accounts. One major firm even cautions brokers against opening such accounts: "Discretionary accounts are open to serious abuse . . . account executives are well advised to refuse discretionary accounts unless they thoroughly understand the client's objectives and financial capabilities." Another firm permits such accounts by only its most senior brokers. Yet another only allows discretionary accounts where the customer is difficult to reach and the investments are very conservative. Most all firms prohibit certain riskier trades from being made in discretionary accounts, like direct investments, limited partnerships, and option or commodity trades.

Time and Price Discretion and Its Abuses

There is an exception to both the NASD and NYSE rules regarding discretionary accounts. It is called *time and price discretion,* and it allows a broker to discuss with a customer a definite amount of a specified security and all of the other requisite discussions about that security (see above), except that the broker will retain the discretion for deciding when he will enter the order (the time) and at what price he will enter the order (the price).

The time and price exception is often misused, not only in the practical world of brokerage transactions, but in arbitration, where it has become a favorite defense to unauthorized trading claims. A number of brokerage firms recognize the potential for abuse and don't allow their brokers to use time and price discretion at all; whereas other firms allow it but discourage its use. We believe that the exception of time and price discretion should be disallowed altogether because of its rampant abuse.

Two scenarios of abuse are seen more often than others. The first is when brokers simply take time and price discretion without discussing it beforehand with customers. This is a violation because brokers must inform customers that they wish to take time and price discretion, explain what such discretion is, and then ask clients if they can have discretion prior to the trade. Time and price discretion may not be obtained after the fact nor may it be based on assumptions. It is applicable only to specific authority for specific trades.

The second area of abuse is in the timing of time and price discretion. Discretion is measured in minutes or hours, not in days and certainly not in weeks. Therefore, time and price discretion that lasts more than a day or two is questionable and is most likely a violation. If a broker wishes to take longer to enter a trade for her customer, she has two other options: call the customer back or use a good-till-canceled (GTC) order.

Tracy represented a customer in an unauthorized trading claim against a small firm and its stockbroker. At the arbitration, much to Tracy's surprise, the broker testified that he was exercising time and price discretion in his client's account and that his understanding of that activity allowed him to enter orders weeks after the conversation took place with the customer. He testified that he handled not only Tracy's client's account in that manner but a number of his other accounts as well. The arbitration panel not only found in favor of Tracy's client but made a specific finding that the brokerage firm had failed to supervise the broker. It is a firm's responsibility to ensure that a broker understands how to properly employ time and price discretion.

It is unfortunate that the discretionary trading rules of the NASD and NYSE do not establish parameters for how long the time and price discretion exception can be exercised. But just imagine the chaos and problems that would result if the industry allowed brokers to have large numbers of orders not written down, not entered, and subject to being entered based on the whim of the brokers. Throw in large, upward spikes or significant drops in the markets to this scenario and picture the conflicts this leeway would create.

One of the more unusual defenses to unauthorized trading came up in one of Douglas's cases—the *Tottenham v. Bear Stearns* arbitration, which received national attention in 1993 because the claimants were one of the wealthiest families in the world and the panel awarded $1 million in punitive damages against Bear Stearns. In that case, the father opened a corporate account after which his son had all of the conversations with the broker about trades and strategy. Because the son had not been given written authority to acquiesce in the trades, the claim was made that all of the trades were unauthorized. Bear Stearns's response to the claim was that it could ignore its own ironclad guidelines and the securities rules mandating written authority from the customer where "apparent authority" existed. The doctrine of "apparent authority" is not generally recognized in this context. The panel rejected this argument and not only sanctioned Bear Stearns $1 million in punitive damages but awarded the claimants $2.4 million in actual damages.[7]

Unauthorized trading is one of the easiest abuses for you to spot. If you are in doubt whether you have granted your broker discretion in your account, call up the firm and ask for a copy of the document in which you granted such authority. If you haven't, then you know you have a problem if every single transaction is not immediately preceded by a detailed conversation with your broker about that transaction. You know you have a problem if you open up your monthly statements or confirmations and, for the first time, see the names of securities previously unknown to you. If this is happening in your brokerage account (and believe us, it happens), consult with a securities arbitration lawyer immediately.

Although unauthorized trading claims may be he said/she said cases when the broker and the customer reside in the same city, these cases take on an entirely different complexion when long-distance phone charges are incurred. If you claim that your long-distance broker made an unauthorized trade in your account, you can prove it if your broker is unable to produce a long-distance phone bill reflecting the time and length of your conversation just prior to entry of the order. We've had cases where the broker produced a phone bill reflecting a 40-second call just prior to the entry of an order; the customer claimed the broker just left a message on the answering machine, and the broker claimed he talked fast! We've had cases where the broker entered orders on days that the customer was camping or out of the country with no phone access. These examples highlight the importance of documenting and maintaining a record of your travels and your inaccessibility.

If your brokerage firm records telephone calls, unauthorized trading claims should be able to be resolved without filing an arbitration claim or visiting a lawyer—that is, if you have a cooperating broker-dealer. Prior to filing an arbitration claim, Tracy attempted to obtain the tapes and the transcripts of her client's conversations with the firm. She wrote:

> I understand that you have transcribed the tapes and have recently received the transcript copies. If there is something in the transcripts that you believe strengthens your defense, you should share it with me in the hopes of possibly precluding the filing of a claim. You probably know that old saying—tape transcripts can either make or break a case.

Because the firm did not comply with the request, Tracy was forced to file a claim against it. When a firm refuses to produce tapes or transcripts, then the only way to get them is to file an arbitration claim and get an arbitration panel to order the firm to produce the recordings.

Remember that not all brokerage firms record telephone calls. In fact, most do not. In late 1998, a new NASD rule was adopted that requires brokerage firms to record all telephone calls with customers when a specified percentage of a firm's sales force is made up of brokers employed within the last three years by a firm that has been expelled from membership or had its registration revoked by the SEC. The NASD monitors these data and notifies firms if they need to start taping. The percentage that triggers the taping varies depending on the size of the firm, from 40 percent for a small firm to 20 percent for a larger firm. Some states require that you be alerted to the fact that conversations are being recorded and others do not. So don't assume that your conversations are not being recorded because you have been given no notice of the fact.

If your firm records telephone calls and you have an unauthorized trading claim, settle for nothing less than being provided a copy of the tape of your conversation about the investment. Sometimes, the inability of the firm to produce a tape recording inures to your benefit. Make sure the tape recording you receive provides the time of the conversation. You need to ask for a copy of the order ticket because, unlike a confirmation, the order ticket shows the time your broker entered your order. Your conversation should not extend more than 15 minutes or so before the entry of that order. If it does, then your broker better be discussing time and price discretion with you on the tape.

Another important step to take if you are the victim of unauthorized trades: complain in writing. Even if you write something like "I just discovered that XYZ Company was bought in my account, but my broker did not discuss this investment with me first nor did I authorize that it be bought in my account. Please advise how I should proceed." That puts the ball into the brokerage firm's court and, at the same time, documents your problem. You need not be specific about the damages or the remedy at this juncture. Just alert the firm to the problem and see how the firm responds.

The reality is that many, many people have no idea that their broker has to have this detailed conversation with them and get their blessing before each and every trade. They believe that stockbrokers can act as licensed professional money managers and make trades as they see fit. New titles sported by stockbrokers, such as "financial consultant" and "financial advisor," do little to dispel this impression. The customer's discovery that unauthorized trades have occurred is often secondary to other complaints voiced against the broker and the firm. The brokerage firms surely don't provide customers with documentation that explains this very basic foundation of unauthorized trades. Consequently, discovery of the problem occurs sometimes years after the wrongdoing. That's okay. Don't be dissuaded if a brokerage firm responds to your complaint with a statement that because you did not complain within ten days, per the instructions on the back of your confirmation, you have ratified the trade. That's hogwash and is a defense that rarely holds water in securities arbitrations. Plus, a customer cannot ratify something without knowing all of the relevant facts. Again, the sufficiency and completeness of the communication between the broker and the client is the determining factor.

Sometimes, brokers try to defend unauthorized trading claims in a bizarre manner. The estate of a deceased man brought a claim against a broker and his firm for churning the account and, in particular, for making unauthorized trades. The estate felt sure it could prove the trades were unauthorized because they took place after the investor had passed away! At the arbitration, the broker testified he was unaware that his client had died months earlier (not that that is a defense to an unauthorized trading claim). The next question blew everyone in the room away. The claimant's lawyer asked if it was true that the broker was a pallbearer at the funeral of the deceased man. The broker admitted that he was!

CHURNING—BUY IT, SELL IT, AND BUY IT BACK AGAIN

More articles and treatises are probably written on the subject of *churning* than on any other type of wrongdoing within the securities industry because of the subtle variations in instructions for performing the mathematical calculations to deduce churning. Churning is probably the third most violated rule in the securities industry, behind suitability and fraud. Churning is also known as excessive trading, which is probably a better term than churning because the title sets the criteria.

NASD Rule IM 2310-2, Fair Dealing with Customers, Part (b)(2) states the following regarding churning:

> Excessive Trading Activity
> Excessive activity in a customer's account, often referred to as "churning" or "overtrading." There are no specific standards to measure excessiveness of activity in customer accounts because this must be related to the objectives and financial situation of the customer involved.

NYSE Rule 345 makes the following statement about churning:

> No member, member organization, or allied member therein shall:
> (1) Effect on the Exchange purchases or sales for any account in which he or it is directly or indirectly interested, which purchases or sales are excessive in view of his or its financial resources or in view of the market for such security.

Why would a broker churn or excessively trade your portfolio? There it is again—that ever present conflict of interest looming on the horizon. Your broker is paid on buys and sells regardless of whether your investment makes money or tanks. The more often your broker can convince you to buy and sell, the more money he will pocket. Buy-and-hold investors are not desirable customers at some brokerage firms. Stockbrokers are like merchandising managers; they know that to make money, they must generate turnover.

Douglas had a similar experience with a car salesman when he bought a Range Rover in 1996. The salesman told Douglas that Range Rover was one of the best-built vehicles in the world as he waved his hand toward a picture of General Rommel crossing the African desert in a Range Rover. "This car is not even broken-in until after the first 100,000 miles," the salesman said. Douglas has been pleased with his Range Rover, but what really irks him is that every time he takes it in to the dealership for one thing or another, the salesmen always tell him he needs to buy the latest model! Yet he's put only 38,000 miles on his vehicle in four years. Turnover is the name of the game for many products.

What do you expect from car salesmen? They are honest, hardworking folks, just trying to make a living. If a stockbroker were to defend her excessive trading in an account by saying, "Hey, I was just trying to make a living," she'd be (or should be) booted from the industry. That never happens, though, because no broker would so readily admit that she succumbed to the conflict.

The very reason brokers churn accounts—extra commissions—is the same reason that the practice is not in your best interest—extra commissions. Buying and selling securities in an account in quick succession creates significant costs to an account. As you learned in Chapter 2, costs impair your capital and reduce your ability to make money because you must first overcome the costs. Even with high-flying Internet day traders, any educated scholar of investments will tell you that short-term trading, scalping, day trading, or similar activities increase your costs significantly and thus lessen your ability to make money.

For those people who think they can make money by short-term trading, we suggest you look at it as you would any other business venture. It's basic Business 101 that to make profits you have to *control your costs*. In short-term trading, commissions and spreads are built in, and you have no control over them. Therefore, those costs are going to hamper your ability to make a profit. We also suggest that you look at the statistics that show the odds are against you in the long run.

There are many other reasons why short-term trading is stacked so heavily against the average investor:

- You are trying to outguess professional traders, who have been doing this for a living all their life.
- Trying to keep track of so much information so quickly is mind-boggling regardless of whether you are doing it or your broker is doing it.
- Almost every treatise written on short-term trading has proven that buying and holding for the long term has a better and more consistent rate of return.
- Because all of your trading profits are going to be short term, gains will be taxed at the highest tax rate as ordinary income.
- Filing your year-end taxes can be something of a nightmare.

Now that we have dispelled any notions that you should trade your own account on a short-term basis, let's turn to how you are to determine if your account is being churned at your broker's behest. The easiest way to start is with the mathematical part. The first measurement to take is called the *cost-maintenance factor*. It's obtained by dividing the total costs in the account (commissions, margin interest, markups, markdowns, and spreads[8]) by the average account equity or net worth over a particular period. The number you get is usually annualized to give it a comparative meaning.

As an example, if you added up the equity each month from your monthly brokerage statements for a year (equity is the amount of money in your brokerage account that you would receive if you sold all of your securities and paid off any margin debt) and then divided by 12, you would have the average equity of your account for that year. Let's say it is $100,000. Next, you would add up all of your costs for the entire year, which may be a problem if your broker does a lot of trades where the commissions are not disclosed. Let's say the total is $20,000. $20,000 is 20 percent of $100,000.

Twenty percent is your cost-maintenance factor, an extremely enlightening percentage because it means that on an annual basis, your return must exceed 20 percent just to pay the broker's commissions and other costs of the account! Stated another way, if your account returns 20 percent, you just break even. The gravy is what your account returns over and above that percentage. And that may not be much, if anything at all. Remember that before the incredible run of the late 1990s, a 10 percent yearly return was considered average for the stock markets. So historically your 20 percent cost-maintenance factor is way out of line and may be an indication that your account is being churned.

The second measurement used to determine excessive trading is *turnover*. Dividing the total dollar amount of stock purchases for a given period by the average equity produces the turnover rate. As in the previous example, let's say your average equity is $100,000. Next, you add up all the purchases in your account but not the sales.[9] Let's say that your total purchases for the year were $1,000,000. You divide the total purchases by the average equity, which gives you the number ten. Ten is the number of times your account was turned over that year.

Arguments and legal treatises abound on what the magic number is that indicates churning. The SEC has found excessive trading with turnover numbers as low as two, three, and four. Another well-known treatise argued that the only proper method to discern a proper turnover rate is to compare the goals of the money in question to a group of mutual funds with similar investment goals.[10] Mutual fund managers don't have an incentive to trade based on commissions because that isn't how they're paid. More aggressively managed stock funds have a higher turnover rate than do more conservatively managed bond funds. The net: if your account has a turnover much over two or three times annually, your account is perhaps being churned.

There are also simpler, more intuitive ways to sense if your broker is churning your account. Does he call and suggest trades often? Does he often recommend you sell an investment you just bought? Could you wallpaper an entire room with the confirmations you've received? If you suspect your broker may be a bit too "trading happy," try to conduct the two trading analyses that we described above on your account or hire someone to do it. Don't ask your broker or anyone at his firm to do it.

Of course, the above analysis is only half of the equation, because a churning analysis hinges on the investment objectives of the account—your investment objectives, not necessarily how your broker described what you wanted on your New Account form. Excessive trading may not be excessive if your true investment objectives were speculation or aggressive growth and you understood the risks you were taking with the money.

The potential for churning is one of the main reasons that discretionary accounts should be avoided. The incentive to churn is just too high when brokers aren't required to run trades by clients and get their permission first. Yet, the vast majority of churning cases involve accounts where the customer and broker talked about each and every trade before it was entered, because there are so few discretionary accounts. This, by the way, is the standard defense of brokerage firms to a churning claim—"You approved each and every trade, so you have no basis to complain now. It's just sour grapes." Just as in defending a suitability case, your broker is going to use *you* as his defense for churning. You were aggressive. You wanted to trade for the short term. You did some day trading before. One of the reasons that so many New Account forms are falsified is to allow brokers to defend alleged churning. Brokers will say that your investment goals are speculation and aggressive growth so that when managers question their active trading, brokers will retort that short-term trading is your goal. Your account documents may also show that your trading history and experience are as a short-term trader to obviate any scrutiny from management.

Again, do not be deterred. In almost every churning case, the broker does talk with the customer before each trade. But because the broker does such an excellent job of choosing his words, you never feel as though excessive trading is taking place. The broker always presents you with a very good reason why you should buy or sell, such as the following:

- "The stock is too high/low."
- "The earnings are coming out and they are going to be high/low."
- "Everyone else is buying/selling."
- "I have an inside tip and . . ."
- "They are coming out with a new product."
- "They just lost a big client."
- "The technicals look good/bad."
- "Our analyst just said . . ."
- "The stock just broke out/down."
- "We made two points; let's take our money and run."
- "We lost two points; let's cut our losses."
- "The stock is going nowhere."

- "I think we can do better by selling and moving our money to . . ."
- "Let's take some tax losses."
- "I just got a hot news story on the company."
- "The stock is down. Let's double up."
- "The stock is moving up. Let's buy more."

Any of these sound familiar? In and of themselves, these comments may be fine, but it is improper when brokers use these and similar comments to convince clients to allow churning accounts. The other reason investors rarely sense the occurrence of churning is because they can never truly grasp the detriment to their portfolio that costs levy as a result of the way monthly statements are written.

Fraud, unsuitable recommendations, unauthorized trading, and churning are enough to make you keep your money in a mattress. With all of these broker-related problems, it's not so surprising that brokerless or online brokerage firms experienced such phenomenal growth. Yet moving your account and taking things into your own hands brings its own unique problems (see Chapters 8 and 9). The better approach is to read this book, acquire a new awareness of your own vulnerability, and employ the tools you've learned about here to make yourself a more informed investor.

MARGIN—AN INCREDIBLE CONFLICT AND PROFIT CENTER

The subject of margin probably contains more brokerage firm tricks than any other subject. The first such trick: many firms have allowed their brokers to employ margin in customer accounts, and when the customer complains, the firm manager points to the language in the customer agreement and says, "See, you authorized the use of margin when you signed this Agreement." Although customer agreements may contain language authorizing the use of margin, your broker is required to discuss with you using margin in your account *before* using it. That means more than just telling you that margin will be used; it means explaining to you the risks and downsides of margin as well as the positives. If your broker suggests employing margin in your account, make sure that he fully explains all of your risks and costs as well as the upside.

Think of margin as a loan from your brokerage firm whereby the firm uses your existing securities as collateral. The money lent you can be used to buy additional securities or to cover personal expenses. The incentive for some investors is that margin can satisfy short-term cash needs. For example, one investor didn't have the cash to make her daughter's college tuition payment, although she knew that she was going to receive a substantial bonus from her employer in several months. Rather than disturbing her stock portfolio, she took a margin loan on 10 percent of her account and paid it off when she received her bonus—an entirely legitimate use of margin.

More common is an investor purchasing additional securities on margin, because she (or the broker) is banking on the investment going up in value. If it does, the investor stands to make money on an investment she didn't entirely pay for herself. For example, if you bought 200 shares of Corporation X at $10 and paid $1,000 in cash and $1,000 in credit, you would have $2,000 worth of Corporation X. If the price then rose to $15 a share, your investment would be worth $3,000, an increase of 300 percent over your initial layout of $1,000. Hence, the benefit of margin. But far too often brokers and investors forget the negatives of margin, a two-edged sword. Using the example above, instead of the stock going up to $15 a share, assume it went down to $5 a share. At $5, you lost your entire initial investment of $1,000. A 50 percent correction in the price of the stock wiped out an entire investment. It is important you let this sink in because it's a point lost on not only a lot of investors but a lot of brokers as well.

You have already learned that brokerage firms charge you a rate of interest that is a tremendous profit center for them but a potentially sizeable bite out of your profits. Margin rates of interest are set forth in documentation provided to you. Some firms, such as Ameritrade, set their margin interest rates as a certain percentage above the national prime rate, which is published daily in the *Wall Street Journal*, so you can check it out and compute the margin rate yourself. Other firms, such as E*Trade, set their margin interest rates based on a base rate set at a firm's discretion with reference to commercially recognized interest rates. Regardless of how it is computed, the interest rate you pay on a margin loan, while lower than that on an unsecured bank loan, is almost always higher than your profit on the investment if you are seeking income-producing investments. This is called a "negative spread." Of course, if you are buying high yield or junk bonds, then your spread may be lowered. Most people use margin to buy stocks, not bonds, and there is no immediate negative spread when you buy stocks. But keep in mind that if your stocks don't outperform the annual interest rate you're paying on your margin debt, you have created a negative spread.

Types of Margin

There are two types of margin: initial margin and maintenance margin. The Federal Reserve sets the initial margin on stocks, which has been at 50 percent for many years. This means, in our example above, that you could not margin more than a $1,000 purchase of Corporation X with a $1,000 cash purchase because, of the $2,000 purchase, only 50 percent, or $1,000, of it can be on margin. If, however, you had securities in your account with a value of, say $50,000, then your margin-buying power would be $100,000. When you make a stock purchase on margin without sufficient collateral (cash or securities) in your account to cover the 50 percent margin requirement, you will get a Reg T margin call requesting you to deposit sufficient collateral.

Brokerage firms are allowed to set what is called "maintenance margin," the percentage the stock price can drop before a margin call is triggered. Through their computer systems, brokerage firms monitor the value of the stock purchased on margin, and when the stock starts to drop in value, usually to around 30 percent, firms issue a maintenance margin call. Both Reg T and maintenance margin calls can be satisfied in a number of ways; investors can send in additional cash or deposit additional marginable securities, or some of their current holdings can be liquidated to cover the margin call.

We promised not to deluge you with investment advice, but we can't help it when it comes to margin. Most people who take a bloodbath from using margin blame it on the fact that their stocks or the market went down. The price movement of stocks is a necessary component of a margin call, but the problem is that no one ever knows when a particular stock or the market as a whole will go down. If you are still dead set on using margin, the trick is to never be *heavily* margined. Far too many individuals figure that if they buy their stock at 50 percent margin, the 20 percent spread between 50 percent margin and the 30 percent margin that triggers a maintenance margin call is an adequate cushion. This is no longer true in these days of volatile markets and volatile securities. It would be wiser to not allow your account to be margined more than 25 percent, as opposed to 50 percent, at least initially. This way, you are more likely to be able to sustain a major drop in stock prices without being forced to liquidate at the worst possible time.

In addition, take a look at the price history of any security you are thinking of buying on margin. This is easy to do on the Internet; review the historical up and down swings in price over the preceding two years on a percentage basis, which should give you a pretty good indication of how this stock might move after you purchase it. A term in the securities industry—*beta*—is a measure of volatility in a security in relation to the S&P 500. Beta can be used as a quick measure of volatility, but it may not let you see the actual swings in price.

Investor inquiries and complaints about margin have ballooned in recent years, certainly as a result of the increasing number of individuals employing margin in their online brokerage accounts. This increase in inquiries and complaints prompted the NASD in August 2000 to approve a proposed amendment to NASD rules that would require member firms to provide retail customers with a written statement that fully describes the risks associated with trading securities in a margin account. The margin disclosure statement must be provided to customers prior to, or at, the opening of an account and annually thereafter; the statement can be delivered electronically or on paper. The NASD permitted firms to create their own disclosure statement so long as it contains the following specific information:

- A customer can lose more funds than he or she deposits in the account if the value declines.
- A firm has the right to force the sale of securities in an account.
- A firm may notify the customer of a margin call and allow the customer a few days to meet the call, but the firm also

can sell a customer's securities without contacting him or her.
- A customer cannot decide which securities should be sold from his or her account.
- A firm can increase maintenance margin requirements at any time.
- A firm does not have to grant a customer an extension on a margin call.

What many would perceive as one of the biggest tricks of the brokerage industry, at both traditional and online firms, is the manner in which firms will "sell out" your portfolio to cover a margin call with no notice to you. This is happening much more often at online firms (see Chapter 11). Even at traditional firms, however, customers are feeling the pinch as a result of the significantly higher numbers of volatile stocks in which they are trading today. The higher the volatility, the more margin calls are issued.

Tracy has a case pending in which her client received an e-mail on a Saturday afternoon from his brokerage firm to inform him that he had a maintenance margin call in the amount of $33,651. The e-mail provided her client with wiring instructions on how to cover the call. Acting promptly, Tracy's client arranged for the wire transfer of $35,000 over the weekend, and the wire transfer process was put into effect first thing Monday morning. On Monday morning, her client began telephoning the firm and after several tries, each met with a busy signal, he finally got through. The firm representative notified her client that his entire position had been liquidated at market. The firm received Tracy's client's wire transfer of $35,000 that Monday afternoon.

Pertinent portions of the firm's Brokerage Account Agreement stated:

> You are responsible for acting immediately on any buy in or sell out notice given verbally or in writing. Your failure to promptly deposit additional money or securities in response to a margin call may result in the liquidation of part or all of the securities in your account. Although we will generally attempt to notify you of a margin call and give you an opportunity to deposit additional equity to secure the account, we reserve the right to institute imme-

diate discretionary liquidation without prior notice and without giving you the opportunity to deposit additional equity.

Tracy's argument is that her client *did* act promptly and it wasn't his fault that the firm's phone lines were busy. An interesting point is that Tracy's client might not have had a case if the firm had simply liquidated the account Monday morning without having sent the Friday e-mail. But the fact that it sent the e-mail and Tracy's client acted as promptly as possible under the circumstances (as the agreement requires) gives rise to a viable claim.

There are also horror stories about brokerage firms permitting customers to purchase stocks on margin well beyond their means, a phenomenon that hardly existed before hoards of unsophisticated investors opened online accounts. If you deal with a traditional firm and call up to tell your broker you want to buy $100,000 worth of XYZ Corporation with your sole remaining $50,000, ideally we hope your broker would say, "Now wait a second, let's take a more careful look at doing this." There's no one to give you any sage words of advice on the Internet.

Even when margin is used on less volatile securities, investors can be severely damaged, as is often the case after a sharp market drop. Often a rebound occurs, and the stocks that plummeted recover, leaving investors who were sold out wringing their hands and full of anguish. The majority of investors who were hurt in the 1987 market crash were those who were forced to sell their investments at severe discounts because of margin calls. This happened again in August 1998 with the Southeast Asian crisis. In both of these cases, the market turned around almost immediately, leaving margined investors with stinging losses.

It is hoped that with firms adhering to required disclosures, a greater awareness will spread that brokerage firms will basically sell you out at whim. Just because you may have gotten margin calls for years and promptly paid them, don't expect that you will get notification of your next margin call. If the value of your stock drops fast, the firm has the right to act fast, with or without you. And the firm can pick and choose which of your securities to sell. We don't agree with this new trend in how margin is being handled. It is mostly online firms that have adopted these new hasty tactics, which deviate from the industry standard and show a total disregard for the interests of the customer. As the rules now stand, you have a tough, uphill battle.

You must be on your toes when it comes to margin. And, for most of you, that means not agreeing to use margin at the drop of a hat. When you consider that the consequence of a margin call could be the loss of your entire portfolio, margin can be viewed as a highly speculative venture. If your stockbroker recommends margin, examine your downside. If, for example, he recommends margin to purchase long-term investments, such as municipal bonds or conservative mutual funds or stocks or bonds you intend to hold, question how the margin cost might be greater than your return in dividends or interest. Question the margin interest and how much more of a return you need to overcome it. The ability to get specific answers is one of the now highlighted benefits of having a human stockbroker, as opposed to entering your own trades online with no individualized input. Finally, if you receive a margin call, *act fast*. Don't assume that the firm will wait for you to come up with the money. It may not, and the language in the customer or margin agreement may support its action.

OVERCONCENTRATION—TOO MUCH OF A GOOD THING?

One of the alarming trends that we both have noticed is a rash of cases where the broker has concentrated investors' holdings in only one or two securities or in a particular industry, such as technology. We both believe that the single most damaging investment practice is the lack of diversification, or overconcentration. You can take the highest-risk investment you can think of, be it shorting options or trading commodities, but if you do it in only 2 percent of your portfolio and lose the entire amount, who cares? Those of us in the securities industry are taught the importance of properly diversifying investors' assets in the most basic training. Most reputable brokerage firms, when they do train their brokers, teach them the importance of diversification and warn them in their compliance and supervisory manuals about undue concentration.

Regulators, and specifically the SEC, have often criticized and sanctioned brokers for concentrating their clients' investments inappropriately, especially in high-risk investments. With this said and done, it is appalling that we are experiencing such a rash of overconcentration cases. Until the industry does a better job of supervising what is admitted to be a serious infraction, we ask you to please heed our warnings. We don't care how good it sounds, how great it may be, how many analysts love it, or the hundred other reasons your broker can come up with for why you should buy more or own such a significant amount of one investment or group of investments, don't do it.

Also, be very sensitive to your stockbroker's becoming too enthralled with a particular security. It often starts out innocently with your broker showing interest in a particular company's stocks or bonds. As the broker purchases and recommends more and more of the security to you and his other clients, he tends to conduct additional research and become more captivated with the stock. This problem is often exacerbated when the broker has personal contact with one of the officers of the company.

The problem of concentration usually worsens if the target security drops in price. Your broker was recommending the security to you at $20 and now at $10 a share he's on the phone urging you to double up or average down. The percentage of his clients' portfolios in the concentrated security grows as the stock continues to plummet and your broker keeps adding to the positions in all or many of his clients' accounts. As a larger portion of your broker's client base becomes concentrated in the security, potential disaster not only awaits you and the rest of his clients but it also threatens your broker's business if the stock doesn't recover soon. For these reasons, your broker is now living and breathing the security. He is the master of all knowledge about it. He ignores all negatives and trumpets any positive news. As the ship continues to sink, he doesn't allow you or any of his clients to get in the life raft. When you call panicked and concerned that you are losing your life savings, he not only talks you out of selling but talks you into purchasing more shares at even lower prices.

Recognize these warning signs. When you hear "average down," "lower your cost," "it can't go any lower," run for the hills because it *can* go lower. If the dot-com bloodbath taught investors anything, we hope it was that not only can it go lower but it can go to *zero*.

SELLING AWAY—WANT TO BUY A BRIDGE?

John Doe was becoming more and more excited about the investment opportunity that his broker had been discussing with him over the last few weeks. It seems his broker had been working very closely with a local technology firm that had designed a revolutionary product that, when added to the fuel tank of cars, would increase fuel efficiency by 30 to 40 percent. His broker knew the company intimately and was on a first-name basis with a number of its key officers. Doe was going to be able to get in on the ground floor of this company! Though he had kept his investing on a small scale, he had been impressed with, and came to trust, his broker and Acme Brokerage Firm. Now his broker was convincing him to make a major commitment of dollars in a technology firm. Based on the other investments Doe had bought from Acme, he assumed Acme felt comfortable with this one, and so he agreed to invest. Doe did think it a bit strange when his broker had him write his check directly to the technology company as opposed to his brokerage account at Acme. But the broker explained that this was common in this type of venture capital investment.

A year later, when Doe's investment tanked to nearly zero, he investigated and found that his broker had lied to him about the financial stability of the company. He complained to the branch manager at Acme; the manager responded that Acme knew nothing of the investment and only recently had found out that the broker, without Acme's knowledge, had been selling this technology company to a number of his clients. The manager told Doe that Acme fired the broker but could not be held responsible for the broker's fraudulent activities because this was an investment that the firm had not approved.

Welcome to the world of *selling away*. The phrase literally means that the broker has sold an investment to a customer away from the brokerage firm with which the broker is licensed. An independent financial planner, a Registered Investment Advisor (RIA), or some other individual not Series 7 licensed rarely gets accused of selling away because these advisors are often independent and thus don't have to clear the investments they wish to sell with a parent firm.[11] Usually, selling away takes place when the customer has an account with the brokerage firm, as in the hypothetical example above. However, it can also occur when the customer doesn't have a brokerage account with the firm, but the broker uses the firm name and affiliation as a lure to entice the customer to invest. Either way, it is almost always damaging for the investor. This is not to insinuate that all the products brokerage firms sponsor are so great, but you can bet that the ones sold behind their backs are worse.

NASD Rule 3040 prohibits brokers from engaging in securities transactions outside the regular course or scope of their employment unless the brokerage firm has acknowledged and approved of the transaction in writing. If the brokerage firm has approved of the transaction, then it undertakes the responsibility to supervise the transaction. In such a situation, you would not get the "We didn't know" response letter from the firm.

This is not to say that a brokerage firm gets off scot-free if it claims it didn't know. Brokerage firms should have written policies and procedures, and systems, in place to detect and prevent the potential of selling away. The question is often whether there were any red flags indicating that the broker was selling away, such as equal sums of money being routinely withdrawn from each of his clients' accounts or the broker's leaving the office every day at 2:00 PM. A branch manager should catch that sort of activity, question it, and uncover the selling away. Most brokers would be fired for selling away without the knowledge of their employer.

The incentive for brokers to sell away is, as usual, the compensation. It's a way for brokers to make not only a little extra cash but often substantial cash. And ask yourself, If this potential investment the broker is recommending is so good, how come someone couldn't convince some brokerage firm to sponsor or market it? The following is a watch list that you can use as your red flags for a broker who may be selling away:

- Is your broker working out of his house? If so, it is easier for him to sell away unnoticed by his firm.
- Does the broker call you from a business other than the brokerage firm he works for? Often, brokers incorporate their own separate businesses, which is a fairly strong indicator of a potential for selling away.
- Do you receive correspondence from your broker that doesn't have his brokerage firm's letterhead? Another warning is receiving personal correspondence from your broker or corre-

spondence referencing your broker's "other" company. However, be aware that your broker may be selling away and just misappropriating the firm's letterhead.

- Is the stock your broker is touting listed on any national exchange? Stockbrokers usually sell away new offerings or other stocks that are not listed on any national exchange or the Nasdaq. Sometimes the investments offered are unregistered securities.
- Does the broker seem to have personal ties or involvement with the company or its officers?
- Do you know how the broker is being compensated on the proposed transaction? If it sounds too good to be true (your broker may brag about his compensation), furrow those brows.
- And the red flag that is so red it's on fire is if you are asked to pay for an investment by making a payment unlike the way you pay for all the other investments in your account, which is typically by writing a check to your brokerage or clearing firm! You should rarely buy investments other than through a fully registered and licensed brokerage firm.

With more stockbrokers working as independent agents out of their homes or in satellite offices, the potential for selling away violations is greater. If you suspect your broker of trying to sell you a side deal or of selling away, first call and ask your broker's manager if the firm is sponsoring the deal. Follow up with a letter documenting what is said. Second, call your state securities division to see if the security at issue is registered. Take these steps before you decide to invest, not afterward, and save yourself a lot of heartache and possibly a lot of money.

OUTSIDE BUSINESS PRACTICES— WORKING BOTH SIDES OF THE STREET

Many of you would not be prohibited from getting a second job if you chose to. You could start a catering company on the weekends or counsel start-up businesses after hours. And as long as you fulfilled your responsibilities at your current job, and perhaps as long as you were not competing with your current job, it would be nobody's business how else you made money. Not so for your stockbroker.

Your stockbroker is required to provide written notice to her brokerage firm of any other employment pursuant to the following NASD rule:

> NASD Rule 3030 Outside Business Activities of an Associated Person
> No person associated with a member in any registered capacity shall be employed by, or accept compensation from, any other person as a result of any business activity, other than a passive investment, outside the scope of his relationship with his employer firm, unless he has provided prompt written notice to the member.

NYSE Rule 346 is similar and in some instances requires written notice to be given to the New York Stock Exchange.

It is rare that you find a stockbroker conducting two separate businesses. It is more common among those who are in the financial industry but are not registered stockbrokers, such as financial planners, CPAs, and the like. Remember that it is not against the rules for stockbrokers to have another job, but the firm must have written documentation of the other job and presumably approved it. We mention the rule only because we want you to be aware of it, as a dual career often leads to selling-away violations. If you suspect your stockbroker has two careers, talk to the broker's manager to make sure the manager is aware of it and ask to have your inquiry confirmed in a letter to you.

INSIDER TRADING—NO JOKES, NO HINTS, NO INFERENCES

Outside business practices, and to some extent selling-away situations, are often teamed with insider trading violations because outside activities sometimes allow a broker to come into contact with material nonpublic information.

Insider trading rules, however, do not apply just to stockbrokers or those working within the financial arena. They apply to everyone who may conduct a trade while in possession of material nonpublic information. The rules prohibiting insider trading are among the strictest; and violations can subject individuals to imprisonment for up to ten years and fines up to $1 million.

Material nonpublic information may include information that something is likely to happen—or just that it might happen. Examples would be the following:

- A pending acquisition or sale of a substantial business or other significant transaction
- Development of a major new product or service
- An increase or decrease in dividends
- A stock split or other recapitalization
- A redemption or purchase by the company of its securities
- Major management changes

You may have heard your stockbroker discuss events like these on numerous occasions. Granted, these events are material, but how are you supposed to know whether they are nonpublic? The primary way that investors get drawn into insider trading violations is when their stockbroker *tells* them that they have privileged, special inside information. Remember that ignorance is no defense to breaking insider trading laws. If your broker simply passes on the information to you, he would be guilty of tipping, which is also illegal. You could also face exposure as the tippee if you act on this inside information. Odds are that if the information is so material and so nonpublic, your broker will be trading on it too.

Information stops being nonpublic when it has been effectively disclosed to the public by a filing with the SEC, a press release, or a newspaper article, for example, followed by a reasonable waiting period for the information to be absorbed in the marketplace. In this day and age, when investors get second-by-second reports beamed into their living rooms from around the world, there is much less material nonpublic information. The recently enacted requirement that analysts disclose their material nonpublic information to the public simultaneously with disclosing it to institutional entities will also cut down the existence of such information.

Customers can pull a trick of their own in insider trading claims. Tracy had a case in which her clients were taken in by a stockbroker who assured them he had the inside scoop, that he was talking to management at the company, and that he was getting information nobody else was getting. The Statement of Claim read: "[I]t does not matter whether or not the broker was lying or, in fact, he was obtaining information from 'inside' sources. The broker either defrauded the Claimants or he violated the insider trading laws. Either way, it is a violation."

The net is that you should have your antenna up when you hear a broker talk of special or inside information. If your broker tells you he has information that is special, privileged, or the inside scoop, ask him directly whether what he has told you is public information. If he says no, run! But before you go, whip off a letter to your broker's manager advising him of the conversation.

CIRCULATION OF RUMORS—
IF YOU DON'T WANT IT REPEATED . . .

The rumor mill has increased by leaps and bounds with the Internet providing the public an easy and often anonymous method of communication to millions. However, the subject of rumors and their interplay with investments existed long before the Internet. NYSE Rule 435 Circulation of Rumors provides:

> No member shall . . . circulate in any manner rumors of a sensational character which might reasonably be expected to affect market conditions on the Exchange. Discussion of unsubstantiated information published by a widely circulated public media is not prohibited when its source and unsubstantiated nature are also disclosed.

According to the rule, a statement is not a rumor if the speaker discloses that she has no idea about the truth or veracity of the statement. This rule has been invoked more often recently because of the posting of unsubstantiated information in Web site chat rooms and is very closely tied to the insider rule, because it relates to the spreading of information that is either nonpublic or unsubstantiated.

ORDER FAILURE AND IMPROPER EXECUTION— VIOLATION OF THE 21ST CENTURY

Claims of violation of the NASD's Rule 2320—the best execution rule—are termed *order failure*. A great majority of complaints of order failure today are against online brokerage firms.

Unlike many of the violations we have discussed, order failure is not done on purpose. Nor is it motivated by any conflict of interest. Just as no broker purposefully loses his clients' money, no brokerage firm purposefully botches clients' orders. These types of errors are not the fault of investors and typically occur as a result of human error, understaffing, or technical problems. This does not alter your ability to obtain a remedy, however. Firms are also liable for simple mistakes.

PROMISES AND GUARANTEES—WORDS THAT SHOULD NEVER CROSS LIPS

Has a broker ever said to you, "I promise you will not lose your money on this one. You stand only to gain." Or after having suffered some losses in your account, has your broker said something similar to this: "Just give me another five months. I guarantee I can make your lost money back." If your broker has said something like these statements, your broker has violated the rules regarding promises and guarantees:

NASD Rule 2330(e)
No member or persons associated with a member shall guarantee a customer against loss in any securities account carried by the member or in any securities transaction effected by the member with or for such customer.

NYSE Rule 352(b)
No member organization shall guarantee or in any way represent that it will guarantee any customer against loss in any account or transaction.

Whenever you hear your broker use the word *promise* or *guarantee*, alarm bells should go off in your head. Watch out, too, for such qualifiers as, "I guarantee if this product takes off as I think it will, you will no longer have to save for your daughter's college education." The "if" clause, however, puts the guarantee in a different light: only guarantees against loss *with no qualifiers* are prohibited.

SHARING IN PROFITS—HOW ABOUT SHARING IN THE LOSSES?

If your broker has tried to make you feel better by suggesting he will bear some of the loss in your brokerage account, don't think he's a great guy. He just violated rules of the NASD and the NYSE:

NASD Rule 2330(f)(2)
No member or person associated with a member shall share directly or indirectly in the profits or losses in any account of a customer.

NYSE Rule 352(c)
No member . . . shall directly or indirectly (i) take or receive or agree to take or receive a share of profits, or (ii) share or agree to share in any losses in any customer's account or of any transaction effected therein.

There are exceptions to the above rules, but they usually won't apply in your situation. Be aware also that registered investment advisors (who are not your average retail stockbroker) *can* share in the profits and losses of your account, although these sharing arrangements must be in writing and meet certain industry standards of fairness and reporting requirements.

REBATES AND COMPENSATION— *KICKBACKS* IS WHAT YOU KNOW IT AS

As for sharing commissions, NYSE Rule 353(a) states:

No member [or] registered representative . . . shall, directly or indirectly, rebate to any person, firm or corporation any part of the compensation he receives for the solicitation of orders for the purchase or sale of securities.

Brokers cannot share commissions with nonregistered individuals nor is it appropriate for your broker to share commissions with you. We occasionally see situations where a broker has worked out a deal with his customer—never in writing—that he will charge full commissions on the front end of a trade and adjust his commissions on the back end of the trade, depending on the trade's profit or loss. This is a violation and would be an example of an indirect rebate of commissions.

If you hear your broker using any of the language listed in these last three rules, it is best that you and your broker part company as fast as you can. He either does not know the rules or, even worse, he does and is violating them.

FRONT RUNNING, BUNCHING, AND POSITION BUILDING—HARD TO CATCH

Front running occurs when a firm or a broker takes action in front of, or ahead of, an incident that favorably affects a stock. For example, a firm might buy up shares in a company just before the firm is about to recommend the stock as a strong buy. Or a broker might buy for himself a large position in a stock just before his firm buys a large block of shares.

Front running can also cover a situation in which a stockbroker trades the same securities as his clients and, in so doing, takes action that benefits himself but unknown to his clients, harms them. Brokers are not supposed to make investments that can conflict with those of their clients. Many investors wrongly think that it is a good thing if their broker, in recommending an investment to them, states, "I have purchased this investment myself." This may not be beneficial for several reasons.

First, the broker's reasons for buying the investment may have nothing to do with your reasons. The broker's financial situation, risk tolerance, needs, and goals may be totally different from those of his customers. The broker may have purchased the investment as the single highflier, speculative investment in his portfolio. Or he may have bought it two years ago at a completely different price than the one at which it is currently trading. Further, many would consider the broker's statement that he bought the same security in his account to be a hype and inflammatory. What's worse is if the broker lied. We have seen situations where a broker stated he had purchased a stock for himself only to discover the security was never purchased in the broker's accounts. You, the customer, have no way to verify such information.

Assuming it's true and your broker has some of your investments in his personal portfolio, let's examine the problems that can arise. A conflict of interest is created that may blind your broker's thinking; he very well may not be able to separate his own interest in the stock from your best interests and may not be able to be objective. For this reason the majority of firms severely restrict and monitor a broker's trading in the same securities as a client's.

If your broker has stooped to front running, then there is a good chance he is also engaging in what may be another abusive act called *bunching*. Bunching typically occurs when a broker phones in an order for a large number of shares of a stock—called a block order—as opposed to separate orders for a smaller number of shares for specific customers. When done properly, at the time a broker phones in a bunched order, the broker should state which shares go to which customer accounts so that all of the shares are allocated at the end of the phone call. Improper bunching occurs when a broker phones in the same large order, does not allocate any of the shares, and later, with the benefit of a price movement, does the allocation. As usual, the conflicts arising from bunching can be likened to a loaf of fresh, steaming bread straight from the oven—too tempting to resist. Let us show you how.

The broker buys 10,000 shares of Fastmoving, Inc., but instead of writing order tickets or punching on his computer the orders for numerous customers, he instead calls the order directly to his firm's trading floor. He tells the order desk, "This is John from the Boca office; buy me 10,000 shares of Fastmoving, Inc., symbol FAST, at the market (at market price)." The order is filled—5,000 shares at $5.00 a share and the other 5,000 shares at $5.50 a share. Before the broker has punched into the system or written a single order ticket for allocation of all these shares, Fastmoving, Inc., moves up to $8.00 a share! The broker is in a real ethical dilemma. Here is where that loaf of bread really causes the broker to close his eyes, lean his head back, and smile. These are the thoughts that may go through the broker's head:

- Do not give any of this stock to my current clients, but instead scurry to call a few hot prospects to say I have a hot stock that I know will go up. This will lock in some new clients.

- Put all of the stock in only my best clients' accounts (best accounts being those that generate the most commissions).
- Divide the $5.50 a share stock among my best clients and put the $5.00 a share stock in my personal account.
- Put all of the shares in my own account and then immediately sell out for a hefty profit, which I could end up blowing at the local casino tonight.

Even if the broker thinks that he's doing the right thing by dividing the stock among all his clients that thought they were buying it and for whom the stock is suitable, who gets the $5.00 a share stock versus the $5.50 a share stock? No matter what the broker does, someone has the right to complain. For this reason, some brokerage firms prohibit their retail brokers from bunching orders at all. If a firm does allow bunching, it should enforce very strict policies governing it.

Also, you can be pretty sure that if a broker has you investing a large amount of money in a stock, a stock that the broker tells you he has bought as well, then the broker probably has a very large percentage of his clients in the stock. At many firms, this practice, called *position building,* is encouraged but is a disaster waiting to happen. Most reputable firms have a policy banning a broker, and even an office, from building too large a position in one stock. It is usually not a problem with a stock like Microsoft or IBM, but you see real problems when you get into thinly traded issues. The broker may have the power to move the price of the stock based just on what he recommends to his clients. If the price of the stock starts to tumble, the broker may have an incentive to keep his clients from selling. Or the broker alone may affect the price of the stock negatively when he attempts to sell. And whose stock does he sell first—his, yours, or his other clients? Which clients get the better price before all the selling starts to drive the stock down?

Front running, bunching, and position building are riddled with conflicts that warrant their inclusion in this chapter. However, these are abuses that are typically not discovered until after a claim is brought and discovery is conducted. We don't have any red flags or warnings for you to detect this sort of conduct, but we want you to be aware of it.

SUPERVISION AND HOW BROKERS DODGE IT—CIRCUMVENTING THE GUARDS

Remember how much fun it was to see if you could break a rule and not be sent to the principal's office when you were in school? As adults, people speed on the highways and hope that a police officer doesn't stop them; they fudge on their taxes and hope the IRS doesn't catch them. These are examples of people versus authority. Don't be misled, however, by this section's title: brokerage firms are not the authority, and stockbrokers are not the people. Some brokers are dodging their firm's supervision, but the firm is leaning back, smiling, and winking. Firms have rules in place for the benefit of the regulators, but when their brokers break those rules, there is leeway in the response. Together, unethical brokers and firms endeavor to bend and break the rules without raising the regulators' eyebrows.

The revered Review and Outlook section of the *Wall Street Journal* on August 11, 1999, published a historic commentary entitled "Morals and Wall Street." The article first slammed the "Clinton age" and continued, "Whatever the standards of the White House, Wall Street needs higher sights . . . . capitalism is not just a question of . . . paying whatever fines. Capitalism only works well when folks play by the rules." The brokerage industry does not always play by the rules.

You might think that the rules and precepts relating to supervision would be of little help to you unless you file a complaint or an arbitration. Not true. Knowing and understanding supervision rules will assist you in monitoring your account and detecting problems. You should also be able to detect when someone is trying to pull the wool over your eyes on a potential supervision problem. Because securities regulations impose a dual duty on your brokerage firm and your broker, both are required to ensure that no trading violations take place in your account—a great idea in theory. The hope is that in addition to the rules of conduct governing brokers, the supervisory backup system will catch and eventually weed out the bad apples.

NASD Rule 3010 (a) Supervisory System
Each member shall establish and maintain a system to supervise the activities of each registered representative and associated person that is reasonably designed to achieve

compliance with applicable securities laws and regulations, and with the Rules of this Association. Final responsibility for proper supervision shall rest with the member.

NYSE Rule 405(2) Supervision of Accounts
Supervise diligently all accounts handled by registered representatives of the organization.

As a retail investor, it is unlikely that you will ever have an opportunity to review a compliance or supervisory manual of a brokerage firm. To us, a securities attorney and a securities fraud expert witness, they are some of the most important documents in every case—the road map that firms are to follow. And in the case of supervision, firms' supervisory manuals spell out the ways a particular firm conducts its supervision. As you can see by the NASD and NYSE rules above, regulators require supervision, but they don't always spell out exactly how it's to be done; that is left to the firms. The firms are required to follow and implement their own rules; and they are required to be able to prove they have conducted proper supervision of all brokers and all accounts. Regular audits by the regulators are designed to confirm this supervision.

It appears that the questionable brokerage firms or poorly run branch offices spend more time trying to prove they are conducting proper supervision than they do trying to make sure their brokers are managing clients' accounts appropriately. Most investors know little to nothing of these requirements. You might have a brush with them when a manager calls to ask a few questions or when you receive a letter from this same branch manager that discusses certain aspects of your account.

One of the primary ways that brokerage firms carry out their supervisory responsibilities is to set up computer triggers or screens to flag accounts that meet certain criteria. Those accounts are then generated on what's typically called an exception or activity report. An account might get flagged on a report in some of the following circumstances:

- Numerous trades
- In-and-out trading (buying and selling the same or similar securities)
- Trading out of approved categories

- High turnover of equity
- Large commissions in relationship to equity of account
- Unusual trading
- Significant losses
- Consistent losses
- Large number of margin calls
- Consistent and similar trading patterns in most of the broker's accounts
- Large number of unsolicited transactions
- Large and uneconomical margin balances
- One account's commissions are a large percentage of the broker's total production
- Large 1035 exchanges (annuity or life insurance switching)
- Unsuitable investments

There is usually a requirement that the branch manager investigate the accounts on the report. The manager's job is to review the account and compare the statistical findings with other information about the customer. For example, by reviewing the net worth and other financial information on the new account form, the manager might conclude that the customer is trading beyond his or her resources. The manager might then talk to the broker about the report and may either call the customer or send the customer a "cover your ass" (CYA) letter—a letter in which the firm states how much it appreciates the customer's business and other laudatory phrases. Somewhere between the lines, the manager may insinuate that the account is trading a lot or that high-risk investments are being purchased. These letters are sometimes watered-down attempts by the brokerage industry to prove to regulators that firms are fulfilling their supervisory duty. Firms try to protect themselves by purportedly putting clients on notice of possibly inappropriate activity, while at the same time reassuring them that even though they are losing a ton of money or there is a lot of trading, everything is okay and management is watching over clients' accounts. For this reason, these same letters are also referred to as comfort or happiness letters.

Alternatively, the communication may come in the form of a phone call that will take the same tack as the CYA letter. There will be lots of thank you's, talk of how great your broker is, and waxing on about how the firm is always there if needed. Clients may also hear "I am sure you are happy with Bob Broker, as he is one of our top brokers. I know that you and Bob talk often, and therefore Bob is doing what you want him to do." The branch manager will follow up this phone call with detailed notes in his file. Omitting the "yeses" and grunts in the phone call, the notes will state that the client said she has lots of money to lose, she discusses every trade in minute detail with the broker, and she loves to do short-term trading of index options.

Be forewarned: the vast majority of these letters and the phone calls will not appear to be much of a warning. Nonetheless, the firm will use them to defend any accusations of wrongdoing by claiming that the firm gave the client notice that the broker was abusing the account. The client didn't do anything about it, so it must have been okay. If you receive one of these CYA letters and buried within it are some sentences that you don't agree with, immediately say so in a letter back to the manager. Do not make the mistake that so many investors do, and that is to call their stockbroker for an explanation. Your broker has every incentive to minimize the branch manager's contact. He might say, "Oh, don't worry about that. The manager has to send those letters to all customers, and it's just a formality." That's not true. The letters typically go only out to customers whose accounts have popped up on the firm's radar screen for detecting potential wrongdoing. Let it be a red flag to you as well and document the misstatements.

If, after you recover from one of these phone calls from the branch manager and in retrospect feel you were caught off guard and maybe agreed to things you shouldn't have, don't just forget about it and go on with life. Write a letter to the branch manager clarifying what you meant to say. This is critical to the effective management of your account. If you don't correct the misinformation, there is a very good chance that your account will suffer.

If your account shows up on an exception or activity report, the branch manager will discuss your account with your broker. You learned in Chapter 2 that brokers have conflicts. Well, branch managers also have conflicts that can hinder proper supervision. A branch manager's conflicts are similar to the broker's conflicts:

- He usually gets an override on commissions your broker produces.
- His office receives perks and benefits based on the total commissions produced by all of the brokers in his office.

- His year-end bonus and promotions are likely based on his office's profit and loss statements.
- If a broker in his office is sued and loses, the firm most likely will debit the branch's profit and loss statements.

The problem with this system is that the inherent conflicts pressure the manager to look the other way—the fox guarding the henhouse conflict. The conflicts also explain why the branch manager's letters and phone calls to you may be somewhat insipid: an unethical branch manager doesn't really want anything to change. And even if you ignore the conflicts, the branch manager's asking the broker if all is okay is like a police officer's asking a man running out of a bank with a bag of money and alarms blaring, "Is everything okay?" If a broker is abusing an account, do you think he is going to admit it to his branch manager just because he's asked?

One of the reasons we harp so much about writing letters and sending them to the firm is that both your broker and his manager are supposed to review your letters even if you address the letter only to your broker. More important, your letter is retained in your file and serves as notice to the firm of what your desires are regarding your account. Your letters are an extremely powerful tool to deter or correct disreputable conduct, and they also serve to ensure proper supervision of your account.

Conversely, all correspondence, including faxes and e-mails, that you receive from your broker or his firm must also be reviewed and approved by management. NYSE Rules 342 and 405 and NASD Rule 3010 require brokerage firms to monitor and preapprove correspondence that is mailed out by their brokers. Individual firm policies almost always require firms to sign off on all outgoing correspondence and retain such proof in a file. You can imagine that it's much easier for a manager to review what comes in than what goes out; all a broker has to do is stick something in an envelope and send it to you, and the manager may never know about it. This is another reason you should keep all correspondence and literature received from your broker.

If you happen to receive something from your broker that seems too good to be true, such as a document touting an investment that is as safe as can be but promises a 33 percent return, there is a good chance the broker sent you the piece without his management's approval. Many firms prepare sales documents for their brokers labeled "For Internal Use Only." These documents often tout only the upside of an investment and omit or minimize the risks. Some firms or managers want their brokers to use such documents to present the investment, because they know that a one-sided presentation will more often result in a sale. It is not uncommon for us to find these "Internal Use Only" documents in our clients' files. Firms prohibit stockbrokers from distributing them, but it happens.

If you ever suspect that your broker is circumventing the regulations governing incoming or outgoing mail, you have reason to be nervous, not only about your broker, but also about the firm.

Another way that brokers and firms dodge supervision is to promote a stockbroker to branch manager and allow him to run the office. Branch managers have supervisory authority over all stockbrokers in the office and over all accounts handled in that office. However, a branch manager doesn't cease being a stockbroker just because he's a branch manager. He may have a cadre of customer accounts himself. Who is supervising the branch manager's accounts and the branch manager himself? It's certainly somebody off-site in some other office somewhere, because the branch manager is top dog in that office.

Tracy and Douglas had a number of cases against a large, well-known firm and the branch manager of one of its offices. The branch manager was also the broker for their clients, and one of the biggest claims in the cases was that the firm allowed this branch manager to work unfettered by any supervision of him or his clients' accounts. At the arbitration, the branch manager testified that *he* supervised *himself* as well as his clients' accounts. This is not permissible under the securities rules and regulations—again, the fox guarding the henhouse. The case settled.

If your stockbroker is also the branch manager of the office, ask your broker who is supervising him and your account, where that individual works, and how often that supervision is performed. Document and keep the answers to your questions just for safekeeping. The mere fact that you have asked these questions might send a message to your broker that he better not try to pull any funny stuff in your account.

In Chapter 4, we discussed the solicited versus the unsolicited trick. Supervisors are supposed to watch for situations where brokers mark a trade unsolicited and yet the investment is on the firm's recommended list. More serious is the situation where a broker marks an investment unsolicited and that same investment is purchased in a handful of the broker's other accounts. That red flag is on fire.

As always, just because we detail these concerns or potential abuses doesn't mean you or your accounts are necessarily being abused. But you never know. One problem in the industry is that it is sometimes very hard to detect improprieties. We hope you are learning more and more in each chapter so that you will be able to spot, at a minimum, the potential problems and, at best, serious violations.

CHAPTER 6

The Regulators
Whose Side Are They Really On?

This chapter will provoke criticism because both the regulators and the industry have a vastly different view of the regulators than we offer. The NASD views itself as "a tough and evenhanded regulator."[1] The NYSE claims it is "the most active self-regulator in the securities industry."[2] The SEC refers to itself as "the investor's advocate."[3] We admit that Arthur Levitt, chairman of the SEC who stepped down in 2001, probably did more over the last seven years than any chairman who preceded him. Though we have not met him personally, his speeches and writings were usually right on the mark for helping and protecting investors.

All of the regulatory agencies will claim great advances in weeding out the bad apples in the securities business. They might claim that year after year there have been larger sanctions and more of them. That may be true, but we liken the claim to the employee who gets better and better in his job but still doesn't cut the mustard; he doesn't get the job done. Although the regulators excel in many of the multifaceted areas for which they have responsibility, when it comes to policing the securities industry, in some ways they fail.

We all must deal with our own peculiar or unique handicaps, whatever they may be. Perhaps the employee mentioned above, who was ultimately fired despite his improvement, was dyslexic, which is what hampered his doing a good job. Or maybe he was caring for his ailing mother, who was on her deathbed, and that distracted him.

For years, regulators have been overworked and understaffed. High turnover at the SEC is a problem. In January 1999, *Registered Representative* published an article that queried, "Is the Securities Industry at Risk of Being Regulated by Rookies?"[4] Many of the regulators' failings may be attributable to these undeserving circumstances.

THE NASD—THE FOX
GUARDING THE HENHOUSE

Apart from the supervisors within each brokerage firm, the next-in-line supervisor of firms and their brokers is the NASD and the NYSE. The supervisory hierarchy looks like this:

SEC

NASD and NYSE

Brokerage firms

Stockbrokers

Between the NASD and the NYSE, the NASD has by far much more responsibility in terms of regulating and disciplining broker-dealer conduct. Although not every brokerage firm is a member of the NYSE, every brokerage firm in the United States is required by law to be a member of the NASD. The NASD's membership is made up of more than 5,500 securities firms that operate more than 67,000 branch offices and employ more than half a million registered securities professionals. On the other hand, the NYSE's membership is composed of firms or individuals who own seats on the New York Stock Exchange. Since 1953, the number of seats has remained fairly constant at 1,366. So you can see that the NASD commands much more authority as a regulator because of the sheer number of firms for which it is responsible.

The NASD also stands out because it is a for-profit company, whereas the NYSE is a not-for-profit company.[5] As long ago as 1943, the president of the NASD reiterated that the NASD "is devoted to the principle that its members are in business to make money."[6] The NASD and the NYSE are referred to as self-regulatory organizations (SROs). As such, they are responsible for developing rules designed to prevent fraud and protect the investing public. And as a self-regulatory agency, the NASD has the power to enforce those rules. We believe there is an inherent conflict in these two responsibilities. How can an organization made up of the very entities that can harm investors benefit and protect them?

The primary way in which the NASD enforces its rules is through field examinations where NASD representatives show up at firms to conduct a review. The NASD examines firms from once every four years to annually depending on the nature of a firm's business activities, method of operation, and type of products sold. The NASD does such things as examine a member's books and records for currency and accuracy; review the firm's sales practices to determine whether the firm has dealt fairly with customers when making recommendations, executing orders, and charging commissions or markups and markdowns; and determine compliance with the antifraud provisions of the securities rules, the advertising rules, and the margin rules.

Many NASD employees who conduct the examinations are underpaid and certainly susceptible to the kinds of things that firms might do to deter focus on problem areas. The NASD president admitted the deficiencies in field examinations in a November 2000 speech:

> As securities transactions become more complex, the burden of regulation has grown. . . . To be frank, historically we haven't done the best job of giving our examiners the cutting-edge tools and training they need to work most efficiently. And because we are tied to a routine cycle exam program, we don't always focus our resources on the riskiest firms—those that require our attention onsite and often.[7]

The bigger problem may be that the NASD does not appear to be willing to slap the hands that feed it to any serious extent. We have long believed that the sanctions and penalties imposed by the NASD when it finds wrongdoing typically pale in comparison to the act itself or the harm inflicted. In our experience, if there are suspensions, they are often measured in days, weeks, or months— not years. That's why you have to take the NASD's claims regarding how many firms and individuals it has sanctioned with a grain of salt. It's like the NASD claiming that the majority of investors prevail in their arbitration system. That may be true, but investors aren't prevailing in terms of recovering their full losses. The awards are often nominal or fractions of the losses sustained, but they allow the NASD to declare, "The investor won!"

Another example of the NASD's limp-wristedness is the Nasdaq system for which the NASD was responsible. In August 1996, the SEC condemned not only many of the market makers in the Nasdaq trading system but the NASD itself for its failure to properly regulate the Nasdaq market.[8] The SEC had these harsh words for the NASD:

> The NASD, during the period covered in the Report, did not comply with certain of its rules or satisfy its obligations under the Exchange Act to enforce its rules and the federal securities laws. It has inadequately enforced rules applicable to market makers while applying, in certain cases, ad hoc standards and criteria not embodied in NASD rules. *This is attributable, in part, to the undue influence of Nasdaq market makers in the regulatory processes of the NASD* [emphasis added].

The SEC did not fine the NASD for its serious violations. Rather, it required the NASD to expend a total of $100 million over the next five years to enhance its systems for market surveillance. The SEC didn't come out the white knight in this story, however. It didn't even uncover the wrongdoing. The SEC was prompted to investigate because two finance professors published an article articulating their suspicions that Nasdaq market makers were profiting from artificially wide spreads on customer trades.[9] Years later, in January 2001, the SEC released a report showing that, for the period covered by the report, the spreads on the NASD-regulated Nasdaq market were higher than similar stocks traded on the New York Stock Exchange.[10]

The NASD is not the only self-regulatory agency the SEC has had to fine for not doing its job. In the summer of 1999, the SEC settled a claim against the NYSE alleging it failed to adequately administer its own regulations against its floor members. It's a good thing we have the SEC to watch over these SROs that often appear to be more concerned with the interests of their dues-paying members than those of the investing public.

NO SECURITY BLANKET

A lot of people may view all of the regulators—the NASD, the NYSE, the SEC, and the state securities boards—as some sort of security blanket. If a problem arises in the handling of an account, the first thing an investor does is whip off a letter to one of these entities, sit back, and wait for the check to arrive. But behind the scenes, an entirely different situation plays itself out. A state securities regulator once told Douglas that because its office was so swamped with complaints, it could only afford to prosecute the wrongdoing that affects the most investors, is easiest to pursue, and that it feels has a very good chance of winning. The Arizona Securities Division sends out a form letter to some complaining customers as follows:

> After reviewing your complaint, we have determined that legal action by this office would not be appropriate at the present time. Division resources generally require that rather compelling reasons, in terms of the nature of the practice, the number of people involved, or the amount of loss must be present in order to justify a lawsuit. We must, therefore, restrict our action to those cases which involve the greatest harm to the public, and which will have the greatest deterrent effect on fraud in the marketplace.

Arizona at least tells it like it is. You may be small potatoes.

What usually happens, at least with the NASD and the NYSE, is that the agency forwards your complaint letter to the offending firm and asks it to reply. The firm then replies in a manner that absolutely contravenes everything you have said. The NASD and the NYSE give great weight and credibility to what the brokerage firm says, because, well, it's one of its own members. The agency may then send a letter back to you that says something like "We have investigated your complaint and have decided to take no action." Letters such as this are known as no-action letters.

If a firm were inclined to deny your claim without a no-action letter, you can bet it will be entrenched in that position with such a letter in its arsenal. If the investor goes on to file a claim and arbitrate it, the firm will waive around that no-action letter like an American flag on the Fourth of July. For this reason, when clients approach us with what appears to be a viable claim, our first advice is "Do not communicate with the regulators." There is simply not much of an upside for you. They won't help in recovering your lost money and an adverse finding or a no-action letter will be used by the brokerage firm as a defense to your claim. Therefore, think twice before complaining to the regulators.

On the other hand, *do* communicate with the regulators if you have no intention of pursuing your losses, if your claim is too small for a lawyer to handle, or if you discover wrongdoing in your account but have no losses. In addition to complaining to the NASD and the NYSE (if the firm is a member), also complain to your state securities regulator and the SEC. The state securities regulators and the SEC can be more objective, generally speaking, as they don't have such a close affiliation with the brokerage industry as do the NASD and the NYSE. Remember stories about the military being ripped off because it was paying huge sums for such things as a wrench or a toilet seat cover? Turns out, the supply companies selling these products consisted of individuals who previously worked for the military. They were selling to their buddies, who were paying the high prices because it wasn't their money!

The securities industry is similar in that few people ever leave the industry. The regulators rarely put individuals out of business or bar them from the industry. Sanctioned individuals just shift around from one brokerage firm to another or migrate to some other type of financial services company. Far too many top officials and enforcers at the SEC, when they leave, "hop the fence and end up working for brokerages or law firms that defend Wall Street."[11]

The common thread here reminds us of Hollywood, where there is no such thing as bad publicity. In the securities industry, a checkered, controversial past may be considered an asset rather than a detriment. It's hard, too, for brokers, to voluntarily leave the brokerage business because the money is generally too good. And they have endless choices of where they can go; stockbrokers who produce can always find a job.

REGULATING QUESTIONABLE FIRMS

How many brokerage firms can you name? We bet you can name only a small fraction of all the firms in the country—5,500 brokerages is a hefty number. One reason for this large number is that it is relatively easy to meet the net capital and other requirements for becoming a broker-dealer. In addition, the net capital requirement is minuscule in relation to the amount of dollars these small firms can reap for themselves.

The following scenario plays itself out all over the country on a regular basis. Con artists raise capital, apply for a broker-dealer license, hire some brokers, and, before you know it, are smiling and dialing. Newspapers routinely report stories about brokerage firms gone awry. In March 2001, 20 people were charged with cheating investors out of $50 million in a stock fraud scheme between 1994 and 1998. Two of the defendants, who were alleged to be associates in an organized crime family, were accused of funneling illicit profits from one of the brokerage firms involved in the scheme—which had since gone out of business—to their mob bosses.[12] All cons have their special tricks to bilk investors. Usually it's a combination of market manipulation, selling unregistered securities, churning and burning, front running, or selling plain ol' junk. As they slowly drain their clients' savings, and at the same time line their own pockets, the complaints and lawsuits start piling up. Finally, some regulator wakes up to find it has thousands of defrauded investors who, by now, have lost millions. The firm sees the handwriting on the wall and slowly starts to shut down its operations, but not too quickly. It knows it will take the regulators months to figure things out and months before any arbitrations kick in, so the firm continues to make hay while the sun shines.

The rub is that you think the regulators are working for you. Things start to unravel, and the NASD finally comes in and shuts down the firm and levies fines on the operators. The regulator's involvement at this juncture is akin to closing the barn door after the horse is already loose. Not surprisingly, only a modicum of capital is left. The scam has worked because all of the illegal profits have been paid out in salaries, commissions, and bonuses to the brokers, owners, and directors. The NASD gets in first and obtains any remaining funds that the firm has and investors slog along in the

NASD arbitration pipeline. Investors who proceed to arbitration and win discover that the well is dry. There is no more money to recover. Seems like a mockery of justice, doesn't it? We feel the money should go to the investors who lost money. The NASD didn't lose any money!

When Stratton was finally put to death in 1996, the NASD publicly declared that it "has rid the securities industry of one of its worst actors"[13] and that "in less than a decade, Stratton Oakmont amassed one of the worst regulatory records of any broker-dealer firm."[14] One of the more disturbing points of the entire Stratton Oakmont issue for investors was how long Stratton was able to remain in business as it continued to defraud investors. Stratton's troubles began in 1989 when it first experienced regulatory problems. *Forbes,* which has a good record of sniffing out wrongdoing early, warned investors about Stratton in October 1991 and again in June 1993. The SEC brought its first proceeding against Stratton in 1992. Yet the firm did not officially close its doors until late 1996 and early 1997. A lot of investors suffered losses during this eight-year period.

We empathize with the regulators. It is always a tough call to know exactly when a broker or brokerage firm should be completely shut down versus the alternative of censures, fines, and additional supervision. In 1994, the SEC required Stratton, through a negotiated settlement agreement, to set aside $2.5 million in a restitution fund for wronged investors and to pay a $500,000 civil penalty. Stratton also agreed to the appointment of an independent consultant who was to advise Stratton on cleaning up their regulatory problems. That didn't last long. So many more problems surfaced regarding Stratton after 1994 that the SEC finally determined to shut the firm down at the end of 1996.

When Stratton filed for bankruptcy in January 1997, there were estimates of over 3,000 individual investors with claims against the firm. Their losses were in the tens of millions of dollars. And Stratton had accumulated a debt of $5 million in unpaid arbitration awards. The assets of a broker-age firm are nominal to begin with—chairs, desks, tele-phones, and computers—and any profit that is generated is quickly paid out to the principals. Therefore, whatever ill-gotten profits may be collectible are in the pockets of the individuals who ran the firm. Though principals can be sued, it is often an uphill battle because they sequester their funds, making it difficult for investors to collect.

Douglas was involved in numerous Stratton Oakmont cases as a securities expert, and many of those investors were never able to obtain a remedy. In addition, there were hundreds, if not thousands, of other customers who lost significant amounts of money in the several-year period prior to Stratton's being shut down. These customers vis-ited securities attorneys about their claims and were told that they had a great case, but collection looked like a problem, so their cases were declined and the investors were sent home without a remedy. Tracy was the bearer of this bad news to several of Stratton's victims.

In the wake of regulator fines against the con artists who now have no money, these same folks who masterminded the scheme just start all over again on their own or walk across the street and operate with another broker-dealer. In the movie *Boiler Room*, one scene depicts an empty warehouse with nothing but dozens of phones lying on the floor. The unscrupulous brokerage firm sensed trouble and had already taken steps to have a new office set up so that the brokers could literally walk across the street and continue their sales pitches. This scene mimicked reality and is probably one of the single biggest injustices of the securities system.

In July 1990 the SEC and the NASD sanctioned a firm called J. W. Gant. Two years later, the firm shut its doors. Many of the bro-kers and managers who worked there simply went to a firm called Dickinson & Co., where soon another rash of problems began to surface. Tracy had a number of cases against Dickinson & Co., which is now no longer in business. When, in the discovery phase, she obtained some of the written scripts the brokers used to make their sales pitches, she was surprised to see that some of them had

J. W. Gant scratched out across the top and Dickinson & Co. written above it!

In the criminal justice system, something like 80 percent of the people who commit crimes in the United States are known to the system. In other words, the majority of criminals already have some kind of criminal record and are repeat offenders. In the same way, the securities regulators know who the bad apple brokers and managers are. They have either fined them individually or know they worked for firms that were shut down for securities violations. They know who they are, where they live, and where they work.

You would think that knowing this, the regulators would do a little supervision of their own. You would think the regulators would be breathing down these folks' necks to make sure they didn't start up where they left off. Think no further—the answer is no. Well, they are breathing, just not down anyone's neck. We are sure to get heated phone calls from regulators telling us that this is not true and they monitor these firms more than the average firm. Remember the NASD's November 2000 admission: "And because we are tied to a routine cycle exam program, we don't always focus our resources on the riskiest firms—those that require our attention onsite and often."[15] The regulators, more than anyone, are in the best position to monitor the bad brokers as they move from one firm to the next. But they don't really do enough.

Questionable firms will continue to defraud investors. It is hoped that the *Wall Street Journal*, *Forbes*, *Business Week*, and the other fine financial publications that have a history of alerting investors to brokerage firm malfeasance will get wind of questionable activities and write about them. Such stories can have a widespread impact in curtailing damage.

TOO LITTLE, TOO LATE

One need only to flip through the *Wall Street Journal* or a number of other financial publications over the last several years or so to be inundated with financial scandal, greed, and rampant violations—enough to make one's head spin. As we mentioned, the culprits are not only the penny-stock firms or bucket shop operations.

The SEC has its own shortcomings in terms of evildoer watchdog. The Prudential scandal happened under the nose of the SEC, and it took place after the SEC was already on notice of similar wrongdoing at Prudential. The SEC had sanctioned Prudential-Bache as early as January 1986, when it required the firm to improve its supervision.[16] When the SEC was investigating Prudential for its sale of limited partnerships, someone must have said, "Oh, and by the way, you are not complying with our earlier order regarding improved supervision."

So when the SEC issued its Findings and Order against Prudential for its limited partnership sales, it had to also sanction the firm for not complying with the 1986 Findings and Order almost a decade earlier! The SEC admitted in the limited partnership Findings and Order that "this matter presents some of the same types of violations and supervisory failures that gave rise to the Prior Order."[17] If the SEC had monitored Prudential's obligation to comply with the 1986 Order, the limited partnership scandal might have been aborted.

Although not funded by taxpayer dollars, the activities of all SROs are subject to federal oversight by the SEC. Employees of the SEC are also overworked and underpaid. In the late 1990s, the SEC revamped its regulation of investment advisors to lop off a huge number of advisors under its regulation because it didn't have the staff or the budget to regulate the growing number of investment advisors. In early 2000, Arthur Levitt was quoted as saying that the SEC "simply cannot pay our staff enough to keep them. . . . Since 1994, we have been experiencing an alarming rate of turnover."[18]

The SEC sanctioned Olde Discount on September 10, 1998, six years after the inception of Olde's wrongful conduct and three years after the conclusion of its investigation. The NASD brought charges against Dean Witter in November 2000 for misstating the risks of various closed-end bond funds that DeanWitter sold in 1992 and 1993—eight years after the fact.

Like brokers, the majority of regulators are hardworking, well-meaning, and honest people. We both know and work closely with many regulators around the country. But we just want to make sure that you don't feel you can trust your brokerage firm because the government or the regulators are watching. The SEC is trying to watch, but it has too big a task. And the NASD and the NYSE are watching, too—but through rose-colored glasses.

CHAPTER 7

Industry Forms and Paperwork
The Hidden Agenda

Although the securities business is perceived as being extremely document intensive, there are actually only a few documents that must be executed by an investor to open a brokerage account. Indeed, investors can open an account over the phone and be trading thousands of dollars in minutes with no documents being signed nor money transferred. But even for those people, the forms will come.

Don't let a stockbroker tell you that the information on any of the forms that relate to your account is not important. All the information is very important during the life of your account and may become even more important after your account is closed. The documents you sign at the inception of your account are supposed to dictate what kinds of investments and recommendations your broker is going to make. In addition, the supervisory and compliance individuals who are supposed to be reviewing your account and your broker's activities will use these documents when making their evaluations. It goes without saying that if the information on the forms is either incorrect or incomplete, improprieties may take place. Also, if you should have a complaint against your broker and these forms contain incorrect information, your brokerage firm may try to use that false information against you.

When you open any brokerage account, whether at a full-service, discount, or online firm, there are going to be a number of forms to sign. And although they may differ somewhat between firms, they are essentially the same. In this chapter, we take you through the forms and paperwork that affect you and your account and help you to understand each of them so that you are aware of the tricks related to these documents.

THE CUSTOMER AGREEMENT— YOU'RE STUCK WITH IT

The customer agreement is the document you sign that looks most like a legal contract. It's full of legal mumbo jumbo in very small print that most people never bother reading. And why should you? There's nothing you can do about it. Actually, Tracy had a client who did do something about it. Her client read the customer agreement and did not like the following paragraph:

> *Arbitration Agreement.* You agree to arbitrate any controversy between you and X Brokerage Firm or any of its officers, directors, employees, agents or affiliates arising out of or relating in any way to your Account.

So Tracy's client just put a bracket next to this paragraph and wrote the word "NO" next to it, as follows:

> *Arbitration Agreement.* You agree to arbitrate any controversy between you and X Brokerage Firm or any of its officers, directors, employees, agents or affiliates arising out of or relating in any way to your Account. } NO

He signed the agreement and sent it back to the firm. No one ever said anything. Years later, when the investor had a dispute with X Brokerage Firm, Tracy filed a claim for him in court. You can imagine how the firm went crazy trying to argue that the case should go to arbitration. The court rightfully concluded that Tracy's client modified the agreement and X Brokerage Firm, by its silence, accepted the modification. The case got to stay in court and quickly settled. This is not a trick we suggest using, though. The vast majority of the time, if you try to adjust or modify the customer agreement, the brokerage firm will refuse to open your account.

Brokerage firms despise being taken to court because in a court case firm secrets are more easily revealed. Not only does the firm have to respond to document requests, answer interrogatories, and give depositions, but everything is open to the public and the press. Firms much prefer to air their dirty laundry behind the closed doors of an arbitration. Therefore, every single customer agreement contains an arbitration clause; and in 1987 the U.S. Supreme Court said that was okay. And except for writing "NO" next to the arbitration clause and hoping the firm doesn't catch it, you are bound to go to arbitration if you have any sort of dispute.

You should also be aware that your customer agreement may not be between you and your brokerage firm. It may be between you and your brokerage firm's clearing firm. Some brokerage firms clear their trades in-house, in which case your customer agreement will be with your brokerage firm. Otherwise, it will be in the name of the clearing firm, which should not concern you. When there is a separate clearing firm, that is the firm that is actually safekeeping your funds and extending credit to you. Therefore, it has more of a vested interest in having you sign an agreement directly with it. Don't worry—your brokerage firm is also bound by that agreement.

The other provision that you should be aware of is the margin provision that firms sometimes sneak into their customer agreements. This is a short, unobtrusive paragraph that simply states that you authorize the use of margin. Firms like to have their customers agree to the use of margin up front so that later, when their broker uses margin in a customer account and the customer complains, the firm can say, "But you authorized it. You agreed to it." That response has probably deterred a lot of investors with valid claims that margin was used in their account without their full understanding of what it was (see a discussion of margin in Chapter 5). Some firms have separate agreements, called Margin Agreements, which specifically address the investor's desire to make use of margin. These agreements are signed at any time during the existence of an account when an investor expresses an interest in trading on margin. Alternatively, some firms, most notably online firms, do a good job of incorporating margin provisions into their customer agreements. Datek Online has a long, nine-page agreement; three of the first four items relate to margin in some form. Appendix A in Datek's agreement consists of a five-paragraph Disclosure of Credit Terms. Of course, for many online firms, margin is the crux of their business, so those firms have more of a desire to highlight the margin provisions. Whether you have a traditional brokerage account or an online account and whether you sign a separate margin agreement or one incorporated into your customer agreement, the important point is that you have a full understanding of what margin is and how it works.

We feel it's fair to say that customer agreements are designed for the protection of the brokerage firm, not the customer. In fact, they are one of the more one-sided agreements you'll ever sign; and some of the online trading firms' agreements are the most one-sided. It's as if a group of online executives (whose average age was probably 20) got together and said, "Okay, we are making tons of money. To protect ourselves, let's put language in our customer agreements that say we can't be held responsible for anything!!" And that's what they did. This is Ameritrade's customer agreement (available online at its Web site):

> DATA NOT GUARANTEED
> Neither Subscriber nor any other person shall hold any Dissemination Party liable in any way for (a) any inaccuracy, error or delay in, or omission of, (i) any such data, information or message or (ii) non-performance or (iii) interruption in any such data, information or message, due either to any negligent act or omission by any Disseminating Party.

E*Trade's agreement (available online at its Web site) says the following:

> You further agree that E*Trade and its affiliates will not be liable for any consequential, incidental, special, or indirect damage (including lost profits, trading losses and damages) that result from inconvenience, delay or loss of the use of the Service even if E*Trade has been advised of the possibility of such damages.
> You also understand that neither any participating national securities exchange or association nor any supplier of market data guarantees the timeliness, sequence, accuracy or completeness of market data or any other market information, or messages disseminated by any party. Neither E*Trade nor any disseminating party shall be liable in any way, and you agree to indemnify and hold

harmless E*Trade and such disseminating party, for (a) any inaccuracy, error, or delay in, or omission of (i) any such data, information, or message or (ii) the transmission or delivery of any such data, information, or message; or (b) any loss or damage arising from or occasioned by (i) any such inaccuracy, error, delay, or omission, (ii) non-performance, or (iii) interruption of any such data, information, or message, due either to any negligent act or omission by E*Trade or any disseminating party . . .

Let's say that you are trying to place a trade in your online account, and you can't access the Web site nor can you get anything but a busy signal when you call. Are you out of luck because of the above language? Not necessarily. Arbitration cases are playing themselves out all over the country where customers are prevailing in the face of the above language. Douglas recently worked on a case against an online firm wherein the firm provided misleading information about some online options. A firm representative confirmed the misleading information on the phone with the customer, who relied on the information to his detriment, and the arbitration panel found in his favor and allowed him to recover.

You are probably familiar with the phrase *contract of adhesion*. Adhesion conjures up images of someone being literally glued to a contract. A contract of adhesion is a contract that is drafted unilaterally by the dominant party and then presented on a take-it-or-leave-it basis to the weaker party, who has no real opportunity to bargain about its terms. You enter into contracts of adhesion all the time: when you rent a car or open a credit card account. There's also the small stub that absolves a vendor of all liability: when you buy a ski pass, enter an amusement park, and take your clothes to the cleaners.

The draconian language in some customer agreements, however, is not always the shield the firms think it is. Firms would probably get a stricter but more beneficial interpretation of the agreement clauses if they were in court because courts often rely on the fact that you can read, you have an education, or you could have tried to negotiate the terms. But arbitration is another story. Arbitrators have often found for the customer in the face of purportedly binding contract language. So if you read your customer agreement and think, "It's a lost cause; I'll never prevail in my claim," you just might.

THE NEW ACCOUNT FORM—
MORE IMPORTANT THAN YOU THINK

Together, as both the lawyer and the expert who have seen hundreds and hundreds of brokerage account documents, we are fascinated by the fact that one of the key documents in virtually every single case is one that the customer has often never seen. It is the new account form.

New account forms are not uniform, as each brokerage firm designs its own, but they typically contain an array of personal information—your age, occupation, marital status, number of dependents, annual income, liquid assets, risk capital, net worth, investment objectives, and your previous investment experience. Your broker is required to fill out the form based on conversations with you from which he derives the necessary information. Prudential calls its new account form a "financial blueprint," and it has begun withholding brokers' commissions until the form is completed. Another firm has begun placing information from a customer's blueprint, such as risk tolerance and asset allocation on the customer's monthly statements, a beneficial practice that more firms should adopt.

It's possible that you don't know what is on your new account form because a considerable number of brokerage firms fill them out for you and then tuck them away in your file. There are no rules or regulations that require these forms to be filled out by customers, reviewed by customers, or even mailed to customers; and few firms require that customers, as opposed to brokers, fill out the forms. Some firms do send a copy of the completed form to customers, and other firms place information from the new account form, like asset allocation and risk tolerance, on each monthly statement.

One of the primary purposes of the new account form is to guide your broker in handling your account. As part of the suitability assessment, your broker is required to know certain essential facts about you; and it's in the new account form that those facts are recorded. Your broker may have hundreds of clients and can't be expected to remember every detail about you when you call or when you are called. Stockbrokers are supposed to continually refer to the new account form so that as new investments come to their attention, they can ensure that those investments are compatible with all of a customer's unique personal investment goals and financial status.

Another equally important role of the new account form is to provide a monitoring tool for a broker's supervisor. At the inception of your account, your broker's branch office manager is required to sign off on the new account form. At that time, any red flags should be detected—for example, if an 80-year-old customer with an annual income of $15,000 and net worth of $80,000 wants to invest $50,000 for trading. Also, throughout the life of your account, your broker's manager is supposed to occasionally review your new account form to ensure that investments purchased in your account and the rate at which investments are being purchased are suitable for you, given your investment objectives and other personal information. The manager is supposed to go through this process when he reviews your confirmations and monthly statements as well.

We have rarely seen a new account form that was filled out completely or properly, which may be attributable to the fact that most of the ones we see, we see because of some sort of problem. As examples, we've seen forms that said the customer had an L.L.M. degree, when he really had a J.D. degree; the customer's age was written as 55 when it was really 45; the customer was single when she was married; and the annual income was $200,000 when it was really $100,000. Almost always, we see portions of the form that are left blank and investment objectives that our clients do not agree with. Errors on the form are the result of customer ego (the customer overstated his net worth or investment experience) or broker negligence or malfeasance.

Brokers have an incentive to bump up the numbers on the new account forms; doing so makes customers seem wealthier or more financially sophisticated than they may really be. This is a benefit to brokerage firms when defending claims brought by customers. For example, on one new account form, the broker had written "10" in the blank for "Number of Years in Stocks and Bonds"; however, the customer explained later that what he told the broker was that his only investment experience was ten years earlier when he had purchased $1,000 of IBM stock. At the hearing, the brokerage firm defended the claim by pointing to the "purported" ten-year investment experience to show that the broker had reason to believe the customer understood the risks of the market, but the investor did *not* have ten years of trading experience; he had purchased only one security ten years earlier.

Whether you are already doing business with a brokerage firm or are opening a new account, ask for a copy of your new account form. Make sure it is correct; if it isn't, correct it and send it back. Write a letter with additional explanatory information. If your broker has inflated, or attempts to inflate, any of the information you have given him for the form, ask for an explanation. Consider that you may be dealing with a broker who is more concerned about protecting himself than looking out for your best interests.

Keep a copy of the new account form, and over time advise your broker of material changes with respect to any of the information on it. Realize that the new account form is merely a guide for the broker; under the Know Your Customer rule, your broker is required to elicit *other* information from you for which there are no neat spaces or boxes on the form. We have never seen any new account forms that had a space for additional comments, which is unfortunate, because some items may deserve more explanation. Just because you have invested for ten years doesn't necessarily mean that you have an understanding of how the securities markets work, how commissions are structured, or what an IPO is. Does your broker know whether your stated investment objective applies to all the money you seek to invest or only part of it? The form may indicate you are employed, but what if you plan to retire next year?

If you discover that your new account form is incorrect, you may have a problem. Seek an explanation; if you aren't satisfied with it, find a new brokerage firm. Don't assume that you can solve the problem by switching brokers within the firm. All brokers within that office will have the same supervisors, and the supervisors may be equally at fault for your problem. Be sure to read Chapter 14 for a detailed discussion of how to determine your investment objectives; the chapter will help you make sure the information on your new account form properly reflects your investment goals.

THE OPTIONS-TRADING APPLICATION— LICENSE TO LOSE

Before you can make an options trade, your brokerage firm must have obtained from you a signed Options-Trading Application, and this document must be signed and approved by a supervisor with a special options license. The reason for this heightened scrutiny is because losing money trading options falls somewhere between easy to a sure thing (see Chapter 14 for information about specific investment products and strategies).

Unlike the new account form, the options application has always had to be signed by the client, but, like the new account form, it too has questions about your investment goals. The options application records your investment goals solely for the money that you plan to use in trading options. The result is that the firm may have two separate documents that have different investment objectives. The new account form investment objective may be growth, whereas the options application objective may be speculation. Brokerage firms like this inconsistency and use it to their advantage when they need to. Here's how. If a customer complains about a stock that tanked, the firm will likely wave the options application in the customer's face to support the proposition that the customer wanted to speculate. Brokerage firms could rectify this problem by simply having a clarification statement on the options-trading application saying that the options-trading objectives apply only to the money traded in options.

Because that won't happen anytime soon, here is our suggestion for clarifying the discrepancy. Take advantage of the fact that you are required to sign, and therefore see, the options-trading application. Next to the list of investment objectives, draw a little arrow to the margin and write something like this: "For options trades only—no more than 10 percent of portfolio, or $20,000, whichever is less." This document is not like the customer agreement, which would cause your account to be rejected if you were to make any changes whatsoever and the firm caught them. The options application is a document that you have every right to clarify, and you have the right to provide the firm with more information about your desires. Just as with the new account form, if you plan to speculate with options, put parameters on that speculation in terms of dollars or a percentage. Doing so adds heightened supervision on your account. Your broker and your broker's supervisor must be careful to ensure that your trading does not violate those parameters, whether at your broker's suggestion or on your own initiative. A specifically tailored objective for options trading also prevents the firm from claiming that you are a dice-rolling, gambling maniac, a resounding theme in many cases.

Even if you check the less aggressive investment objectives on the options form, you are nonetheless agreeing by signing the form that you have read a whole host of other documentation advising you of the risks of various options strategies. For this reason, it is important that you understand these strategies, which are also listed on the form for you to check. If you don't understand these strategies and their attendant risks, tear up the options form and don't trade options. We have a client who checked income and safety on his form, but then the broker marked strategies that were much more aggressive. No one at the brokerage firm ever caught this obvious contradiction.

The options form will also include various questions about your investment experience. Don't allow anyone to write, or convince you to write, anything but the absolute truth about your experience. If you traded options ten years ago and have not traded them since then, don't put down ten years of options experience. You are well advised to not overstate the figures on this form.

As with your new account form, every year ask your broker or brokerage firm to send you a copy of your current options-trading application to review it for accuracy. If anything is incorrect in any way, find out why it is incorrect and correct it.

ORDER TICKETS—DINOSAURS BUT STILL KEY DOCUMENTS

Other than your new account form, the order ticket is the second most important document regarding your account. Your broker writes up an order ticket for each and every transaction in your account. Formerly, brokers would write each order ticket by hand, but that practice is almost obsolete now for larger firms. As firms computerize, brokers enter orders directly into the computer, which has done wonders to speed the process of routing orders through the system.

Order tickets have always been considered one of the more important documents in the brokerage industry. If there is a dispute, problem, or complaint relating to your order, the investigation begins with the order ticket, which embodies the specific conversation you and your broker had relating to a specific order. If you trade on the Internet, there will be an electronic order ticket or blotter. Regardless of its form, order tickets are regulated and specific information is required to be on them; the information is not the same as what you input when you enter an online order. Nor is it the same as the information you see on your confirmation. What follows is a list of the information that is on most order tickets (options, bond, and mutual fund tickets will differ somewhat):

- A buy or sell
- Name and account number of the customer
- Name or symbol of the security
- Number of units to be traded
- How the trade is to be handled as to price (market or limit order)
- A day order or a GTC (good-till-canceled) order
- A time stamp indicating when the order was placed
- A second time stamp indicating when the order was filled/executed
- Whether the trade was solicited or unsolicited
- Whether discretion was used if it's a discretionary account
- Whether the order was read back to the client (to catch errors)
- The commission and how it was calculated if different from the firm's standard
- How long the security has been in the account if it's a sell order
- The manager's initials indicating his review

Brokerage firms are required to keep these order tickets or some type of trade blotter for six years. Firms are also required to keep any changes to any order tickets, such as cancellations, changes, or corrections. If you do a lot of trading with a broker, and he is entering all of the orders, we suggest that you ask him to give you a copy of all the types of order tickets he may be using in your account. It can be an eye-opener and should help you communicate with the broker when orders are being placed.

Keep in mind that brokers are required to write a ticket or input an order into a computer program and enter that ticket as they are talking to you or immediately after hanging up the phone (see Chapter 5 for a discussion of time and price discretion). If you suspect that this is not happening with your order, find out why.

CONFIRMATIONS—A NONEVENT IT'S HOPED

When we ask the firm to produce the order tickets for the account in arbitration cases, the firm often responds that there is no need to because the confirmations show the same information. You are probably familiar with the information on a confirmation because you receive a confirmation in the mail after every transaction in your account. You can compare the confirmation to the order ticket list above and will quickly conclude that the information is not the same. For example, your confirmation will not tell you the time the order was entered (what if it was an hour after you spoke with your broker?) or how the commission was arrived at (you will see just the commission).

The confirmation slip is a summary of your securities transaction. Although your trades are summarized on a monthly statement you receive in the mail, the confirmation of a trade is sent to you days after the trade. Review your confirmations immediately, while the conversation with your broker is fresh in your mind. Always note if the confirmation is marked unsolicited, meaning the trade was your idea. If you had not heard of the investment before your broker brought it up, then it cannot be an unsolicited purchase. If you receive a confirmation incorrectly marked unsolicited, whip off a letter to your firm pointing out the error.

MONTHLY STATEMENTS— WHO REALLY READS THEM?

It is our firm belief that for many years, brokerage firms purposefully made brokerage statements difficult, if not impossible, to understand because of conflicts of interest. The more a customer understands what's happening in the account, the less the firm can get away with. And often, just when you think you've figured out how to read your statement, the firm changes it, and not always for the better. Our proof is that we have been forced to read thousands and thousands of monthly statements over the years, a daunting task indeed. We admit that some firms have made vast improvements in the readability of these documents, but there is so much more they could still do.

Most monthly statements are just plain confusing. A person should be able to discern in a matter of minutes the following information:

- The bottom line—the net worth of the account
- How the net worth figure changed from the previous month
- The realized P&L (profit and loss) in the current month and year to date
- The unrealized P&L in the current month and year to date
- Margin charges, if any, in the current month and year to date
- Total commissions (including markups, markdowns, and other fees) in the current month and year to date

We challenge you to find a monthly statement that displays all of the above information.

Charles Schwab was one of the first firms years ago to show on a monthly statement how the account had changed from the previous month's statement. You can understand why many firms have no incentive to show you this information, because they fear that the results may prompt you to close the account.

Some firms now list your investment goals (from your new account form) on your monthly statement. Pay close attention to these statements. If you don't agree with the order of the list or the list itself, immediately type out a letter stating your disagreement and demand that the list or the goals be changed. And if the form lists "speculation" as your last goal, and you don't want to speculate at all, then send a letter to the branch manager to say that you want this "goal" of "speculation" removed from your account. Save a copy of your letter.

Depending on the brokerage firm and the size of your accounts, you may be able to get fancier statements with more information. Ask your firm for statements that allow you to evaluate your account as much as possible. Otherwise, you have to pay your CPA or someone like Douglas to tell you what is going on.

The better monthly reports today provide you with the following information in addition to the typical information and the information listed above:

- Your cost basis in each investment and whether the holding is long term or short term

- Your unrealized gain or loss
- Your realized losses and gains for the year to date
- Commissions, fees, and margin costs for the year to date
- A breakdown of your portfolio by investment type and the percentage of your portfolio those types represent

Read your monthly statements. If you can't understand them, ask your broker to explain them over and over until you do understand them, especially if you are paying full commissions. Never let your broker know you are not reading your statements or your confirmations, as that only invites improper activity. If you travel or live outside the United States, don't let your statements go anywhere where your broker could have access to them.

When you see something on your statement you don't understand or seems out of place, circle it, write your question on it, make a copy of it, and send it to your broker. Demand a full explanation. If you suspect something improper, make sure your questions and his response are in writing. And make sure that a copy of both your question and the answer goes to the branch manager of the firm.

Duplicate statements sometimes make good sense. If your elderly mother-in-law has a broker making investment recommendations or decisions for her, have her broker send you duplicate statements and call once or twice a year so that he knows you are reviewing them. A CPA or a person who is giving you second opinions on your investments should also get duplicate statements.

Save your monthly statements and your confirmations for six years. Your CPA will thank you for it. And if you ever seek a second opinion or have some sort of problem, you will need them.

In conclusion, do not take your brokerage firm forms and paperwork lightly. If you never lose money or never have a problem or complaint, then an incorrect or misleading document may be inconsequential. But you will only know that with the benefit of hindsight. Nobody knows what will happen in the future, least of all what will happen in your brokerage account! Take protective measures now to ensure that all documentation is current, complete, and accurate. Doing so will lessen the potential for problems and will assist you if a problem should arise. Remember: all the documents that govern your brokerage account were written by the firm (and their lawyers) to protect them, *not you!*

CHAPTER 8

Online Trading
Are You on Your Own?

The legal landscape is just beginning to catch up with the advent of online brokerage firms. Although you may not have been aware of the host of duties traditional brokerage firms owe to their customers, you may be surprised to discover that the law is still unclear regarding what duties an online brokerage firm owes to its customers. Because online firms have eliminated the "broker," many of them take the position that they do no more than execute unsolicited trades. So, their argument goes, their only duty to the customer is to execute those trades properly—nothing more. SEC reports show a steady rise in complaints over the last four years regarding online brokerage services, from 259 in 1997 to 1,114 in 1998, and 3,313 in 1999 to 4,271 in 2000. You, like these thousands of others complaining about online brokerage services, are realizing that regardless of the firms' advertising, you really are on your own in dealing with online firms—at least from their standpoint.

THE NO-DUTY STANCE—WOW!

In an online brokerage case in which Douglas served as the expert, the claimant was permitted to buy over $400,000 worth of stock when his account equity was only $96,000. Because the purchase was for a stock that was not yet trading, the online firm had to hand-calculate the margin buying power of the account. Therefore, before the trade was executed, the firm should have known that the purchase could far exceed, not only the equity in the claimant's account, but the claimant's net worth as well. The firm took no steps to cancel or limit the trade, nor did it notify the claimant that such an event was about to take place for either margin or suitability reasons. The firm said it had no duty to do any of these things.

One of Tracy's online arbitration cases provides a good example of the no-duty stance many online firms take. This particular online firm allowed her client to buy over $4 million of securities in his account over a roughly three-month period when he had only deposited $12,200!! According to her client, he misunderstood how buying power worked, and he says that his screen kept telling him he had additional buying power. Tracy's demand letter to the online brokerage firm stated: "You allowed this to happen in an account in which the individual had little prior experience trading options and no prior experience trading on margin. In fact, my client has a net worth of not much more than his total deposit." The online firm has denied the claim and there is no resolution at this time. Cases not too dissimilar from these are playing themselves out all over the country.

In two arbitrations in which Douglas was the expert witness, an executive at an online brokerage firm provided testimony that two of the most sacrosanct guidelines of the industry did not apply to this firm, including the NASD suitability rule and the NYSE "Know Your Customer" rule. The executive stated:

> . . . that is why our firm assumes no duty with regard to protecting the customer—who knows if we are protecting the customer or hurting the customer. Our manager [a licensed trading manager at this online firm] is there to protect the firm, and our firm has made this very clear to its customers.

These statements merit review. The first sentence states that this online firm "assumes no duty with regard to protecting the customer." Throughout the hearing and through various witnesses, this online firm repeated this same no-duty theme. The only duty this online firm acknowledged was the duty to process orders accurately and timely. The firm contended that because the firm only takes unsolicited orders, the duty to protect the customer does not apply.

The second part of the online firm's quoted sentence—"who knows if we are protecting the customer or hurting the customer"—essentially takes the position that an online firm has no way of knowing, for example, if a customer's trades are suitable based on the investment experience, net worth, or investment objectives of the customer. Not withstanding that position, if an online firm has obtained a completed new account form from a customer, the firm *could* determine if the customer is being hurt.

Let's say a customer has a net worth of $150,000, an annual income of $25,000, and an investment objective of long-term growth. If the customer margins himself to the tune of $300,000, this online firm could conclude that harm lurks on the horizon. In addition, this same firm fairly easily could program its computers to catch and even prevent this obviously unsuitable trade or trading pattern. But why should this online firm go to this effort and expense if it feels it has no legally recognized duty to do so?

The last sentence of the quotation, "Our manager is there to protect the firm, and our firm has made this very clear to its customers," borders on the comical in view of the fact that one of the claims in Douglas's case was false advertising. The claimants not only supplied the arbitration panel with numerous print ads disseminated by the firm but also played a number of its television ads. In his client's view, none of those ads stated that the firm's policies, procedures, and employees were there merely to "protect the firm" and not the customer.

Then why, might you wonder, are you often asked all of that personal information when you opened an online account? Customers who open online trading accounts are frequently asked to provide information about their net worth, trading history, and investment goals. Why do some of the online firms obtain this information? According to at least this online firm, it's simply because the firm is required to obtain it. Both the NASD and NYSE rules require the gathering of this information by brick-and-mortar firms so that they can fulfill their suitability duty. Although the online firm in Douglas's case has admitted that it gathers the information, it continues to take the position that it had no duty to make any use of it.

We say "Wow," because it seems to us that online firms have attempted to create the ultimate brokerage firm—all money falls to the bottom line and there is little to no liability because the broker has been removed. Online firms rely heavily on the language of the NASD suitability rule that says, "In recommending to a customer the purchase, sale, or exchange of any security, a member shall have reasonable grounds for believing that the recommendation is suitable." Because there is no broker to recommend, online firms contend there can be no rule violation.

This issue has been raised and fought long before online firms appeared. If a little old widow in tennis shoes walks into a brokerage firm and lays $10,000, all the money she has in the world, on the table and says she wants to risk it all on index options, should the brokerage firm accept this unsolicited order? Can a firm knowingly let a customer blow herself up, or can a firm knowingly let a customer make unsuitable trades? Some court decisions say no. And many experts and regulators say no; the firm has a duty to not enter that trade for that customer despite the NASD rule's reference to recommending.

In addition, NYSE Rule 405 does not limit its applicability to recommendations, as the NASD rule does. Nor does it carve out an exception for accounts in which customers place their own trades. The duty of suitability has always been a dual responsibility on the part of the broker and the brokerage firm. We believe that just because online brokerage firms have removed the broker, the requirement for the firm to make sure the trades are suitable should not be lessened.

Brokerage firms are licensed and, like doctors, they cannot allow a customer to do something they know is not in the customer's best interest—that is, unsuitable. For years, major brokerage firms have launched similar arguments in traditional suitability cases. For example, they argue that the broker presented a number of investments to a customer, some safe and some risky. It was the customer who chose the risky investments, so it's not the broker's fault. That defense typically does not fly. A doctor cannot line up a row of medicine in front of his patient and say, "You pick the one that you think might cure your ailment." Isn't that like what the online firms are doing? They have solicited investors' business and then said to them, "Hey investor, here at your disposal is an entire laundry list of investments to choose from and an easy and cheap way to buy them." We don't believe that Buyer Beware should have any place in the securities industry.

We also say "Wow" because some brokerage firms that offer online trading have taken a different stance. The *Wall Street Journal* on June 7, 1999, reported:

> Merrill says its normal customer "suitability" rules will apply to the fee-based program because those customers are still "full-service clients"—even if they do some online trading. "Merrill Lynch generally takes a more responsible position when servicing investors than simply allowing them to commit financial suicide," says Assistant General Counsel Kevin Moynihan. "There are some levels at which you don't stand by and let that happen," he says.

Registered Representative magazine, a brokerage industry publication, reported in its September 1999 issue:

> Both Merrill Lynch and Prudential supervise clients' online trading activity. Merrill Lynch won't say just how it oversees client trading other than flagging accounts with high turnover—those making 250 trades or turning over more than five times a year. Prudential, for instance, will not allow a client to make a trade representing more than 25 percent of his net worth to buy more than 10,000 shares in a single order, or to make more than 20 purchases in a day.

How is it that these traditional firms comply with these traditional brick-and-mortar duties where so many of the pure online-only brokerages feel they don't have to?

Even those online firms that have taken the position they have no suitability duty whatsoever have assumed a suitability duty with respect to certain investments. For example, at least one of the "we have no duty" firms we're aware of disseminates information about its offering of IPOs. Its Web site states, "Public offerings are considered speculative investments and can be extremely volatile . . . eligibility will be based on responses to your Customer Profile regarding your investment objectives [and] financial background. . . ." Now, wait a second. The firm admits it performs a suitability analysis for some investments but not for others? If an online firm assumes a duty to protect the investor from IPOs, then what about day trading, options trading, excessive trading, excessive margin, and a host of other trading activities that are just as risky as IPO investing, and in some cases riskier?

THE REGULATORS' INPUT

As of this writing, the latest pronouncement on the part of the NASD was on March 19, 2001, in its Notice to Members 01-23.[1] In this notice, the NASD made clear that there certainly exist situations in which the suitability rule would apply to online brokerage firms, thereby eliminating a blanket "the suitability rule never applies to us" defense. But this notice is not as beneficial to investors as one might think and not as clear. The NASD says that the suitability rule applies when an online firm "recommends" securities, and the NASD gives some guidelines as to what can be considered a recommendation. However, issues still remain whether a certain set of facts would combine to constitute a recommendation. The NASD recognized that "many forms of electronic communications defy easy characterization" and that "the 'facts and circumstances' determination of whether a communication is a 'recommendation' requires an analysis of the content, context, and presentation of the particular communication or set of communications."[2] In other words, "there remains a lot of gray area."[3]

A disconcerting inference made by the NASD notice, and one that Douglas has personally heard at least one NASD regulator espouse, is that solicited does not mean recommended. The NASD notice does not use the words *solicited* or *solicitation*. In the securities industry, a solicited trade is generally treated the same as a recommended trade.[4] A departure from this standard may result in part from pressure from online firms that want to expand their product lines and services to investors without the restrictions that would result if the suitability rule applies. We believe that this is a very, very dangerous interpretation. It could lead to mottos from online brokerage firms such as, "We solicit everyone for every investment, but we make no recommendations" or "If you want to blow yourself up, we'll supply the dynamite. But don't blame us."

In its notice, the NASD described some scenarios that would *not* constitute recommendations, such as a Web site's research pages or electronic libraries that contain research reports (which may include buy/sell recommendations from the author of the report). Interestingly, the SEC characterized the NASD notice by saying that "these common-sense guidelines suggest that if a communication is not a recommendation on paper, it is probably not a recommendation online." Yet it has always been accepted that the mere mailing of a research report by a brokerage firm is considered a recommendation and solicitation. A number of major brokerage firms' compliance manuals specifically state that if the mailing of a stock commentary or research report results in a purchase, the broker must mark that order ticket as solicited. Under the NASD notice, what is a recommendation on paper is not necessarily a recommendation online.

Conversely, the NASD described situations that would constitute recommendations—for example, if a firm sent an e-mail or a pop-up screen to a targeted customer or targeted group of customers encouraging the purchase of a particular security. Critics charge that "no online broker is currently engaging in the kind of practices that the NASD says might give rise to a suitability claim."[5] So, for the time being, as drafted, the NASD guidelines would have no negative impact on most of the large online firms.

On at least one occasion, the NASD backed off proinvestor stances originally taken on this issue. For example, in 1996 the NASD put its foot down in Notice to Members 96-32 entitled, "Members Reminded to Use Best Practices When Dealing in Speculative Securities"; a section entitled "Suitability" stated:

> Members are cautioned to take special care with respect to their suitability analysis where the securities involved are low-priced or speculative in nature. . . . Members' responsibilities include having a reasonable basis for recommending a particular security or strategy. In addition, the know-your-customer requirement . . . requires a careful review of the appropriateness of transactions in low-priced, speculative securities, *whether solicited or unsolicited.* [Emphasis added]

The above language was a huge step forward for investors. The NASD declared that both the suitability and know-your-customer rule apply regardless of whether the trade is solicited or unsolicited.

Perhaps in part in response to its members' reactions to the notice, the NASD issued Notice to Members 96-60 entitled, "Clarification of Members' Suitability Responsibilities under NASD Rules with Special Emphasis on Member Activities in Speculative and Low-Priced Securities." The notice specifically says that it was issued as a supplement to the above notice to "clarify certain issues addressed in that notice." It stated:

> A member's suitability obligation under rule 2310 applies only to securities that have been recommended by the member. It would not apply, therefore, to situations in which a member acts solely as an order-taker for persons who, on their own initiative, effect transactions without a recommendation from the member.

Investors who effect transactions on their own initiative are, by definition, making unsolicited trades. In its clarification notice, the NASD threw out the window pro-investor language about suitability obligations in speculative, low-priced securities applying *"whether solicited or unsolicited."* The mere fact that the NASD made the original proclamation tends to support that the NASD felt it would protect investors' interests. That it later qualified it almost out of existence is unfortunate.

The SEC apparently didn't think that the NASD's March 19 notice went far enough. It stepped up to the plate with a broader interpretation, stating, "The Commission notes that although NASD Notice to Members 01-23 does not expressly discuss electronic communications that recommend investment *strategies*, the NASD suitability rule continues to apply to the recommendation of investment *strategies*, whether that recommendation is made via electronic communication or otherwise [emphasis added]."[6] The SEC's statement arguably encompasses situations that NASD Notice to Member 01-23 did not describe—for example, if an online firm advertised on its Web site or encouraged customers to participate in IPOs, to trade on margin, or to trade in options, each of which could be considered investment strategies.

There already exist suitability obligations that are triggered by the nature of the activity, as opposed to whether the firm provided a customer-specific recommendation. On October 16, 2000, the SEC approved day trading rules that are now embodied in NASD Rules

2360 and 2361. These are wonderful, proinvestor rules. Rule 2360 imposes the obligation on any firm that promotes a day trading strategy to make a threshold determination that day trading is appropriate for the customer. A firm makes this determination by exercising reasonable diligence to ascertain the essential facts relative to customers, including their investment objectives, investment and trading experience and knowledge, financial situation, tax status, employment status, marital status and number of dependents, and age. Firms are also required to prepare and maintain a record noting the rationale for approving a customer's account for day trading.

Strong support exists for regulators to go further than they did in NASD Notice to Members 01-23. An online firm may not promote day trading, but it may promote other equally risky activity, such as margin or options trading. In December 2000, the state of Virginia published its report on Broker-Dealers Who Provide Discount Brokerage Services.[7] Among other things, the report identified best practices for online firms and had the following to say about suitability determinations:

> Brokerage firms should not limit the suitability determination to recommendations and solicitations. . . . Suitability determinations should serve as an effective screen when deciding what trading privileges various investors should receive. In terms of margin, determining whether a margin account is suitable for a customer is one best practice that may prevent individuals without the financial capacity or experience from trading with margin. Furthermore, since margin is a type of loan, on-line and off-line brokerage firms may want to lower the risk of defaults by limiting margin to those investors with the financial capacity to sustain a substantial loss in their portfolio. The same is also true for options trading. However, the investor's trading experience is also a characteristic that the firm should evaluate before granting options and margin trading privileges because these styles of trading can be highly technical and complex. Thus, options trading and margin are not suitable for all investors. When determining whether to grant special high-risk trading privileges, it is imperative that discount brokerage firms gather information describing the investor's investment

objectives and financial capacity. In light of the suitability information gathered, the on-line and off-line brokerage firms may make better-reasoned decisions to match the investor's objectives and financial capacity with the trading privileges and services offered by the firm.

Virginia also advocated that "if technically feasible, on-line firms should utilize the collected suitability information to provide an automated suitability warning service available at the option of the on-line investor."[8] A similar sentiment was echoed in a law review on the subject of online firms' suitability obligations: "Regulators should require suitability checks for unsophisticated customers entering trades online. . . . A suitability check or suitability review is when an online broker monitors the trades customers place online and stops the execution of any trades that are unsuitable for a customer's financial situation. . . . With this type of review, online brokers could identify unsophisticated online investors attempting to purchase securities that are too risky for their financial position and notify the investors about their findings."[9] It is true that advances in technology allow online firms to perform automated suitability checks. Traditional brokerage firms have been using similar technology to generate active account reports for years. As a representative of the Vanguard Group poignantly stated, "The benefits of online technology in the future should accrue to the investor, not to the online companies that offer the service." We agree wholeheartedly.

At the time of this writing, the debate continues. The NASD notice had been published for comment in the Federal Register and will likely generate an intense and voluminous outpouring of both opposition and support. We have yet to see whether the notice will evolve into a rule approved by the SEC. Our hope is that broader rules will be passed, rules that will protect the multitude of unsophisticated investors who venture online only to lose significant life savings.

So now that we have made you aware of many online firms' position that they have no duties relating to certain of your online activities and that the regulators are still debating how the suitability rule is going to be applied, how can you put all of this to use? Until these debates are worked out, we suggest that you be very, very careful and very vigilant, and perhaps a little paranoid, in all of your dealings with your online firm. If you have an online account, assume that the firm is recommending nothing, that nothing is individualized or tailored to meet *your* needs, that the firm is not monitoring or supervising your account in any way, and that the firm takes little responsibility except for best execution. In other words, assume a worst-case scenario in this interim period.

CHAPTER 9

Online Trading
Step into My Web Site,
Said the Spider to the Fly

Bookstores are currently jammed with investment books about Internet and online trading, but our topics on online trading are very different from the ones found in most of those books. We set aside "technogarb" for straight talk about what's going on behind the scenes at your online brokerage firm. If you bought this book because you're an online trading maniac and immediately flipped to Chapters 8 and 9, we believe you'll get your money's worth. You may decide, however, after reading the other chapters, that you're motivated to abandon online trading and return or switch to a traditional stockbroker. Why? Because knowing traditional firms' secrets, you'll have more control.

You learned in the last chapter that one of the core philosophical questions, and one that certainly impacts investors, regulators, and online firms, is what the overriding duties of online brokerage firms are. In this chapter, we address some of the hotter, more topical issues concerning online trading. These are issues of which you should be keenly aware, whether you are evaluating your current online brokerage firm or are thinking of opening an online account.

Online trading has been around for a number of years. Well before anyone even used the terms *online* or *Internet* trading, Schwab implemented a system called Schwab Link that allowed investors to trade via their computers. Douglas has had accounts with Schwab for over 20 years. He vividly remembers having to borrow $10,000 from his father to meet the $20,000 minimum to open a money market account in the 1970s at Schwab. The real online explosion has come recently with two events. First, a number of firms, such as Brown & Company and TD Waterhouse, that had previously not offered online trading have now expanded into that market. Second, new brokerage firms have sprung into existence for the sole purpose of providing online trading (E*Trade, Ameritrade, Datek, etc.). Of course, none of this growth could have occurred without a large and growing base of investors with computers equipped for online access. It comes as no surprise then that right alongside the phenomenal growth of online shopping is the ever expanding market of online trading.

We have been critical of online firms for employing marketing campaigns that try to convince investors that they don't need a broker. Online brokerage firms have taken the human broker or advisor out of the picture. *There is no one on your team at an online brokerage firm!* There is no one to sympathize with you or to go to bat for you when there is a problem, error, screwup, or complaint about your account. Like a thousand other analogies in life—life insurance and seat belts, for example—you never miss something until you need it.

We have both heard variations of the following story from a slew of investors. You enter a limit order of $70 a share to sell 500 shares of Cisco. You keep thinking your order should have been filled because you see the stock, at least momentarily, go above $70 on your computer screen. Yet you see no report of an execution. You even go so far as to call your online firm and talk with a representative, who advises you that your order was not filled. Although this call might be recorded, don't count on ever seeing the tape. Based on this purportedly accurate and reliable information, you cancel the trade and re-enter the order to sell 500 shares of Cisco but now at $65 a share because that is the current price. The firm acknowledges the cancellation and reorder, and all appears to be okay.

The next day all hell breaks loose. The firm informs you electronically that not only was your original order to sell Cisco executed at $70 a share but so was your second order! So you now have a short position in your account. And as is so often the case with an order error, the markets always tend to complicate the matter. You guessed it; Cisco has moved up to $80 a share and your short has cost you $15 dollars a share for 500 shares, or $7,500. And it's not your fault!

Which brings us round to why stockbrokers remain a very important ingredient within the brokerage industry. First, it is extremely unlikely that this mistake would have ever taken place if you had been dealing with a live broker. A stockbroker would have known if your first trade had been executed. The second point is that if your broker admitted that he misinformed you about your initial trade execution, he would most likely take immediate responsibility for the screwup and agree to take the losses out of your account. And a final point to keep in mind: Even if your broker didn't admit that he misinformed you about the trade, it is highly likely he would nonetheless intervene on your behalf and argue that his firm, not you, should eat the loss on the short position.

First, consider why a stockbroker would stick up for you. The answer should be because you are his client. You are the one who pays his house and car payments. Without you, he is out of business. He is fully aware of the competition for your commission dollar; and it's hoped he has worked for years to gain your trust and loyalty and relies on you as a base for referrals. As we explained earlier, a broker's real value is his book of clients that he can take to almost any brokerage firm in the country. His loyalty should be to you, not his firm.

Now consider the other side of the equation. Whose client are you at your online brokerage firm? No one's! Because no particular individual or even group of individuals share commissions on your trades, there is no one loyal to you. Worse yet, there's a pretty good chance that anyone who has contact with you concerning an order error is likely to run for cover. He has nothing to gain in trying to help you get to the bottom of your problem; and he might get blamed. And because he gets no benefit from your trading, he has no reason to argue with his employer on your behalf.

You might hope that threatening the online brokerage firm with taking your business elsewhere will prompt the firm to put forth a good-faith attempt to rectify your complaint. Don't bet on it. Although the pace of online trading has slowed somewhat, the loss of a couple of, or a couple dozen, accounts won't even show up on the firm's radar screen. Not a comforting thought, is it?

Despite this, the growth of online brokerage firms has produced a number of fabulous benefits for the American investing public. Online firms have put intense pressure on the entire industry to lower commissions, a significant and positive event. Leaving the potential negatives aside, online firms have done what Merrill Lynch's motto has been for decades: "To bring Wall Street to Main Street." Millions of investors are now able to quickly and cheaply participate in the American dream of building net worth by investing in stocks and bonds in the comfort of their living rooms and in their pajamas without the high pressure and sometimes intimidating sales tactics of brokers. Online brokerage firms have done an excellent job in providing you full and accurate information that is both current and fairly reliable. This has been a goal of the securities regulators since the enactment of the 1934 securities act. Competition for your investment dollar is at an all-time high. You now have more options for how and where to invest than ever before.

MARKETING—YOU NEVER KNEW YOU WERE WORTH SO MUCH

Advertising has been a part of modern man's life ever since the first Babylonian yelled "Bread for sale!" 3,000 years ago. Procter & Gamble (P&G) sponsored soap operas with Tide ads blaring across every television set in the 1960s. The dot.comers took advertising to new levels in the late 1990s with the outpouring of untold millions to get their word out. And now the online brokerage firms are spending millions of dollars to get you.

What we think is so novel is how much money these online firms are willing to spend to attract a customer. Sure, Procter & Gamble was the largest advertiser in the United States for years, but calculations of P&G's advertising cost per bottle of Joy dishwashing liquid measured in cents per bottle, not hundreds of dollars per person. The following are some statistics for you to ponder:

- The average amount spent by brokerage firms in advertising dollars for a new customer is between $250 and $350. Some pay over $400 to attract each new client.[1]
- In the fourth quarter of 2000, Schwab spent $77 million in just two months of advertising. In one month, November 1999, it added 94,000 new accounts.
- E*Trade spent $5 million on two ads for the Super Bowl in January 2001. For the second year in a row, E*Trade was one

of the sponsors of the Super Bowl's half-time show. E*Trade spent $521 million in marketing in 2000.

- TD Waterhouse said it opened 165,000 new accounts in the third quarter of 2000 at an average cost of about $133 per account, down from about $160 a year earlier. For all of 2000, Waterhouse opened about 1 million new accounts at an average cost of $109 per account.[2] Yet acquisition costs at Waterhouse are running about $200 per new account, up about 45 percent from levels in November 1999 through January 2000.[3]

- At the beginning of 2001, customer acquisition costs at Ameritrade were running about $477 per new customer, based on estimates. The firm spent approximately $59 million in advertising in the fourth quarter of 2000 and supposedly added 123,000 new accounts. Amertrade's acquisition costs jumped 177 percent from the first three months of 2000.[4]

Of course, the real question might be whether there is anything wrong with these firms spending so much money on advertising to attract new investors. If E*Trade's stockholders don't care, why should we? But we do care, because we think that much of this advertising is leading people to move accounts or open new accounts with these online brokerage firms for the wrong reasons. A CBS Market Watch article echoed these sentiments when it reported: "So when smart and sophisticated investors go online to trade, they expect the experience to be like advertisements promise: quick, safe, and easy. That's not the case."[5] Regardless of what the ads say, these firms are not necessarily cheaper or better or an easier place to make money than a traditional brokerage firm. We think you'll come to the same conclusion through firsthand experience.

You would hope that online brokerage firms will treat you with considerably more respect once you arrived at their online door. After all, they paid considerable money to attract and get you there. They don't. You are a commodity, an account number on a screen, a grain of sand on an endless beach. Try complaining about an error on an order you placed at one of these firms, and see if the response you get comports with the claims in the ads. It probably won't. Read on and learn what Mr. John Doe experienced at one major online brokerage firm.

AN ONLINE FIRM STORY—WE HOPE
YOU'RE PLEASED WITH OUR DISSERVICE

One of our favorite online brokerage stories we think is of interest because it combines two of the more prevalent attitudes in the online brokerage business: aggressive marketing coupled with a denial of responsibility when there are errors.

Can you imagine going to the doctor and being told that you have a cancerous growth in your arm and you will die if you don't have your arm removed? Based on the doctor's representation, you have your arm removed—only to find after the operation that the doctor was wrong. You were merely suffering from tennis elbow. When you confront the doctor, he says, "Hey, we make mistakes all the time. We can't be held responsible. You're just out of luck. I hope this doesn't mean I can't still be your doctor."

Sound like a nightmare? Well, something similar happened to an online investor. The investor, whom we shall call Mr. Doe, entered an order through his account at an online firm to sell short 400 shares of a stock after the market closed. Shortly thereafter, he says he received a written notice on his screen saying that his order had expired, so he re-entered the exact, same order. The next day, much to his shock, he discovered that *both* orders were executed, thereby doubling his trade. To complicate matters, a debit balance was created in Mr. Doe's account, and he received a margin call. Mr. Doe couldn't afford to pay the margin call. So the firm not only sold the duplicate order, but they wiped out the entire equity in his account.

Mr. Doe wrote a letter to the firm, in which he succinctly laid out his recitation of the facts and asked that he be put back in the position he was in before the duplicate order.

The response from the firm's regulatory specialist was somewhere between comical and ridiculous. First, the firm admitted in its response letter that "[t]he Internet site may have temporarily reflected an 'expired' notification for [the] order." Okay, this is not exactly an admission that the expired notice appeared, but not exactly a resounding denial either. Notice the distancing that the firm employed in referring to "the Internet site," as if it were some independent, unrelated entity. The remaining three pages of the firm's response was much like the doctor's response above . . . even if the expired notice did appear on the screen (but we're not admitting that it did) we make mistakes all the time and we aren't legally responsible. What made the firm's response amusing is that intermingled with the brush-off of the client was its continual bragging about being "the most customer-friendly discount brokerage service." In a crowning blow just after telling Mr. Doe he was responsible for both orders, the firm closed with the following: "I am sure you will agree that [the firm], through its use of technology, has helped you gain a powerful command over your investments and lowered your cost of investing. But I also want you to be assured that we are here to provide the highest level of services on a personal basis."

It would appear that the regulatory specialist closed with the firm's standard form language, which in this case was quite offensive to Mr. Doe. Mr. Doe is clearly powerless. His cost of investing was not lowered—he lost thousands of dollars through no fault of his own. And Mr. Doe's opinion of the firm's service level is . . . well . . . not fit to be published.

In another unbelievable arbitration case, in which Douglas was the expert, the client made an online purchase. According to his client, immediately after making the purchase and the trade was executed he realized that he had mistakenly purchased 9,000 shares instead of the 900 shares he meant to purchase. Douglas's client testified that he called the firm immediately to alert it to his error and to find out what should be done about it. He was shocked—you may be too—when he heard the firm's response. In a recorded conversation, the transcript of which was entered as evidence in the arbitration, the firm representative told him that if the stock went up, the firm would keep the profit, but if it went down, the client's account would be debited for the ensuing loss. The law is not so clear on this issue. We should all apply to be in a business where we get to keep all profits from mistakes and stick somebody else with the losses. The investor received a partial award in that case.

Back to our doctor story, you can rest assured that as a lawyer, Tracy would be filing a medical malpractice case and the jury would be awarding large sums of money for the missing arm. As a securities attorney, Tracy can say, if her client's story is true, that the firm's defense that it can't be held responsible for its own negligence shouldn't fly. Yet, this defense is one that is being used throughout the Internet's securities industry. The results of the debate are still being tabulated, but in our experience not too many arbitration panels have bought into it.

ORDER FAILURE—BUT THEY PROMISED THEY WERE BETTER

Order failure, simply put, is when an order to buy or sell a security is mishandled, screwed up, or botched. It doesn't matter if the order is placed by an individual on a computer screen or through a stockbroker on the phone or in person, the order must be handled correctly and in a timely manner. Thus far, in the few years that online trading has mushroomed, we have seen the following types of order failure complaints.

Botched Orders

The best example is a recent case, in which Douglas was the expert against an online firm. The investor testified that he had canceled a limit order, yet the firm filled the order 45 minutes later. The firm could not explain why the order had been filled and not canceled. The documents produced in the arbitration showed that the stock did not hit the limit price at any time between the initial order and the cancellation, so the firm had no legitimate excuse for the fill. The client arbitrated and won, because the firm refused to honor the cancel order. The client also recovered his attorney's fees and Douglas's expert fees.

System Failure

An investor's inability to enter an order may also fall under the heading of system failure rather than order failure. System failure can impact an investor who simply cannot log on to place an order, and it can also affect the investor who has placed an order but never gets a fill. This is not the same as an investor claim of an improper fill. For years, brokers have occasionally made mistakes filling orders. Arguments over the timeliness of executions are why order tickets are time stamped and why time and price sheets are prepared each trading day.

What is new is that now online firms advertise and draw investors by proclaiming a cheaper, more efficient system for entering orders, when, in fact, the process has been anything but faster or more efficient for many investors. And if your order is filled at a price far from the one you expected, the process is anything but cheap.

You've no doubt heard about the outages sustained by online firms. You couldn't pick up a newspaper a year ago without reading about a brokerage firm's computer trading system going down. There are hundreds of stories about investors who, on a fairly regular basis, have had problems making an online connection to a brokerage firm, getting someone to answer a phone in less than an hour, and not being able to check their order status. You can imagine the damage that can be done when investors can't enter a trade or check their account status because the system wasn't working. The NYSE fined TD Waterhouse $225,000 for repeated outages that left investors without the ability to enter trades.[6]

Online firms have two distinct problems with their systems. The first was, and continues to be for some, an inherent inability to handle the volume of business. Operations departments were not adequately staffed, and the limitations of computer systems were being exceeded. The irony is that online firms themselves are responsible for the huge volume they attracted. This reminds us of the brokerage firms who sold real estate limited partnerships in the 1980s and, after the partnerships failed and investors sued, defended by saying that the real estate market had collapsed and that was not their fault. In fact, the huge amount of capital that brokerage firms poured into poor real estate investments through limited partnerships was part of the reason for the decline in the real estate market.

Likewise, online firms have marketed like crazy the last few years to attract new customers. You could hardly connect to the Internet or buy a software product without some discount being offered for signing up with an online firm. Also, the marketing was very convincing in contending that the benefits of online trading far outweighed trading at a traditional brokerage firm. Clients and their accounts flooded in. Yet online brokerage firms were unable to handle the volume that their marketing departments created.

The problems created by this influx of accounts include customers unable to connect as a result of busy lines or a firm's Web site going down; customers unable to enter a trade or check an account's status because of some glitch in the Web site; and customers unable to call their online firm when its Web site malfunctioned or, alternatively, waiting on hold for an hour or more.

A January 25, 2001, report by the SEC was critical of a number of aspects of online brokerage firms. In addition to findings that some of the online firm's advertising is misleading, the report found that some online brokerages weren't adequately assessing the quality of order executions.[7]

The second problem centered on an online firm's design of its system more than on the system's inadequacy. Traditional brokerages have *screens*, a term that doesn't refer to computer screens but rather to computer programs that monitor the trading in customer accounts. The screens are a compliance and supervisory requirement so that unsuitable or improper activities can be investigated. At first, online brokerage firms had few, if any, screens. As the errors, complaints, and arbitration claims piled up, the better online firms slowly created screens, though they are still not adequate.

Best Execution

One of the biggest mistakes being made with the flight to online trading is that individual investors incorrectly believe the playing field between themselves, on one side, and the professional and institutional traders, on the other, has been leveled. They feel that their access to information, lower commissions, and the best execution is the same. No doubt, $8 a trade is an even lower commission than the one most institutional and professional traders pay. But what these investors are missing is that the commission is no longer the highest cost in trading securities—at least at online firms. You don't think that online firms make a lot of money at $8 a trade, do you? They are making a lot of their money on margin interest and spreads. If you buy 1,000 shares of a stock at the offer of $10 and the bid was $10.75, whoever picked up the spread picked up $250.

Firms may be more concerned about picking up the spread than making sure you get filled at the proper price. The stock exchanges, as well as the NASD, have rules and guidelines governing the timely filling of orders. Brokerage firms must prove that entering an order was done on an immediate and timely basis. Anything short of that is a violation.

MARGIN AND SELLOUTS—YOU TAKE THE RISKS, THEY TAKE THE MONEY

Allow us to reinforce once again our contention that one of the reasons online firms charge pittance commissions is because they hope to make additional profits in other areas, such as margin debt. For online firms, margin is where the action is. Margin debt at online brokerage firms has quadrupled since 1995 and continues to swell at alarming rates. When we compare margin debt levels at on-line firms with levels at traditional firms, well, there's really no comparison. Online firms hover around four times the margin debt of more traditional firms.

Adding fuel to the fire is the frenzy with which investors have opened online accounts and employed margin. Some are borrowing money from their credit card company or their mortgage company to serve as collateral and to increase their borrowing power—a disaster waiting to happen. For many, margin is a way to borrow without having to stand in line at the bank, fill out myriad forms, and divulge every detail of their financial status. A customer can borrow double the amount of money she has in her account and use that borrowed money within a span of minutes at an online firm. Think of it: with margin, you can buy double what you ordinarily would be able to buy. That's like a two-for-one sale at the supermarket, but many investors don't factor in the effect of the margin interest they pay.

And, of course, online firms love margin. It's not *their* money they're lending to customers. The firm is simply borrowing the money from the bank at one rate and lending it to you at a higher rate. Therefore, the simple act of your utilizing margin puts money in the brokerage firm's pocket. You hope it puts money in your pocket too. But if the margined stock takes a nosedive, the firm is protected with no risk whatsoever so long as you have enough equity in your account to cover the margin call. Even if you don't, online firms will stop at nothing to make you pay, going so far as to report your debt to credit companies.

That is not to say that brokerage firms have no exposure when a customer can't pay back a margin debt. It is rumored that one customer racked up a $4 million margin debt at several firms. Two of the firms were able to take the hit, but the third firm couldn't meet its net capital requirements and, as a result, had to shut its doors.

This is an extreme situation, though. The vast majority of the time, online firms have themselves covered when it comes to margin issues; they have backup and protection.

To further protect their downside, online firms are doing something not previously done. Formerly, firms would routinely calculate margin debt at the close of the trading day, so that any margin calls would be made at the close of that day or the next morning. Previously, you had five days and later only three days within which to meet the margin call. Now, firms are not only creating margin calls midday, but they are also selling out customers midday based on the market activity during the day. We are critical of this new margin practice that so many online brokerage firms have implemented because it creates an incredible hardship for investors.

Let's say you get up early one day and place a trade to purchase 1,000 shares at $10 a share of Floopercom Technology. You make your purchase and then leave for work, knowing that you have enough money in your account to meet the initial Regulation T margin call of $5,000. Later that morning, while you are snoozing through a company meeting, the stock drops to $7 a share, which creates an additional maintenance call on the security because of the intraday practice of some firms. You don't have enough money in your brokerage account to meet this additional maintenance call. No one from the brokerage firm attempts to call you at work or home, nor does anyone e-mail you to relay the events. The firm panics and sells your position at $7 a share. In the span of a few hours, you lost $3,000 on your initial $5,000 investment. You are fuming because if only someone had contacted you at work, you could have transferred money from your checking account to meet the additional maintenance call. Worse yet, you find out after work that Floopercom Technology's stock closed for the day at $12 a share. And to add salt to the wound, over the next week it soared to new highs. How utterly unnerving.

Intraday sellouts force investors to constantly monitor their portfolios for price movements and margin calls. In our view, intraday sellouts should not occur without some attempt to notify the customer. We have seen far too many situations where a simple phone call could have prevented the damage.

Another practice we have seen at online brokerage firms is an abandonment of monitoring customers' credit status. Most traditional firms will not permit a customer to carry substantial positions while in a margin call unless the firm believes the customer has the financial means necessary to satisfy any deficit that may be incurred. So it should be at online firms.

If you are considering using margin in an account where you call the shots, educate yourself. Read the terms of the margin agreement so that you are familiar with what the firm can and cannot do. Print out all of the documentation on margin that you can access online, date it, and save it. Investigate if, how, and when the firm notifies you of changes to maintenance margin requirements or if there is a place you can go online to review those changes. Lately, some online firms have been either increasing the margin significantly or prohibiting any margin at all on certain stocks. Monitor the value of your account so that you will be on top of dramatic changes and can possibly prevent margin calls. And of course, do not consider using margin unless you have the resources to absorb the losses that could result from a downturn.

ONLINE TRADING TIPS— DID SOMEONE SAY TIPS?

We know. Everyone has a tip. But our tips are different from the majority you read in financial books.

Gain Some Respect

If you trade a lot or have a sizeable account—say, over $500,000—use these to push your weight around. An old saying is that brokerage firms get 90 percent of their business from 20 percent of their clients. If you are lucky enough to be among that 20 percent, use it to your advantage. Almost all online firms and some in-between firms have special perks for "better" clients. And, of course, "better" means more money in the account or lots of trading. Shop around and get a list of the special perks. As your volume of trading or the size of your account increases, the perks improve. You may want to combine all of your accounts at one firm if it helps you to reach the necessary level for perks. Level II quotes, streaming quotes, access to research and IPOs, and special toll-free numbers are just some of the benefits.

The benefit we would like to stress is that of having a specific person assigned to you. Remember we began this chapter discussing how there's no one to care about you at an online firm. At most firms, like DLJ, Morgan Stanley, and Schwab, you can demand that a person or a couple of people be assigned to your account if you meet certain criteria. Make sure they are senior people. Ask them about their background and number of years in the business. If they haven't been in the business at least five years, ask that someone else be assigned to your account. Get a phone number that goes directly to your broker's desk or to a team desk. Get to know everyone on your team. Only deal with these people. Let them know from the very start that you are relying on them for personal attention. And if you don't get the attention you deserve, then move your account. You can get the attention you deserve elsewhere easily.

Market Orders

Tracy had a 21-year-old client who had $7,000 in his online account. He entered a market order to buy an over-the-counter (OTC) security that was being offered at eight cents a share. He entered a 30,000 share market order that, in his young mind, would have resulted in a $2,400 purchase. Fifteen minutes later, his order was filled at a $1 per share. Needless to say, the $7,000 in his account fell woefully short in covering the $30,000 purchase price. The stock then plummeted, wiping out his account and leaving him with a $23,000 debt to the firm.

The above scenario has been played out all over the country. There's a presumption that market orders are filled almost immediately. Tracy's client assumed that if his order was not filled at eight cents, then it would be filled at something reasonably close to eight cents. A market order is an order to buy or sell a security at the security's market price—not necessarily the market price when you decide to place your order but rather the market price when your order hits the system. In today's fast-paced market, stock prices can jump up and down like a kid on a pogo stick.

Volatile Stocks and Volatile Markets

When dealing in volatile stocks and volatile securities markets, market orders can be dangerous. If you are considering entering a market order, you should first assess whether any of the following scenarios apply to you. First, if you are trading in OTC stocks, be aware that market orders tend to be less instantaneous, because the order is first routed through one or more market makers. Second, if you are dealing in a thinly traded security, that is, one where the average volume of shares traded on a given day is limited, your market order may not go through as you planned. Third, the securities markets are much more volatile than in the past. For numerous reasons, up and down prices of the entire market for the last several years have experienced large swings, so individual price movements on a given stock have increased. Fourth, the particular security that Tracy's client was trying to buy was a volatile stock, that is, one with large price swings on a percentage basis on any given day. A stock that goes from eight cents to $1 in 15 minutes is, by definition, about as volatile as you can get. The technical term for measuring a stock's volatility, as noted in an earlier chapter, is called its *beta*. If a stock has a high beta, then it has high volatility.

Volume Issues

The volume of trading can also be reason to pause before entering a market order. If other market orders are in front of yours (orders entered at the same time as yours or before yours), those orders will be filled before yours. If you are trying to buy 30,000 shares and the offer was 5,000 shares at eight cents, you should recognize that there are only 5,000 shares to be bought at eight cents and the next set of shares could be at a significantly higher price. In addition, the offer may still be only a few thousand shares. Depending on the sophistication of the trading software or the firm you are trading with, you can get the size of the bid and ask in addition to the price.

Another problem in entering a market order arises when your order is for a large number of shares in relation to the average daily trading volume. Tracy's client entered a trade for 30,000 shares when the average daily trading volume of that security was 15,000.

In this scenario, your market order could be filled at a price vastly different from the then prevailing price. For this reason, when a person owns restricted securities, the selling shareholders are restricted from selling so many shares based on daily average volume. If the shareholders try and dump too many shares, they will depress the market.

Limit Orders

If you decide to play in these fast markets and trade in volatile stocks, our suggestion is that once you've gotten a real-time quote for the bid and the offer, put in a limit order rather than a market order. A limit order is an order to buy or sell at a specified price or better. Your limit order should reflect the maximum you are willing to pay for the stock or the minimum for which you are willing to sell the stock. Most people don't understand that if a stock is selling for a $1 and you put in an order to buy it at $1.20, your order should be filled at $1 (assuming that when your order hits the system, the offer is still $1 in the size that you are trying to buy). It is not true that if you put in a limit price of $1.20, you will get filled only at $1.20. In the "old" days, this type of order was called "limit or better." Anyone who is buying is always willing to buy it for less and anyone who is selling is willing to sell it for more. The limit is the most you will pay or the least you will accept. Most online firms do not have the words "or better" after the word "limit" on their order screens, although this is the way that firms should treat a limit order. If you need to clarify this with your particular brokerage firm, do so before entering a limit order.

Stop Orders and Stop Limit Orders

Stop orders and stop limit orders can be excellent tools with which to play the volatile markets. Like a limit order, they provide significant control over the price at which your order is executed. On the buy side, a stop order is an order to purchase a stock above the current prevailing price. You enter a specific price per share, and when the stock goes up and trades at your specific price, your order immediately changes to a market order and you are filled in line with other market orders at the then prevailing price. This means that your order could be filled at a price other than your stop price, just the same as when you enter a market order.

A stop limit order is also an order to buy above the then prevailing price (if when you place the order you place it above the current trading price of the stock). The difference is that when the stock trades to your limit price, your trade is executed but only at the limit price you set.

These orders are best used on stocks that trade up to or down to certain prices. If IBM is trading at $100 and you believe that it's on an uptrend if it trades to $105 and will go to $120, you might put in a buy stop order at $105. Let's say that IBM moves from $100 to $120 and that you got filled at $107 (your order converted to a market order once IBM hit your stop of $105). You are happy because you benefited from the uptrend. For that, you were willing to take the risk of the price fluctuation. If you had instead put in a stop *limit* order at $105, then you can eliminate the risk of not knowing what price you will get filled at. You know that either you will get filled at $105 or not at all. (Actually, you could buy the stock for less than $105 on a stop limit order of $105 if IBM hit $105, which triggers your stop, and the next trade is $104, so you could get the stock at $104.) The risk of using the stop limit order is that you may not get filled at all. If, at the time your order goes through, the volume of shares you specified at the price you specified is not available, your order will not go through and you would have missed the uptrend.

You can also use stop orders to sell stocks below the current price. We usually refer to these types of orders as "stop loss" orders. Why would you enter a trade to sell something for less than what you can sell it for today? Let's use the IBM example one more time. You own a hundred shares for which you paid $100 a share. It is now selling for $110 a share. You think it is going to go higher, but you are smart enough to know IBM could go back to $70 a share. You are busy and don't have time to watch it every day. So you decide to enter a sell stop order at $95 a share. If IBM starts to crater, your order will be triggered, when the price hits $95 a share. It will then become a market order to sell 100 shares at the market. Because you didn't enter a limit, you won't know exactly what you will be sold at, but you will be sold out, which is what you wanted.

Now you could enter a sell stop limit order at $95. Like the earlier stop order, nothing will happen until IBM hits $95. When

IBM hits $95, your order will be triggered but this time, because you have a limit at $95 a share, your order will be filled only at $95 a share or better. Of course, if IBM hits $95 and keeps going down like a rock, there is a good chance that your order never got filled, and thus you didn't protect yourself from the slide.

We know stop orders can be a bit confusing, but try to think of it this way. Basically, stop orders are when you try to sell below the current price or buy above the current price. Because in both of these trades you are trying to make a trade that on its face looks contrary to your best interest (i.e., buy higher or sell lower), you need to use the term *stop*.

If you want to buy lower than the current price, you use a plain limit order below the current price. If you want to sell higher than the current price, you use a plain limit order above the current price.

If you have a job, the limit order, the stop order, and the stop limit order can be useful tools. You can enter trades and go to work without sneaking furtive glances at your online account all day. But if you enter orders to buy at the market in volatile stocks, you had better stay put and watch that monitor because you don't know what price you might get filled at.

PAYMENT FOR ORDER FLOW—
HELPS THEIR BOTTOM LINE, NOT YOURS

The *New York Times* published an article that implored Harvey Pitt, the new chairman of the Securities and Exchange Commission (as of this writing, yet to be confirmed) to ban payment for order flow. It reported:

> The practice of a brokerage firm receiving money for sending its customers' orders to a specified trading firm or market maker has been going on for years. In any other business, it is called bribery and is illegal. On Wall Street, it is given an innocent-sounding name and allowed to proliferate.[8]

Now, in addition to market makers, we have electronic trading centers, also called electronic communication networks (ECNs), which match customers' trades. Firms route their customers' orders to market makers or to ECNs. In exchange and as compensation for directing the trade to that firm, they receive a portion of the spread. Brokerage firms have found another way to ratchet up their profit from order executions. Brokerage firms, including online firms, are buying interests in the market makers or ECNs. Recently, Merrill Lynch bought Hertzog, one of the largest market makers in the securities industry. Charles Schwab bought Mayer Schweitzer, a large market maker, years ago. When brokerage firms own market makers, they retain all the spread when they direct their orders through these subsidiaries.

You should be concerned about payment for order flow because your firm may not be directing your order to the market maker or ECN that will most likely get the best execution for your trade but rather to the entity that will pay it the most. Some online firms have derived revenue in payment for order flow that rivals commission revenue. Don't be wowed by the promises of trade executions in 60 seconds or less when the price you receive is something less or more than the current best price.

One last tip. There may be times when you would like to document something that you see on your online account and displayed on your monitor, but there are often views and screens that you cannot print. If you want to document what is on your screen, just whip out your videotape recorder and record it! Tracy had a client who, after a problem occurred, later videotaped numerous screens from his online account as well as e-mails from the firm. The images came out great.

SUPERVISION OF YOUR ONLINE ACCOUNT—AN OXYMORON

As you learned in Chapter 4, the brokerage industry has a dual duty. First, the firm has a duty to supervise its brokers and the firm's accounts, and second, the individual stockbrokers have duties to know their customers. In doing away with the stockbroker, online firms seem to have forgotten the first duty. This is again one of the disadvantages of trading with an online firm: there appears to be little to no supervision.

The computer programs, or screens, that traditional brokerages use to monitor trading in customer accounts were discussed in an earlier chapter. Their purpose is to flag activity that, after further investigation, may or may not be proper.

So-called collars, on the other hand, are actual restrictions that prevent activity from taking place, such as commodity accounts that are precluded from going over certain trading limits or clients prevented from using margin improperly or in excess of a firm's margin requirements. We sympathize with brokerage firms' conflict of interest when they want to make commissions, but they can't have their cake and eat it too. Firms cannot allow the clients to take positions that may be highly leveraged and risky and shortly thereafter blow the clients out ("blowing out" or "selling out" is when a brokerage firm liquidates stocks or a portfolio to meet a margin call). If the firms refuse to limit the trades with collars, they should at least generate an automatic warning that notifies clients of the negative and somewhat arbitrary consequences.

Thus far, we have seen limited screens or collars being implemented by online firms. Many of the order problems with online firms could have been easily prevented with proper screens or caps built into the firms' software systems. The problem seems to be that screens are not in place, not functioning properly, or ignored.

If the proper systems (collars, restrictions, screens) were put in place, they would be able to disallow many of the following situations:

- A person with a listed net worth of $100,000 should not be allowed to enter an order that could result in a $50,000 net order.
- A person whose new account form indicates a desire for growth should not be allowed to make speculative investments.
- An investor whose account form indicates limited means should not be allowed to invest in speculative trading programs.
- A person with no options experience should not be allowed to short naked options.
- An investor whose account is already margined to the hilt should not be allowed to enter orders that will result in almost immediate margin liquidations.
- Early warnings should be sent to clients who continually flirt with margin calls.

The real problem here is that online firms appear to ignore the information they have on the new account forms. Again, what is the point of asking all these personal and investment-oriented questions if they are not put to any use? As we stated earlier, many online firms do not feel compelled to conduct any supervision because they feel they have no duty to the customer except to fill the order.

AFTER-HOURS TRADING—FOOLS RUSH IN, WHERE ANGELS DARE TO TREAD

There are a number of reasons for the phenomenal growth of online brokerage firms, one of which is the number of markets and firms that have begun after-hours trading. Maybe in the not too distant future we will have 24-hour trading. Even with some of the older online trading systems, an investor always had the ability to enter a trade when the markets were closed, and the firm would enter the order when the markets opened on the next trading day. What differentiates after-hours trading is that individuals can actually execute their orders when traditionally the markets would be closed. For the majority of Americans who work from nine to five, they now are able to trade for a few hours before or after work; many people find these hours their only free time to dabble with their investments. The flexibility that an individual has in determining when to enter trades or conduct research has also fueled the growth of online trading.

A word of warning for those who are considering trading in the after-hours market: it can be dangerous to the naive investor. The whole point and supposed benefit of the merging of markets that you hear so much about is that spreads will be reduced and the investor is more likely to get the true best price. Trading in the after, or secondary, market basically runs contrary to this whole line of thinking.

Thinly traded securities always add additional risk to a transaction. Securities trading after hours have nowhere near the volume of trades that those same securities have during normal trading hours. Because of this, the spreads between the bid and the ask tend to increase. Whether you are buying or selling, wider spreads increase the cost of trading. In addition to widening spreads, sometimes the prices are out of line with where those securities were trading the day before or will trade the next day. The following is an example, which was quoted in the *Wall Street Journal* in January 2000:

> Many individuals who bought shares of merger partners America Online and Time Warner in pre-market trading Monday morning got a rude awakening to the dangers of buying stocks on private networks before financial markets open. Had they waited for the regular session to begin on the New York Stock Exchange, the early-bird investors, who only recently got access to these pre-market forums long used by professionals, might have been able to buy their stock for less. Investors were trying to get a jump on news that Time Warner, the world's largest media-and-entertainment company, and AOL, the No. 1 online-service provider, which agreed to merge in an earthshaking $166 billion stock transaction that would be the biggest corporate merger ever. Shares of AOL and Time Warner were quoted as high as 90 and 115, respectively, on Instinet, an electronic communication network, or ECN, operated by Reuters Group, where investors can trade stocks before the exchanges open. But when trading began on the Big Board at 9:30 a.m. EST, AOL was quoted at 75$\frac{1}{8}$ and Time Warner was at 97. As the day wore on at the NYSE, neither stock came close to their pre-market highs. At 4 PM on the Big Board Monday, AOL traded at 71, while Time Warner was at 90$\frac{1}{16}$.[9]

So our advice: unless you want to live dangerously, at least at this stage, we suggest you conduct your trades only during regular market hours. And if you must trade in the after markets, do so with limit orders, not with market orders where you can get killed.

In summary, we can say that a large percentage of complaints about online trading we have seen are compounded by investors' lack of understanding of either the securities markets or the online trading system. Margin is just one example. Online firms have directed their marketing to the masses—novices as well as the financially sophisticated. So the firms knew or should have known that they would attract inexperienced investors as well as knowledgeable ones. It has been a long time since the enactment of the Securities and Exchange Act of 1934 and there have been a world of changes since then. But the heart of the 1934 act is still in place—the recognition of a naive, investing public. In terms of the number of people investing, there are probably more naive investors today than ever before. Having totally removed the stockbroker from the picture, online firms may have brought down the cost of executing trades, but they have also eliminated the one safeguard for many individuals. In an ideal world, we should see online firms paying more attention to the inexperienced, unsophisticated investor. Yet that is not what we are seeing. Rather, many online firms would simply prefer to maintain a hands-off relationship with its customers, a distressing thought.

CHAPTER 10

Bucket Shops
and Boiler Rooms

With the proliferation of financial products, services, and professionals, words unique to the securities industry seem to be proliferating. How are you supposed to know what they all mean? If there are any with which you should be familiar, the two in the chapter title would be near the top of the list.

LEARNING THE LINGO—A PRIMER

Are you smart enough to know whether the broker who cold calls you is working for a bucket shop or a boiler room? These two terms are similar in meaning. The term *bucket shop* is the oldest and derives from the literal manner in which securities were sold at some firms. Every morning, the branch manager would walk among the brokers with a bucket, in which were pieces of paper that had on them the stock the firm was pushing that day and a number of shares written next to it. The broker would draw from the bucket and learn what stock at what allocation he was required to sell that day. Bucket shops were also known as places where investors' orders were never executed. Instead, the brokers and the firms just pocketed the money.[1]

Such dictates on what a broker can and cannot sell and in what quantities fly in the face of the NASD's and NYSE's suitability rules and create a high likelihood that the broker will be forced to sell shares to customers for whom the investment is not suitable. Although the use of the bucket was done away with many years ago, similar practices prevail today. You may recall the cover of *Forbes* in its February 24, 1997, issue featuring a large, rusty bucket with "Wall Street Sleaze" emblazoned across it.

Today, the term bucket shop has given way to the term *boiler room*, popularized by the movie of the same name.[2] A boiler room is similar to a bucket shop and has been defined as "a place devoted to high-pressure promotion by telephone of stocks, bonds, diamonds, commodities, etc., which are of very questionable value."[3] You may also hear references to microcap firms, which are firms that specialize in small, little-known, thinly traded, and undercapitalized stocks. No brokerage firm would ever refer to itself, at least publicly, as a boiler room or a bucket shop, but a good number of firms advertise themselves as microcap firms. Many of these once specialized in selling penny stocks, but after the penny stock rules went into effect in 1990 and greatly restricted the marketing of penny stocks, many of the penny stock firms just switched their operations to pushing microcap stocks.

The list of firms that have run boiler rooms is a long one: Hibbard Brown, Blinder Robinson (later jokingly referred to as "Blind and Rob 'Em"), G.W. Gant, Duke & Company, A. R. Baron, First Jersey, Stratton Oakmont, and Sterling Foster.[4] Though many of these firms had only one or two office operations, several, such as Sterling Foster, grew to have multibranch offices. The NASD has recognized that certain types of activity are more commonly associated with boiler rooms, such as lack of supervision, lack of research, nondisclosure of information about the true nature of a stock, and baseless price predictions.[5]

Hibbard was a classic boiler room operation. It perpetuated fraud by recruiting young, inexperienced brokers and training them to use highly aggressive, cold-calling techniques to sell low-priced, speculative securities. Supervisors encouraged Hibbard's brokers to use misleading sales literature and scripts during sales presentations. The NASD found that the firm committed egregious sales practice abuses, including providing baseless price predictions, misrepresentations, and unwarranted hyperbole about the securities they were selling.[6] Hibbard was expelled from the NASD in 1994.

HERE TODAY, GONE TOMORROW—
WITH YOUR MONEY

Bucket shops and boiler rooms employ unique strategies to build their wealth and, at the same time, decimate their customers. We will show you how those strategies may impact you so that you can protect yourself. In our section on cold calling in Chapter 3, we listed 11 reasons why you should hang up on a cold-calling stockbroker. Following are some of the tricks employed by bucket shops, boiler rooms, and microcap brokerages to get their hands on your money as well as some of their characteristics:

- The first call will almost always come from a prequalifier (a person who, prior to calling you, was fixing flats at a bicycle shop). The prequalifier will hold no securities licenses and will almost always be male and young. But he will be very convincing and professional sounding.[7]
- The prequalifier will "qualify" you by asking whether you buy stocks and how much money you usually invest (this is so the firm will know if it's worth its brokers' supposedly valuable time to call you back).
- You will probably not recognize the name of the brokerage firm.
- The brokerage firm will most likely be located in New York, Florida, or southern California (these types of brokers love warm weather; they tolerate New York because the food is so good).
- The gist of the first call is a focus on the caller, the broker, or the firm rather than investments. You'll feel good about this, because you'll hang up thinking, My, he didn't even try to sell me anything.
- Within a week or so, a licensed broker will call you from the firm with a hot stock idea.
- He will also be male and young and will talk fast and in an exciting tone.
- The broker will use almost every trick known to mankind to convince you to buy his hot stock.
- The number of shares or dollar amount he wants you to commit will almost always be higher than that you have ever committed in the past.

- The initial recommendation is usually a blue chip company. You are familiar with the name and hence feel good. You may even make a profit on this first trade, which will further engender your trust in this faceless, previously unknown broker and his firm.
- Additional recommendations will be in progressively lower-quality stocks.
- If you ask for documentation regarding any of these investments, you won't get any.[8]
- If you want to sell to cut your losses in a declining stock, you'll be talked out of it.

The reluctance of brokers to allow a declining security to be sold deserves an explanation. Perhaps you've owned a junky security that has run up in price, followed by a precipitous fall. You attempt to track down your broker to demand that the security be sold to save what little equity you have left. It is taboo for a broker to refuse a direct order from a client (although it sometimes happens), so what does your broker do? He does one of two things. First, he either talks you out of selling with statements like, "This is the worst time to sell" or "You should be buying not selling" or "This stock is going to rocket up any day now and you will miss a great opportunity. Trust me." These tactics often work because customers think, My broker knows something I don't. He's the one in the business, not me.

Alternatively, your broker will avoid you. You will call and call and leave message after message. All of a sudden, you'll not be able to reach your broker. You may be told that he is at the funeral of his grandmother (a ploy used for the fourth time in six months). Meanwhile, you're watching your stock's price creep lower and lower. If and when you finally get through and *demand* that your stock be sold, you should be successful. If that still doesn't work, we have another suggestion.

Fax a letter to the brokerage firm with your sell order. The nice thing about a fax is that, depending on your fax machine, you have an immediate record that you sent the fax, at what time, and to what number. Be sure to keep a copy of your letter and of the evidence that it was faxed. Although it may be easy to sidestep a telephoning customer (there's usually no record of the call, much less the conversation), it's very difficult for a firm to circumvent a letter you've faxed.

One characteristic practice of boiler rooms is an attempt by a firm's officers, directors, and many lead brokers to gain control of the publicly traded shares of a particular, typically lower-quality company. This is relatively easy to do, because the "float" (the outstanding number of shares available for public trading) is usually very limited in lower-quality companies. This practice is known in the industry as "domination" and "market manipulation" and is a direct violation of securities regulations. Firms employing this tactic will usually concentrate their brokers' efforts in only a few stocks at a time.

The objective is twofold: drive the stock up in price as quickly as possible by first getting customers to buy and then preventing them from selling. Stockbrokers at Dickinson & Company told Tracy that if their customers wanted to sell a stock that they had been directed to not sell, the office manager would simply not approve the ticket. Other brokers were threatened with their job if they so much as presented a sell ticket to the manager. The second objective is for the officers and other key employees to dump their shares on the unsuspecting public while the price is high. The insiders profit handsomely while the purchasers are stuck with a stock that invariably tanks. Such a program works as long as the firm can find new suckers to whom they can sell the shares. Suckers are a dime a dozen, a number we hope that our book will decrease.

In December 1997, the New York attorney general issued a compelling report that detailed certain indicia of microcap manipulation schemes as follows: (1) control of the stock by one broker or a small number of brokers; (2) manipulative public offerings where post-IPO purchases are tied to a small allocation at the lower IPO price; (3) matched purchases and sales of the stock to drive the price up; (4) unauthorized purchases to drive the price up or to "park" the stock; (5) large and excessive spreads between the bid and the ask price; (6) false and misleading representations about the stock; and (7) dumping the stock at an inflated price by the brokers, insiders, and others involved in the scheme.[9]

Many of the firms that deal in microcap securities employ brokers who jump from one firm to the other. Some of these brokers may have a history of criminal convictions, arbitrations, and an excessive number of customer complaints. Not only is broker turnover high in these firms, customer turnover is high as well. The reason is quite simple: either the broker loses all of his investors' money or, better yet, the investors finally wise up. Either way, the broker must look for new clients.

You may wonder how firms like this stay in business. The answer for the majority of them is that they don't. They are often here today and gone tomorrow. A firm's demise is part of the plan. Here's how it works:

The owners of the firm have little capital invested in the firm, certainly when compared with the quick profits that can be made. When the heat increases from the regulators, it's easy to walk away. The officers, managers, and brokers all know from day one that the business will quickly fail, so building a long-term business or making money for investors is neither a goal nor of any import, because within a year or two everyone will be working at a new firm. The regulators are almost always one step too late. By the time they act, the millions lost by investors will have been skirted away or spent by the owners and employees. The regulators rarely fine or suspend the wrongdoers. And when they do, it's usually minuscule in relation to the amount of the ill-gotten gains. Customer complaints and lawsuits may eventually reach incredible levels, but by that time the firm is out of business. Again, investors are left holding the bag with no one to collect the money from even if they should win their lawsuits and arbitrations.

The practices of bucket shops and boiler rooms continue today. The continued existence of these types of firms is yet another one of our reasons for generally recommending that you stick with larger and more recognized brokerage firms.

CLEARING FIRMS AS LIFE SUPPORT

You may have been in the situation of your stockbroker working at a firm different from the one listed on your monthly account statements and confirmations. In this situation, the firm where your broker works is known as the "introducing firm." The firm on the monthly statements is the "clearing firm." It is not uncommon for brokerage firms to delegate back office functions to clearing firms. Roughly 86 percent of brokerages clear their trades through the approximately 80 to 90 clearing firms; approximately 750 to 800 brokerage firms clear their own trades.[10]

Some of the services that a clearing firm offers to an introducing firm are the following:[11]

- Opening, approving, and monitoring the customer's account
- Accepting the customer's order
- Executing the customer's order
- Extending credit (in a margin account) to the customer
- Providing written confirmation of the executed order to the customer
- Receiving or delivering funds or securities from or to the customer
- Maintaining books and records that reflect the transaction, including rendering monthly or periodic statements of the account to the customer
- Safeguarding funds and securities in the customer's account
- Clearing and settling the transaction in the clearinghouse

For bucket shops and boiler rooms, clearing firms are a life support. Without them, they could not pull off their lucrative schemes
because all bucket shops are generally undercapitalized and therefore
cannot afford to perform the services listed above themselves. The
clearing services require expensive computer equipment and staffing.
The clearing firm will pony up significant capital to a brokerage firm,
allowing the firm to do business with a relatively small deposit, usually a minimum of $250,000. Without the clearing firm's help, many
bucket shops and boiler rooms wouldn't get off the ground or survive.

For the clearing firm, money is also the name of the game. The
clearing firm gets to use the introducing broker's deposit interest
free. For every transaction executed by the brokerage, the clearing
firm reaps a "ticket charge" per trade. The clearing firm also charges
interest—typically 1 percent a month—on customer debit balances
carried on the clearing firm's books. The interest meter starts ticking the day a trade is done, which is where the real money in clearing
is made. Clearing firms also have free use of customers' credit balances.

Another compelling reason why bucket shops and boiler rooms
enjoy the services of clearing firms is that the recognizable name of
the clearing firm often lends a certain cachet to the little-known,
and often new, broker-dealer. The broker-dealer can lure in more
clients with a facade of respectability and ride on the coattails of
the clearing firm's recognition. Therefore, you may feel that your

money is in safe hands and that the big firm, like a big brother, will somehow protect you. Not!

In February 1997, *Forbes* published an article about Bear Stearns and its clearing business.[12] It told the story of a man who was pleased when his broker informed him that he was moving to a new brokerage firm—A. R. Baron & Company. The man had never heard of Baron, but then the broker mentioned that Bear Stearns would be involved in the account as the clearing firm. The man later said, "I felt we were in excellent hands. . . . Bear Stearns was a household name." Almost immediately after the move, the man began to get confirmations for trades he never authorized. He promptly complained and, after receiving no help from Baron or his broker, he turned to Bear Stearns for assistance in reversing the trades. Bear Stearns advised him to address the issue with Baron, because it claimed to be "just the clearing firm."[13]

In trade magazines for brokers and firms, Bear Stearns was running full-page ads that said, "We clear just about everything for just about everybody." Bear Stearns cleared for Sterling Foster, a now defunct penny stock firm. Its president pleaded guilty to bilking investors out of more than $100 million.[14] As for A. R. Baron, it was shut down in 1996 and a number of its executives and employees either pleaded guilty to or were convicted of charges in connection with their activities while employed by the firm. Prosecutors said A. R. Baron lied to investors, manipulated small stocks and initial public offerings, and misled regulators about the firm's financial stability.[15]

The man described in the *Forbes* article sued Bear Stearns in arbitration, claiming that in keeping A. R. Baron alive for almost a year, Bear Stearns enabled the firm to harm investors with its fraudulent sales practices, although the arbitrators found no liability on the part of Bear Stearns. For years, the state of the law has insulated clearing firms from liability claims.

LOTS OF PROFIT AND LITTLE LIABILITY— WE SHOULD ALL CLEAR

The clearing business is one of the most lucrative on Wall Street, with profit margins running as high as 25 percent. The tasks are largely administrative. Costly compliance duties, such as investigating customer complaints, traditionally have been left to the introducing firms. In fact, the written agreements between clearing firms and introducing brokers typically specifically state that the clearing firm will have no responsibility for the introducing broker's firm's mismanagement in the handling of an account. Case law follows suit, rarely finding clearing firms liable for the misdeeds of brokers whose trades they process.

Bear Stearns is regarded as one of the industry leaders, clearing more trades than many other firms on Wall Street. An August 1999 report stated that Bear Stearns processed 12 percent of all trades executed on the New York Stock Exchange; the business accounted for about 25 percent of the firm's record fourth quarter net income of $269.1 million.[16] When approached to be interviewed by *Forbes* for the 1997 article mentioned above, a Bear Stearns spokesperson responded, "Clearing is a very, very proprietary business for us, and we don't want the public knowing about it."[17] Sorry, Bear Stearns—we think the public has a right to know what's going on behind the scenes at clearing firms and how it impacts investors.

While Bear Stearns denied any wrongdoing related to its clearing operations for A. R. Baron, the SEC investigated their relationship to determine whether Bear Stearns ignored signs of A. R. Baron's fraudulent activity.

Richard Harriton, the head of Bear Stearns's clearing division, was also the subject of regulators' inquiries. The SEC claimed that he aided and abetted fraud in connection with the A. R. Baron matter.[18] His attorney said in a statement that the SEC charges were "baseless" and that Harriton "expects to be fully vindicated."[19] As it turns out, Harriton's attorney was incorrect. In April 2000, Harriton agreed to one of the largest fines ever against a senior Wall Street executive by the SEC—$1 million—and was suspended from the securities industry for two years.[20]

After a long and protracted battle, while Bear Sterns made no admission of liability, it agreed to pay $38 million to settle the matters concerning its relationship with A. R. Baron;[21] $30 million of that amount went to a restitution fund for A. R. Baron investors. A news report by Dow Jones said that "SEC officials and prosecutors from the Manhattan district attorney's office characterized the case as an object lesson for clearing firms, saying they should be on notice that they will be held responsible if they don't take steps to head off fraud by their clearing clients."[22] "Senior officials can't insulate themselves from wrongdoing," said William Baker, the SEC's associate director of enforcement, who led the investigation. "When they become aware of fraud, they have to act quickly to end the fraud and bring it to the attention of the appropriate authorities."[23]

Regulators made further headway in laying more responsibility on clearing firms. In July 1999, the NYSE and NASD adopted rules that require each clearing firm to furnish promptly any written customer complaint it receives regarding an introducing firm to that firm and to regulators. In addition, the clearing firm must notify the customer that it has passed the complaint on to the introducing firm and the regulators.

Bear Stearns is hardly the only clearing firm that has cleared for bucket shops. JB Oxford also makes the list. It cleared for Greenway Capital, a firm, like so many others, that is no longer with us today. Douglas participated as the expert in a case in which the investor sued both Greenway Capital and JB Oxford, its clearing firm, claiming that Oxford had responsibility for Greenway Capital's wrongdoing. When Douglas returned from the arbitration, one of his first comments was that based on everything he saw and heard in the arbitration, it was hard to say which of the two firms was more responsible. It turns out that Oxford was the subject of a white-collar criminal investigation as a result of its business relationship with a convicted Canadian stock swindler.[24] Greenway Capital had had many run-ins with securities regulators, and its president was suspended from the securities industry for four years.[25]

The compliance director of Greenway testified that JB Oxford was aware of Greenway Capital's compliance problems and the violations of its former president. Yet Oxford continued to do business with Greenway Capital until the day that Greenway was shut down. Like any clearing firm, Oxford had much to gain from clearing trades. For example:

- The more activity in the client accounts of the Greenway Capital brokers, the more money JB Oxford made.
- The more Greenway Capital brokers margined their clients' accounts, the more money Oxford made on the margin balances.
- If Greenway Capital brokers' clients traded in securities in which Oxford made a market, Oxford profited handsomely.[26]

The final outcome of this arbitration: the arbitration panel awarded damages against Greenway Capital only and none against its clearing firm. It was a hollow award because Greenway had ceased to exist, the sad conclusion of too many claims against an introducing brokerage firm such as this.

You now realize why we said that we should all get into the clearing firm business. It is incredibly profitable with seemingly few liabilities. The various courts around the country have tended to agree that the clearing firms have very limited, or no, liability. Perhaps the proceedings the SEC brought against Bear Stearns and Richard Harriton signal the start of a regulatory change on the liability issue.

Indeed, in 2000 a panel of arbitrators who heard a clearing firm case issued a 39-page arbitration decision (a rarity) explaining why it rejected the no-liability argument of clearing firm Hanifen Inhoff (also known as Fiserve Correspondent Services, Inc.).[27] The panel found that the clearing firm materially aided the broker-dealer in the transactions that caused extensive losses to the claimants. It held that a clearing broker cannot turn a deaf ear to, and consistently ignore, clear evidence of its corresponding broker-dealer's fraudulent practices.

What a victory for investors! It was in 1997 that the president of the North American Securities Administrators Association (NASAA), the agency that embodies all of the state regulators, said, "Clearing firms are a vital component in the business of a cold-calling boiler room operation."[28] Although this statement may still be true today, it's hoped a decision like Hanifen Inhoff signals a change, and clearing firms may worry more about their potential exposure. We hope this is a trend that continues.

We took so much time to discuss clearing firms to hammer home a few important points. Don't fall into the trap of opening an account with a second-tier or bucket shop operation based on a false sense of security because you recognize the name of the clearing firm. You may garner no benefit from this relationship. And don't think that your small brokerage firm must be on the up-and-up or else the big firm wouldn't associate with it. We think the questionable activities surrounding the business of some clearing firms is yet one more example of how far too many within the securities industry care little for you but are instead concerned only about their bottom line.

After writing ten chapters about the conflicts, scams, and horrors in the securities industry, we hope you have gotten the point: *don't be so trusting*. Now you're armed with knowledge to allow you to be a better watchdog over your broker and your accounts. In the next several chapters, we're going to offer help in case you ever have a complaint against your broker, advisor, or online brokerage firm. In the final two chapters, we arm you with valuable information on how to pick a broker or advisor and how to simplify your options. Please don't skip these chapters even if you are in love with your current financial professional; the information will help you to improve what may be a wonderful relationship.

CHAPTER 11

What to Do
When Things Go Awry

Now that you know the rules, what do you do if you find your broker violating them? Let's say you have caught your broker red-handed (or, more appropriately, green-fisted). She made a trade in your account that you and she didn't discuss completely beforehand. She made an unauthorized trade, and you confront her with the facts. If she denies it or tries to justify it, close your account. If she admits the mistake but refuses to have your account credited with any losses you sustained, close your account. And if your broker begs you not to write a complaint letter or call her manager and promises to make it up to you somehow in the future, close your account.

Many people stay with their broker after learning that they were misled or deceived. The decision to leave is easier when there is a specific trade and specific losses. It becomes much grayer when you suspect your broker of not having your interest at heart when your account losses or trading has increased, and you don't know why. We often hear stories from clients who confronted their brokers with questions of concern only to have the brokers convince them that all is well, the losses are merely a short-term aberration in the market, and that millions in profits are just around the corner.

You learned that stockbrokers are good salespeople. You don't think that this silver-tongued devil can talk you into trusting him just one more time, do you? How about multiple times? He talked you into opening an account with him and trusting him with trades. Talking you into *keeping* the account with him is even easier. Resist the temptation. Close your account! Do not pass go. Do not collect $200. Just close your account!! If you insist on staying with the advisor that has wronged you and thus whom you should now mistrust, promise us that you will document the problem and watch your broker like a hawk.

WHEN TO WRITE A COMPLAINT LETTER

A common response to Tracy's standard question to clients, "Did you ever complain?" is "You bet I did. I called the broker and his manager and gave them an earful on the phone." Tracy then looks at her client with pursed lips and sad eyes. She knows that she may never see any documentation of that verbal complaint; it will be the firm's word against her client's. Oral or verbal complaints are somewhat meaningless in the securities industry. We have the NASD to thank for that, because its rules require that firms document and respond to only *written* complaints.[1] This requirement was probably to accommodate the brokerage firms that were already inundated with written complaints. One can only wonder how many oral complaints they receive.

We are not crazy about investors writing complaint letters. Generally speaking, they are fairly worthless and do little to advance the interests of the investor. As you learned in Chapter 1, complaint letters rarely result in money in your pocket or a resolution you'll be pleased with. Though brokerage firms may respond to your complaint letter, almost invariably you'll receive a denial.

In addition, investors, not being lawyers (usually) and not knowing the intricacies of the system, can sometimes write complaint letters that hurt. We have had client-authored complaint letters come back to bite the client in the arbitration, because (1) the client didn't complain about *all* of the wrongdoing in the letter or (2) the client asked for reimbursement in an amount *less* than the damages actually suffered. Usually, arbitrators don't hold these sorts of things against the client, but some do.

We do, however, have a few limited scenarios in which we would recommend you write a complaint letter. The first is when you are planning on continuing to use the broker and keeping your account at the firm. In this letter, your main goal is to put the broker and his manager on notice of the wronging and try to gain assurance that the infraction will not take place again. If your broker has apologized for the infraction and verbally assured you it will not happen again, then craft your letter so that you are thanking him for his magnanimous gesture. Send a copy not only to your broker but to his branch office manager and, of course, keep a copy in your vault. There is a fairly good chance that you will receive a response. If the firm takes a position different from your broker's or refutes your version of events, close your account.

The second situation in which you would write a complaint letter is to document your complaint in a timely manner. It may take six months or more to determine your losses, have your case analyzed, hire a lawyer, and get a claim filed. That the investor waited too long to complain is one of the brokerage firms' standard responses and defenses. Take it away from them by documenting what went wrong in a letter, but we do not recommend going into great detail regarding the nuances of your claim. This letter should do nothing more than state what happened and ask for a response. It can be short and simple. You might say, "This past Monday, I received a confirmation for a trade that did not match my order. Please respond." Or "I have just learned that Fly-By-Night Airlines was a risky investment. This is not how my stockbroker described it to me." Writing this sort of letter is particularly important in online trading disputes because often the information you see online you will never see again.

The third situation in which you would write a complaint letter is when your case is so small that your only hope of resolution is dealing with the brokerage firm on a one-on-one basis, as opposed to getting a lawyer involved. The reality is that below certain amounts, it will be difficult for you to find a lawyer to take your case. This will vary lawyer to lawyer, but generally speaking, we think that if your losses are under, say $50,000, you will likely be stuck handling your own case. Be sure to include the following in your letter:

- All of the pertinent facts—dates, times, prices, identities, and so on
- Specifically what the broker or the firm did wrong and why you feel it was wrong
- A request for reimbursement in a certain amount and an explanation of how you calculated that amount

- A request for a response by a particular date, usually no later than 30 days

If you write a complaint letter to the firm, do *not* send a copy of it to the regulators. After reading Chapter 6, we hope you understand why. Chances are they will do little, and at the end of doing little, they will find no wrongdoing on the part of the firm. Even if your case doesn't go to arbitration, the brokerage firm will consider the regulators' finding a feather in its cap and will offer you less to settle your claim.

HIRING LAWYERS AND EXPERTS

Hiring a lawyer is a necessary evil for all of those situations when your claim is good enough and big enough to warrant pursuing it. The primary reason you need to hire a lawyer is because without one, you will probably not recover your losses, and if you do, you won't recover much. A person who represents himself or herself is said to be pro se. You've heard the phrase "A person who represents himself has a fool for a client"? We have coined our own phrase: "Pro se? No way." The statistics bear that out. Publications that report awards in arbitration claims reveal that individuals who pursue their claims pro se often lose their cases. It's no surprise really. Pro se claimants are pigeons for the industry's highly paid securities attorneys who do nothing but defend these types of cases.

Another reason you may find you need a lawyer is because you have reached the inevitable dead end. Perhaps you've sent a detailed complaint letter with a demand for compensation, you received the "Just Say No" letter in response, and you don't know where to turn. You know that continuing to jockey with the firm will get you nowhere, but you don't want to give up, so you may have to consult a lawyer.

These, then, are reasons why you find yourself in a situation where a lawyer may be necessary. The downside is that other than the initial consultation, which may be free, you'll have to pay for the lawyer's time. As you may know, many lawyers and securities arbitration lawyers work on a contingency basis, which means you don't pay them for their time unless you recover something, and their payment consists of a percentage of your recovery. For many

victims of securities fraud, this type of arrangement is the only feasible one as a result of the loss of funds.

Tracy handles the vast majority of her cases on a contingency
basis. From the client's standpoint, a contingency fee case is often
preferable to an hourly rate for two reasons. First, there is no outlay
of money by the client to pay the lawyer's hourly rate. Second, and
perhaps most important, a contingency arrangement aligns the
client's interests with the lawyer's. Lawyers will not want to undertake a contingency case unless they believe there is a good chance
of recovering. Lawyers are risking their time in exchange for a potential fee that will adequately compensate them. They hope for a
windfall—that is, the contingency fee will be more than the value
of a lawyer's time on an hourly basis. A lawyer's risk is that the
client recovers nothing and the lawyer, consequently, is paid nothing.

You can expect to pay a contingency fee of anywhere from 33 to
45 percent and even as much as 50 percent, depending on the facts
of the case. Sometimes clients are surprised to hear that the contingency fee is higher than 33 percent because they may have some
knowledge about personal injury lawyers charging 33 percent as a
standard. Higher contingency fees are accepted and are the standard in securities arbitrations because securities arbitrations require
such particular expertise, not just in securities but in the procedures
of the regulatory forums that administer the cases. But there are always lawyers willing to enter into hourly rate arrangements and
even hybrid arrangements to accommodate the needs of clients.

If you need a securities arbitration lawyer, we cannot stress
enough how important it is to find one who is experienced in handling securities arbitration cases because the lawyers who represent
brokerage firms do so on a regular basis and usually know the ropes.
We are known for saying that an experienced trial lawyer would be
a fish out of water in securities arbitration. It's an entirely different
ball game with an entirely different set of rules. In addition, brokerage firms routinely use attorneys who do nothing but securities
arbitrations. These lawyers are extremely gifted at attempting to
thwart your lawyer's every effort.

One thing that makes arbitration a different ball game is that
lawyers like Tracy can represent clients all over the country. It's
not necessary that she be licensed to practice law in the state in
which the client resides. She has represented clients all over the
United States and even abroad. Unlike a court case, the only per-

sonal appearance necessary in securities arbitration is at the arbitration itself. And because most cases settle, distance from the client is rarely an issue. Of course, if you or someone you know has a potential claim involving a brokerage firm, you can contact Tracy (<www.brokeragefraud.com> or 719-783-0303).

Sometimes, clients turn to experts before lawyers. Potential clients often contact Douglas to perform a churning analysis, to calculate damages, to analyze certain investments, and to offer advice on what rules and regulations the broker or firm broke (<www.securitiesexpert.com> or 719-783-3230). In most securities cases, an expert witness is critical to prove up certain aspects of the case. Experts are often referred to as the "gladiators" of arbitration. Unlike a court case, where experts are excluded from the courtroom during the trial, experts in arbitration are permitted to attend the entire arbitration and listen to all of the witnesses. This is a tremendous benefit in that it allows your expert to testify to such things as, "When Barry Broker testified that bla, bla, bla, he was wrong. The rules state bla, bla, bla." Just like lawyers, there are good and bad experts. Choose carefully.

FORGET YOUR RIGHT TO A JURY TRIAL

In a landmark case—*Shearson/American Express Inc. v. McMahon*, 482 U.S. 220 (1987)—the U.S. Supreme Court ruled in 1987 that it's okay for brokerage firms to require their customers to arbitrate any dispute they may have with the firm. As testament to the fact that this was a good thing for the brokerage industry is that every brokerage firm agreement contains such an arbitration clause. They didn't have to do it. The Supreme Court didn't issue an edict that all brokerage firms *must* require their customers to go to arbitration. It was a choice the brokerage firms were given. But we have yet to see a brokerage firm agreement that didn't contain an arbitration clause. And we bet we never will.

Not only did all brokerage firms choose to insert an arbitration provision in their agreements, but they used to do it in such a way that you could barely read the provision—it would be buried among the legalese in difficult-to-read type. Those problems have been cured, but the arbitration clause today remains non-negotiable. If you say you want it stricken, your broker will just laugh and suggest you go elsewhere. As you may recall from an earlier chapter, Tracy had one client who bracketed the arbitration clause in the customer agreement and wrote "NO" next to it. Nobody at the firm caught it. Years later, Tracy filed a claim on her client's behalf in court— not in arbitration. The firm argued vehemently that the case had to go to arbitration. The judge correctly ruled that Tracy's client modified the contract and the brokerage firm accepted the modification through its silence. The case got to stay in court.

The brokerage industry fought long and hard for mandatory arbitration because it recognized that one of the biggest threats to its financial well-being was a jury verdict. Juries can issue what are termed *run away* verdicts, that is, verdicts that have no relationship to, or have run away from, the actual damages. In this same vein, the brokerage industry realized that no matter how small the actual damages in a case, the real harm could be inflicted with punitive damages— damages designed to punish (hence the origin of the word).

One of Douglas's earliest cases involved an elderly blind woman, who had been a nun for roughly 30 years. She left the nunnery to work in a school for the blind to help others like herself. Because nuns earn very little, she came into the working world penniless. She realized that at her age she had only a few years to earn any savings for retirement. So she began to scrimp and save every penny she could. After ten years of working for the school, she was able to save roughly $80,000, which was not only her life savings but her entire net worth. She sought out a broker to help her invest her money so that she might have it grow at a slightly better rate than she could get from her bank's CDs. The broker put almost 100 percent of her money in two high-risk, illiquid limited partnerships. Shortly thereafter, the former nun lost all but a few thousand dollars of her life savings. The arbitration panel awarded her all of her losses, most of her attorney fees, and Douglas's expert fees. But the panel declined to award any punitive damages. If ever a case deserved punitive damages, this was the case. Not only did the broker blatantly disregard the wants and needs of this woman, but he left her almost destitute as a result. The broker and the firm should have been punished for its wanton acts. If this case had been in court, a jury would have awarded punitive damages and sent a strong message to the firm that such conduct would not be tolerated.

When a jury considers an award of punitive damages, it is allowed to examine all of the details regarding the financial status of the firm, because the jury's job is to assess a financial penalty that will truly hurt. Brokerage firms cowered at the thought of their financials displayed in newspapers for the world to see, much less facing the potentially large verdicts and punitive damages that might be assessed against them.

The Supreme Court's 1987 decision stripped you of your right to a jury trial. Wait a second—aren't you entitled to have a jury of your peers decide your case? Isn't the right to a jury trial one of the inalienable rights guaranteed by the U.S. Constitution? Yes, it is. The Seventh Amendment of the Constitution states:

> In Suits at common law, where the value in controversy shall exceed twenty dollars, the right of trial by jury shall be preserved, and no fact tried by a jury, shall be otherwise re-examined in any Court of the United States, than according to the rules of the common law.

Interestingly, the Supreme Court did not even address in its opinion every individual's right to a jury trial granted by the U.S. Constitution. Across the country, in industries beyond securities, businesses seek to benefit themselves by inserting arbitration clauses into their agreements. On March 21, 2001, the U.S. Supreme Court cleared the way for employers to require arbitration of all discrimination claims.[2] Effective June 1, 2001, Citibank inserted an arbitration provision into its credit card agreements requiring arbitration of all claims "that arose in the past, or arise in the present or future."[3] At the same time, we are seeing a backlash in consumer complaints about mandatory arbitration.

ARBITRATION—FAIR SHAKE OR MILK SHAKE?

Investors are filing arbitration claims at the NASD at the rate of one every 20 minutes. That's 15 percent more than in the year 2000. 2001 probably will be the NASD's biggest arbitration year ever.[4] The SEC reported that in 2000, complaints against broker-dealers for sales practice violations rose approximately 8 percent to 4,476 from 4,152, reversing a five-year decline. Overall complaints in 2000 jumped to 13,599 from 12,463 in 1999. Since 1995, the complaints and questions received and responded to by the SEC have risen 88 percent.[5]

The regulators would have you believe that arbitration gives investors a fair shake. They cite statistics evidencing that claimants win in arbitration a majority of the time. What they don't tell you is that in the year 2000, for example, claimants won NASD arbitrations 53 percent of the time. In 2001, through the end of April, claimants won 55 percent of the time.[6] Certainly not a landslide "majority." What's more deceiving is that to the NASD, the word *won* means that the claimant received some money, no matter how little. Though Tracy has a very good track record in recovering her clients' money, far too often investors fall short of recouping their full losses after costs and fees. Hence, to the brokerage industry, arbitration is a way to limit awards to investors.

Arbitration can be more like a milk shake than a fair shake for many. Some of the Justices in the *McMahon* decision mentioned above pointed out one of the primary problems with the arbitration of securities disputes. They wrote:

> The uniform opposition of investors to compelled arbitration and the overwhelming support of the securities industry for the process suggest that there must be some truth to the investors' belief that the securities industry has an advantage in a forum under its own control. . . . The [brokerage] houses basically like the present system because they own the stacked deck.

The deck is stacked not only because the industry runs the arbitration system, but also because on every three-member arbitration panel, one member is what is called an "industry" arbitrator—a person employed by a brokerage firm or otherwise connected in some way to the brokerage industry. Critics charge that the industry panelist often sways the other members of the panel to rule in favor of the brokerage firm.

Arbitrators who have participated in many arbitrations are another problem. In a court case, a jury does very little comparative analysis. When arbitrators hear many of the same types of complaints over and over, they become anesthetized. It's like the difference between the people who drive by an accident, straining their necks with widened eyes to see what happened—they're shocked and concerned—and the ambulance driver seeing these same events—he looks as though he's making copies. He's seen these same events many times before and so is less impacted, as it is so often with arbitrators who have a lot of arbitrations under their belt. Experienced arbitrators may discount a claimant's damages because the facts of the case are not nearly so bad as the facts in a different case they heard a month before.

Many securities attorneys agree that arbitrators often scrutinize a claimant's conduct and testimony more closely than they do brokers' and managers' conduct and testimony. Puffery and aggressive sales tactics are a part of many stockbrokers' daily routine. Therefore, when brokers use these same tactics in arbitration, the panel tends to expect, or gloss over, it. Claimants' attorneys jokingly say: "If the stockbroker lies on the stand, it's okay. He's expected to lie. But if the claimant lies on the stand, he loses."

Another travesty that befalls investors in arbitration is the manner in which many brokerage firms deal with the production of documents. More than a decade ago (1990 to be exact), we authored an article entitled, "Forced Arbitration—Perfect Justice? Discovery in Arbitration," published in the *Securities Arbitration Commentator*. We were critical in that article about how brokerage firms abuse the discovery process to the detriment of investors. The sad fact is that not much has changed since that time.

In a court case, discovery consists of depositions of all witnesses, requests for production, interrogatories, and requests for admission. In arbitration, the only discovery permitted is requests for production of documents. For an investor, many times all of the documents needed to prove a case are in the possession of the brokerage firm. Many brokerage firms object, stall, and simply fail to produce documents pertinent to the case; defendants in court cases do the same thing. However, in a court case, when the judge orders a defendant to produce documents, the defendants hop to and do it! They know that to disobey a judge could lead to severe financial penalties and even the striking of some of their defenses.

In arbitration, most arbitrators' rulings have no teeth, just gums. They may order the production of documents, but the firm may disobey the order, knowing there is little downside in doing so. Brokerage firms often treat arbitration rules no differently. Tracy had a case where a brokerage firm failed to file an answer to the Statement of Claim for six months after it was due. The arbitrators didn't do a thing about it, despite Tracy's request that the firm's answer be stricken or other sanctions imposed.

Douglas returned from an arbitration in March 2001 where one of the witnesses testified that the firm's operations and procedure manual should be in the branch office a few miles away. Unknown to this witness, the investor's lawyer had expended untold hours attempting to obtain this very document from the firm. Two prehearing conferences were held on the subject and the chairman of the panel had ordered the production of the manual. The firm had asserted that the manual couldn't be found. On hearing the witnesses' testimony, the chairman once again ordered that an attempt be made to find the manual at the branch office. Miraculously, the very same manual that for months no one could find was found in two hours and brought to the arbitration hearing.

Arbitrators are empowered to issue monetary and other sanctions for discovery abuse, but they rarely do. Brokerage firms and their lawyers know that arbitrators rarely issue sanctions, and this has exacerbated the problem. Some brokerage firms reason that the benefit of not producing harmful documents is outweighed by any fallout in the arbitration process for failing to produce them.

Finally, another prevalent problem in arbitration is what we refer to as the "split the baby" mentality of many arbitrators. Some arbitrators believe they are doing the right thing by awarding the claimant roughly half of his losses if they have found liability on the part of the firm. They don't factor in that the claimant will typically pay a percentage of his recovery to his lawyer and also have other costs to bear. Some critics voice concern that arbitrators shy away from giving large claimant awards for fear that brokerage firm lawyers will strike them from future arbitration panels.

We cannot have a section that refers to arbitration as "milk shake" without sharing with you some of our own personal war stories that depict arbitration, and particularly arbitrators, well, in not the most favorable light. Recognize, though, that these stories involve what we hope are a minority of arbitrators. Just as with stockbrokers, there are always a few bad apples. A November 1996 *Money* magazine article titled "Wall Street's Stingiest Judges" discussed many of the shortcomings of arbitration and some arbitrators.[7] We don't intend to direct our criticism at all arbitrators; after all, we are arbitrators too.

Perhaps the most egregious travesty that we have ever experienced involved a case lasting several weeks against a small brokerage firm and its manager, whom we'll call John Doe. When Tracy was cross-examining Doe, he testified that on a monthly basis he or another principal in his office reviewed Tracy's client's monthly statements for excessive trading and to ensure the investments were suitable based on her client's investment objectives. He testified that the evidence of his review was a signature notation that he would place on the monthly statements. Tracy thought this odd, because she had specifically requested that the brokerage firm produce any and all documents evidencing that the firm performed any supervisory review of her client's account. Nothing responsive had been produced, so she asked Doe about the whereabouts of those initialed monthly statements. He said that he didn't know why they were not produced.

Two days later, Doe walked into the arbitration hearing with an armful of Tracy's client's monthly statements. He testified that he had received the statements at lunchtime from another supervisory manager at the brokerage firm. Scattered throughout the monthly statements were the original initials and a few notations by John Doe. Tracy was suspicious. She requested permission to take the monthly statements for the purpose of having an analysis performed to determine when the initials were placed on the documents—several years earlier, when they should have been or in the last week after Tracy had begun asking Doe questions about them. The panel granted her request, and she noticed that Doe appeared to be squirming.

The next morning, Doe's attorney entered the hearing room with a grave and concerned face. He advised the panel and the parties that he had called the supervisory manager, who admitted that Doe telephoned her in the past week to ask her to take Tracy's client's monthly statements and randomly place his initials throughout. The supervisory manager went further than that, however. She used pens of different colors and occasionally circled things and drew arrows to make it look as though some sort of analysis had been done.

Two wrongs had been committed. Not only did Doe and the manager together manufacture critical evidence for the arbitration—evidence that went to the very heart of the case—but Doe lied about it under oath. Tracy requested that the panel make a disciplinary referral to the NASD to sanction these two licensed, supervisory individuals, the only avenue for punishment available. The NASD, in turn, could investigate the matter and fine both Doe and the manager, suspend them for a period of time, or yank their licenses, thereby prohibiting them from working in the securities industry. The panel responded that any such referral would be made in the written decision of the panel.

When Tracy reviewed the arbitrators' decision some months later, not only did her client lose the arbitration, but the panel failed to make any disciplinary referral or even comment on the misconduct described above. What is it that caused the arbitrators to ignore such egregious conduct? Because arbitrators are not required to make any findings or provide any support for their decisions, we will never know.

Douglas was an expert witness in an arbitration where the industry arbitrator kept butting into the examination by the claimant's attorney of his witnesses. The arbitrator made personal attacks on the claimant and, at times, mocked his testimony. Finally, a very heated verbal battle ensued between this industry arbitrator and the claimant's attorney. There were accusations and name calling. The claimant's attorney accused the arbitrator of being biased. It was agreed that the arbitration would be adjourned and would start over on a future date with new arbitrators. While everyone started packing up, the chairman of the panel went to the phone and called the NASD. He came back into the arbitration and announced that the NASD said that the parties should not stop the arbitration so long as the industry arbitrator would state on the record that he was not biased against the claimant's case. Of course, the arbitrator so stated for the record. And the award for the claimant? Maybe it's just chance, but he got a big fat zero.

Then there was the sleeping arbitrator, who was asleep for the vast majority of the hearing. It was sometimes comical because his head would slump forward, and he would snore a time or two. But there was nothing funny for the claimant because, as in court, the burden of proof is always on the claimant. If one of the finders of fact is asleep, then he is clearly not hearing the facts. The claimant's attorney decided not to complain, reasoning that the other two arbitrators knew the third arbitrator was sleeping and thus, when it came time to deliberate, they would not give much weight to his input. But matters became more complicated.

Whenever the sleeping arbitrator would awaken, he would do so with a flurry of questions, almost as if to make the point that he had not been sleeping and had been paying attention all along. Unfortunately, this occurred primarily during the claimant's testimony, and so the claimant bore the brunt of the sleeping arbitrator's wrath. What a predicament. Does the claimant's lawyer dare state a complaint and risk ticking off the sleeping arbitrator? The parties had lengthy discussions about what to do. Finally, the pain became too great, and the claimant's lawyer convinced himself that the other two panelists would do the right thing and ask the sleeping arbitrator to remove himself from the panel. But no, the other arbitrators vetoed the attorney's request and the arbitration continued. The claimant received an award but not nearly a make-whole award. Perhaps the outcome would have been different had the sleepy arbitrator stayed awake throughout the proceeding.

There are many other horrible arbitration stories but our horror stories about arbitrators should, we hope, not scare you into thinking you'll never bring an arbitration claim. Between them, Tracy and Douglas have participated in over 600 arbitration claims; their horror stories constitute but a handful. Thankfully, the system has improved dramatically in terms of the arbitrator pool and the selection and training of arbitrators. Tracy recently had a prehearing conference in an NYSE case wherein the arbitrator made some comments, which Tracy thought showed his bias against the investor and in favor of the brokerage firm. Tracy objected and asked that the arbitrator excuse himself. He did, but the NYSE went even further. It permanently removed him from the arbitrator pool.

The NASD and the NYSE are always looking to increase the number of arbitrators willing to hear arbitration cases. Personally, we would love to see more individuals become arbitrators who do not have ties to or a bias toward the brokerage industry. Even many arbitrators characterized as "public arbitrators" have ties to the brokerage industry. If you do not have ties to the brokerage industry and have an interest in this book, think about becoming an arbitrator! No specific background or qualifications are required. In fact, arbitrators should constitute a broad cross section of people, diverse in culture, profession, and background. Before being assigned to a case, you will attend a one-day arbitrator skills-training program to familiarize you with the procedures. NASD arbitrators receive $200 for four hours or less (for example, a prehearing conference on the telephone) and $400 per day for each day of arbitration. Most arbitrations last two and a half days. To become an NASD arbitrator, you can download an application and get all of your questions answered at the NASD Alternative Dispute Resolution Web site at <www.NASDADR.com>. Just click on Recruitment & Training. To become an NYSE arbitrator, click on the Arbitrators tab at <www.NYSE.com/arbitration>.

We think it's appropriate to end this chapter noting some of the benefits of arbitration. The biggest benefit is that an arbitration case will be resolved in significantly less time than a court case. Court cases are often postponed and postponed simply because of the court's overloaded docket. Not so in arbitration. The case is usually set for arbitration within eight to ten months or so from filing, and parties are required to pay a fee if they want a postponement. Arbitration is also generally much less expensive than a court case. Although the filing fees are greater in arbitration, you may get a refund of a portion of that fee. There are no depositions in arbitration; and depositions can really run up the costs in a court case. An arbitration is much less formal than a court case, often taking place in a hotel conference room, a setting far more relaxed than a courtroom and very comforting to many investors. The award by the arbitration panel should be received within 30 to 60 days from the close of the hearing. And the losing party is required to pay up within 30 days. Appealing an arbitration award is next to impossible and can be a double-edged sword. But generally this is a positive because the losing party can't drag out the inevitable.

For many investors who are abused by Wall Street, filing an arbitration is often more than just trying to obtain the dollars that were stolen from them. Investors feel betrayed by the system and the broker they had put their faith in. Arbitration allows these abused and defrauded investors to have their day in court and an opportunity to tell their story of how they were wronged and how it has affected their life. The vast majority of arbitrators are interested in your story and will do what's fair at the end of your arbitration.

CHAPTER 12

Inundated
with Choices
Distinguishing the Players

You can't turn on TV these days without being inundated by advertisements from financial services firms. Traditional brokerage firms, online brokerage firms, commodity trading firms, and mutual funds are all on a nonstop marketing blitz for your investment dollar. As you now know, the financial services industry is an incredibly profitable one, so spending hundreds of millions of dollars on advertising is a mere drop in the bucket compared with its bottom line. To complicate your life even more, the choice of investment periodicals and newspapers is staggering and ever growing. Yet their growth is put to shame by the vast array of investment research, educational content, news, and opinions found online in cyberspace.

Having read 11 chapters of our special insights, secrets, and warnings about the securities industry, you are now better armed to control your destiny when dealing with the securities industry. In the next two chapters, we focus on the myriad players within the securities industry, many of whom are stewards of your money.

If you are a sophisticated and experienced investor, then you may be tempted to skip these chapters as of no use to you. We beg to differ. With Douglas's 20 something years in the securities business and Tracy's 12 years as a securities attorney, you would be shocked to learn how many supposedly knowledgeable and sophisticated investors we have come across who can barely cough up enough money to buy a house.

In this chapter, we discuss various alternatives for finding investment advice and help. At the conclusion, we hope you won't feel inundated. In the following chapter, we concentrate on choosing and evaluating stockbrokers and brokerage firms.

ONE-STOP SHOPPING—CAN'T TELL THE PLAYERS WITHOUT A SCORE CARD

This chapter would have been a lot easier to write a number of years ago, when it was far simpler to distinguish between the players. For over 20 years, we have been witnessing both a consolidation and an expansion of sorts within the securities industry. Blurred now are the demarcation lines that sharply distinguished who did what. Perhaps it all began in the early 1980s when Merrill Lynch introduced its cash management account, or CMA, and, in so doing, got into the banking and credit card business. We have also seen a rash of mergers of various financial services firms, firms that were fierce competitors just years before.

At such stores as Wal-Mart and Sam's Club, you can buy your groceries, your prescription glasses, and your car tires, and afterward eat lunch—all under one roof. Financial firms have followed suit (or maybe Wal-Mart and Sam's copied—we aren't sure). Buy your stocks, manage your 401(k), refinance your house, pay your bills, and buy your life insurance all in one place. This one-stop shopping concept has benefits for both the purveyor and you, the consumer. From a business standpoint, it is a tremendous economy of scale. As brokerage firms have discounted their commissions to lure customers, they have been forced to find other ways to maximize their profits. The addition of fee-based services, wherein one fee provides you a variety of services, is an obvious path. For you, the consumer, being able to conduct so much of your financially oriented business in one place is a real time-saver. If you need a loan, you may be able to pick up the phone and call your broker as opposed to filling out a slew of paperwork. In addition, you should become a more valuable asset to your brokerage firm and broker when they are tapping you for a number of fee-based products and services. Just make sure you demand and receive the added attention that you now deserve.

We see little reason to deter you from grouping many of your services at one firm. We simply offer a few caveats to keep in mind:

- When only one person wields so much influence over so many of your financial affairs, you run a risk of financial havoc if that person doesn't deserve your trust and is all the more reason to have in reserve an unrelated and unbiased second opinion when dealing with an "all-in-one" firm.
- Though you may concentrate all of your investments and financial dealings at one firm, that does not necessarily mean you should concentrate your investments as it relates to products. Stay diversified with different types of investments and remain diversified *within* the various types of investments.
- Make sure the firm that you choose is financially sound and nationally respected.

Let's back up and not assume that you are looking for a one-shop-fits-all kind of relationship. Where do you go for good old-fashioned investment advice? We hate to throw the ball back in your court, but before we can answer that question, *you* have to make some decisions that pertain to *you*. Many different entities are competing for your investment dollar, and one distinguishing factor among them is how much involvement you have. The main question you need to address is, How involved do you want to be in the entire process of managing your money? If you don't know the answer to that question, we are here to help.

Generally speaking, we think Americans should learn more about their investments—and we mean everyone. Far too often, investment decisions are left to the husband; when he dies, his living wife is left with no clue as to what to do. Unscrupulous advisors often prey on widows because they view them as easy targets. If individuals had a better understanding of investments, they would be better able to evaluate their current advisors and their current situation, even when unexpected responsibility pops up. But let's be realistic; we run hectic lives and have little time to second-guess our CPA, lawyer, doctor, and stockbroker. And as we stated earlier, you should be able to trust and rely on these professionals; that's what you hired them for in the first place. There's a happy medium. We think you should stay involved enough so that you basically understand what your broker or advisor is doing with your money. The advisor should be in control, in making both recommendations and decisions but with input, understanding, and monitoring from you. That's the ideal.

Though the lines of distinction can sometimes be gray, you have basically four choices for having your money managed and receiving investment advice. We explain them in order, starting with the one requiring the least consumer involvement and moving toward the one requiring the most consumer involvement.

MUTUAL FUND MANAGERS AND FAMILIES OF FUNDS

Most people have a fairly good understanding of mutual funds. The most elementary explanation is that a mutual fund is a company that obtains money from many different people and then invests that pool of money in stocks or bonds pursuant to certain guidelines. People invest in a mutual fund when they want their money managed in the same manner as all of the other people who have bought that mutual fund. Whether it's an open-end or closed-end mutual fund, an investor's money is commingled with other investors' money, and the investors have no input as to how or in what their money is invested. What you pay for with this form of management is very easy to calculate these days. Mutual fund prospectuses spell out in detail all of the charges associated with the mutual fund. Be sure to add up all of the fees, and read our subchapter on mutual funds in Chapter 14. As for control, you have none. You either have your money in the fund or you take the money out of it.

Diversification among various types of mutual funds does not necessarily mean that you must have relationships with ten different mutual funds. Firms such as Investors Diversified Services (IDS) and American Funds helped pioneer a concept called families of funds. Firms like Vanguard, Fidelity, and T. Rowe Price offer investors all the choices they will ever need in one family of funds. You can keep your savings in a firm's money market fund (remember our advice not to mix your checking account with investments), your retirement account in another fund, the bulk of your money that you want to grow in index funds, and a small portion of your money in more aggressive growth funds. If circumstances dictate a need for cash flow, you can move money into taxable or tax-free income funds.

The benefits of staying within a family of funds are that you get one statement that summarizes each account, and you can get all of your questions answered at one 800 number or Web site. If you choose a load fund (and why would you), you can move within the same family of funds at no additional fee.

Most brokerage firms have created a large family of funds managed by their own in-house managers. However, be sure to do your homework. Historically speaking and on a comparative basis, these funds have been underperformers. In addition, they have above-average costs, especially when compared with a true no-load family of funds.

MONEY MANAGERS

The term *money manager* is used loosely within the industry and by investors because no license is needed to be a money manager. Anyone can call himself or herself a money manager. Most legitimate money managers, though, are also Registered Investment Advisors and should proudly display the acronym RIA after their name or on their business card. The designation RIA means that these advisors are licensed with their state securities board and with the SEC if they manage more than $30 million.

A money manager can be either an individual or a firm that manages your money according to your overall guidelines. Once the guidelines are established, the money manager invests and manages the account without any input from you. Having your money managed by a money manager can feel similar to having your money in a mutual fund because neither requires input from you.

What distinguishes a money manager from a mutual fund is that with a money manager your money is usually not commingled with other investors' money. You have a separate account. The obvious advantage over a mutual fund is you have an account that is more specifically tailored to your needs and can change as your goals and needs change. That benefit has a cost, though. What you'll pay a money manager in annual fees, costs, and commissions can be higher because of the costs of individualized statements and more client interaction. Money managers don't benefit from the economies of scale that mutual funds do, economies that result in reduced spreads and commissions. Money managers are mainly in the business of managing assets, not giving a lot of broad investment advice. The vast majority of money managers charge for their management of your money by assessing an annual percentage of your assets. Of course, as your assets go up or down in value, so does the fee you pay.

Money managers represent one of the few investment relationships in which one option is to pay the manager on a percentage of the profits made in the account on an annual basis. This type of payment arrangement has both positives and negatives. Sure, it sounds good you reason; if your account doesn't make any money, you don't have to pay the money manager. And you may think that the incentive for your money manager to make money for you is a good thing, that perceived benefit is what we have found to be the cause of trouble. The incentive creates big conflicts of interest for a money manager: far too often, a money manager makes higher-risk investments, hoping to hit a home run and thus reap a big payment, which is usually not in your best interest.

FINANCIAL PLANNERS

Like money manager, *financial planner* is a term used liberally with no requirement for a particular license. Financial planners come in every color in the rainbow, so it is hard to put a label on them. Through course work and an examination, individuals can earn the distinction of Certified Financial Planner (CFP), a title that is not bestowed by any securities regulatory organization. It's similar to the difference between an interior decorator and an interior designer. The latter requires a college degree and license, whereas the former may be usually a frustrated housewife looking for a reason to get out of the house.

If your financial planner is also your stockbroker, then you are on safe ground in terms of licensing. Your stockbroker has a Series 7 license that allows him or her to make trades on your behalf. The problems we see arise when individuals who call themselves financial planners give investment advice without the requisite licenses. Other than Series 7–licensed stockbrokers, anyone who gives advice about stocks and bonds must have an RIA license. Make sure that your financial planner does.

Unlike money managers and mutual fund managers, financial planners rarely take control of your funds. Your money is usually deposited with a financial institution and the planner merely issues instructions on how the money is to be invested. Unless you give the financial planner discretionary trading authority, planners, like stockbrokers, must discuss with you each and every trade or investment idea.

So if you want to be involved in the day-to-day management of your money, choose a planner or broker, not a mutual fund or professional money manager. Put another way, planners and brokers are in the advice business, whereas money mangers and mutual fund managers are in the management business.

A strong word of warning when dealing with smaller, independent money managers, RIAs, and financial planners: *Their conflicts and your risks generally increase with these types of smaller businesses.* This warning also covers stockbrokers who are basically working out of their own office or in a very small satellite office. You learned earlier about the rules of supervision, so remember that these smaller types of operations are less supervised. We also warned you about the likelihood that these smaller operations will push you into private investments that may be less than sound. And last, in this day and age it is not a good idea to deal with advisors or brokers who are limited in the product lines they can offer. Even a firm as large as Merrill Lynch has evidently felt the heat to compete with Schwab and now offers no-load funds, an unheard-of proposition just a few years ago. When brokers and advisors are limited in the products they can offer, you are inevitably shortchanged.

STOCKBROKERS

The stockbroker or broker label, as you know, is used most often to describe an individual who works for a brokerage firm and gives investment advice. But when you meet brokers these days, they usually don't call themselves stockbrokers. They call themselves financial advisors or financial consultants, thus confusing you even more. Firms used to routinely call their brokers registered representatives, as that is the term used by the NASD and the NYSE in their manuals. But the term was eventually dropped in practice because it was too much of a mouthful. Most people's relationship

with a broker is when the broker makes individual investment recommendations one at a time. If you ever give your broker power of
attorney or discretionary authority to manage your account based
on your guidelines without talking to you before each and every
transaction, then you have in essence turned your broker into a
mini–money manager.

Below we discuss a number of types of accounts you can have
with your broker and brokerage firm.

BROKERAGE FIRM WRAP ACCOUNTS

Wrap accounts have been around for years, but lately firms
like Merrill Lynch are bringing money into them by the billions.
Assets in individually managed accounts grew by 29 percent in the
first three quarters of 2000 to $660 billion. Gone is the term *wrap
account*. Now these investments are called *flat fee accounts*. The concept is simple. The customer pays a flat percentage per year on the
total assets of the account; firms advertise that customers need not
be concerned about commissions because there are none. No brokers are pushing products driven by commissions, and customers
can trade as much or as little as they like and still pay the same percentage fee. Flat fee accounts are on the rise because they are the
traditional brokerage firms' way of competing with discount commission firms. Most large brokerage firms have myriad options to
choose from with these flat fee–type accounts. Unlimited trading
with no commissions is not always as clear as one might think. Make
sure it is spelled out in writing and you fully understand exactly
what you are getting in services and exactly how and what you are
going to be charged before you sign up.

But if wrap accounts are as great as brokerage firms say, then
why as early as June 22, 1992, did *Forbes* publish an article on wrap
accounts entitled "Rip Accounts"? *Forbes'* primary criticism was
that wrap account investors were paying an above-average annual
fee with no particular benefit. Flat fee accounts may suffer from the
same problem—the same investment program in different clothing.

The sad reality is that much of the money flowing into flat fee
accounts is not money that is traded actively. If a large percentage of
your portfolio is in fixed-income investments, such as CDs, municipal bonds, and government bonds, you should not be in a flat fee

account. All you have done is guarantee the brokerage firm an above-average percentage return in fees on your account. Why should you pay a brokerage firm 2 percent or even 1 percent to hold investments you rarely ever trade and on which you are only earning 6 percent a year? Clearly, such a portfolio needs little management.

One rub with these flat fee accounts is that though you may be lured to them by the promise of no commissions, you may still pay some fees, just as you would in a traditional brokerage account. For example, when you buy an IPO, you are paying extra fees to the firm. When you buy a mutual fund, the firm and your broker still may reap a portion of the 12(b)-1 fees.

When firms argue that these flat fee accounts are great because of the lack of conflicts, let us alert you to one conflict that has been raising its head lately. Major brokerage firms are allowing their brokers to encourage the use of margin in these flat fees accounts. A big conflict? You bet. The brokerage firm and broker now benefit three ways:

1. The firms calculate their annual fee not on your equity but on the entire leveraged/margined amount.
2. The firm collects the profits it makes on lending you the money to buy on margin.
3. With more buying power, you can buy additional products that have additional or hidden fees.

One of the worst abuses in flat fee accounts occurs when you pay 1 percent to 2 percent to a brokerage firm to manage your portfolio and then your firm places your money with a money manager or a mutual fund that charges a fee to manage your money. This practice was introduced mainly in the 1980s when mutual funds grew like weeds. *Fund of funds* and *manager of managers* were terms used to describe this business. The structure varied but the concept was always the same: the investor was charged twice on his dollars. Many of these same concepts are sadly still alive today. Here is how it plays out.

First, your broker tells you that she specializes in monitoring and screening the best investment advisors and mutual funds in the country. She will recommend that you place your money with one or a number of these money managers. The broker may get paid two ways. First, she may get paid because the firm that she recommends that you place your money with has an agreement to run all of your trades through your broker's firm. So your broker may be getting her percentage of the commissions as if she were doing the trading herself. The main problem with this arrangement is that fairly often, your broker charges you slightly reduced retail commissions, which are much higher than you would pay if you hired a professional money manager without going through a brokerage firm.

The other way your broker can be paid is by the brokerage firm charging you a percentage of your total assets. So now you are paying twice. You pay your brokerage firm a flat fee and you pay a management fee to the mutual fund or money manager. Of course, even large funds pay spreads, commissions, markups, and the like. And there is a decent chance they are paying them back to the very firm that is charging you a management fee.

Flat fee accounts can serve a useful purpose when the fee is very low and the services very high. And because the conflicts that come with pushing commission-based products is reduced, flat fee accounts don't suffer from many of the same problems that traditional accounts do. As with almost everything within the investment world, flat fee accounts are not without their downside.

BROKERAGE FIRM IN-HOUSE MANAGEMENT

You have yet another option for who can manage your money. It is someone in your brokerage firm, other than your broker, managing your money on a discretionary basis. (Merrill Lynch, for example, refers to this department of managers as Merrill Lynch Asset Management [MLAM].) Your account falls somewhere between your broker managing it on a discretionary basis and your buying one of the brokerage firm's in-house mutual funds. You have less input than if your broker managed your money but more input than if you just bought an in-house mutual fund.

We have never really liked this type of management because it is too much in the gray area for us. It is not a mutual fund and thus comparing results and performance is harder. You are not going to get the personal attention that you would from your stockbroker or a small investment advisor. And last, on a comparative basis, the returns are lower generally than those obtained by the better independent manager.

In summary, here is the rundown on how your money can be managed when parked at a full-service brokerage firm:

- You can make all investment decisions and trades.
- Your broker can make all investment decisions and trades.
- You and your broker can share calling the shots.
- You can place most of your money with nonaffiliated money managers or mutual funds.
- You can invest your money in mutual funds that are owned and managed by your brokerage firm.
- You can have a professional in-house manager at the brokerage firm manage your money.

FACTORS TO USE IN CHOOSING FROM THE OPTIONS LISTED ABOVE

You know the old saying that the three most important factors in selling a house are location, location, location? Well, we seek to ingrain another threesome into your head regarding how to go about deciding which of the above options is best for you: cost, performance, and conflicts. Realize that the choices listed above, with some exceptions, are all trying to do the same thing: manage your money in some way. Sure, firms offer other, peripheral services and benefits, but the bulk of a firm's business, and where the majority of where your fees and commissions are going, is in managing your money. Once you have decided how involved you want to be, the next step is an easy one. Hire the firm to manage your money that has (1) the lowest total costs, (2) the best long-term track record, and (3) the least amount of conflicts of interest. Let's look at each.

Costs

One of the greatest anomalies of the securities industry is that you do not have to pay more for better performance. We could list hundreds of mutual funds that year after year have beaten the pants off 90 percent of their competition, including money managers, brokers, and planners, and yet their fees are the lowest. For example, Vanguard's S&P 500 index fund has consistently outperformed

80 percent of professional money managers and other mutual funds, and it has one of the lowest annual fees of your options, one-quarter of a point a year. That's right, .25 percent a year. Compare that to what you have been paying in fees and commissions over the last ten years. And if you really want to do some investigating, compare the annual rates of return for the last ten years from the Vanguard S&P 500 index fund to your returns.

We find fault with any financial planner or advisor or stock-broker who charges you a percentage of your assets on an annual basis and then puts your money with *another* money manager or mutual fund that charges you an additional annual percentage fee. Do not pay twice for the same money. It is stupid and counterproductive. If you go the mutual fund route, continue to keep costs at the forefront of your selection process. Study after study has shown that mutual funds that charge hefty front-end or back-end charges to purchase their funds perform no better than do no-load funds. So why would you not buy no-load funds and put every cent of your hard-earned money to work?

A money manager who charges you based on profits he makes in your account is a rare exception to the standard, but let us repeat our warning. This option can create damaging conflicts of interest; we've seen accounts wiped out because of the conflicts. Let's say that for one or two years this money manager's performance is flat, and thus he is paid little to nothing for his services. He has bills to pay like everyone else, prompting him to start increasing the risks he takes in your portfolio from his need to make some home runs so that his fees will jump up to make up for the lean years. Not a situation you want or ever need to be in.

If you want and need to be involved in every trade, then your choices are a stockbroker or going it on your own. Just remember that going with a broker is usually the highest cost relationship you can have. You are charged a retail commission on every trade, both the buy and the sell, along with the spreads or markups or markdowns.

Performance

You should almost always choose an advisor or fund that has an excellent track record. When it comes to mutual funds, the job of choosing is done by numerous rating agencies such as Morningstar. Also, such publications as *Forbes, Money* magazine, and *Consumer Reports* provide an annual rating of various mutual funds. The only caveat is that just because one type or group of funds has performed well over the last couple of years doesn't mean that it will continue to. Janus is one of the largest family of funds, and a number of its funds performed fabulously on both an individual and comparative basis in the late 1990s as a result partly of Janus's concentrating in technology stocks. Yet when the tech stocks cratered, Janus funds turned out to be big underperformers in late 2000. Still, when comparing similar types of funds, you should generally go with a proven winner. Excellent books have been written about the issue of mutual funds, which can be of great assistance. One is by John Bogle, the past president of Vanguard Mutual Funds, and is entitled *John Bogle on Investing—The First 50 Years*.

When you do a performance analysis of most any investment other than established mutual funds on both an individual and a comparative basis, the going gets tough. Most large money management firms have comparisons for you against such traditional indices as Standard & Poor's (S&P) 500. The problem with most of these comparisons is that you aren't comparing apples with apples. If friends tell you that their portfolio has beaten the S&P 500 (after all fees, of course) in three of the last five years, the question you ask then is, "But did you take greater risk to obtain that performance?" If the response is, "Yes, our risk levels were higher," then you must decide whether you're willing to take that greater risk for better performance. If your friends' portfolio didn't outperform the S&P 500, then you should just buy the Vanguard S&P 500 index fund and pay only 0.25 percent a year in management fees.

And if your friends say they beat the S&P 500 in three out of five years, what about those two other years? Also, what were the tax ramifications? Did the investing by your manager or broker result in your paying a lot of taxes on your gains? Be sure to deduct that from your net returns.

When you are considering money managers, financial planners, or stockbrokers, remember that the vast majority of them manage money in separate individual accounts, so conducting a thorough comparative analysis is almost impossible. You can imagine how easy it is for an advisor to brag how some account he manages has done and then prove it by showing you the records. But what about the performance of the other 200 accounts he manages? You can bet he won't show you those results.

And do the majority of brokerage firms give you a year-end statement that not only shows your annual return in dollars and percentages but also a comparison of your return with the Dow Jones Industrial Average or the S&P 500? No! One of the main reasons firms don't do this is because the majority of investors' accounts don't perform as well as many of these indices. Surprisingly, even most mutual funds underperform when compared with the S&P 500. So you have the right to ask, "Why shouldn't I just put my money in the S&P 500 and not worry about all of this stuff?" You won't hear any argument from us. You may wonder, If the majority of brokers and managers underperform, how is it that they stay in business? The answer: They are not compensated based on how their clients' portfolios perform, and firms do a pretty good job of keeping clients in the dark about indices and charges, making it difficult for clients to perform the proper comparisons. Therefore, most investors don't realize how much their portfolios are underperforming. Think how easy it would be for you to do these needed comparisons if firms were to spell out their full fees, returns, and conflicts on a comparative basis the way mutual funds do. Don't hold your breath for that to happen any time soon.

Before we leave the subject of comparative performance, we must share with you an old saying that "cream always rises to the top." This is apropos in discussing the securities business. Although stockbrokers can have superior incomes as retail stockbrokers, those who are unusually adept at managing people's money on a comparative basis are likely to start their own money management firm or mutual fund. Or they might apply for a job at a large mutual fund as a portfolio manager. These jobs offer even more compensation than the highest-paying brokerage position. Keep this in mind when your broker is highlighting his performance and brags how he makes hundreds of thousands of dollars a year.

Conflicts

We need not repeat the conflicts of interest entailed in trading individual stocks with a stockbroker. You have also learned that mutual funds engender few conflicts, and we listed the few they do.

That leaves money managers and financial planners. If you plan to have a money manager and a financial planner manage your money on a discretionary basis for a flat percentage fee, the conflicts are lessened, certainly when compared with a stockbroker on a nondiscretionary basis.

In the final analysis, you need to make adjustments for your needs using the three criteria—costs, performance, conflicts—and we hope you make the right decision. A preferred decision is to not go with any one option 100 percent. For the vast majority of us, using our criteria or your own, mutual funds are a logical choice. Why do you think mutual funds have enjoyed such phenomenal growth over the last ten years? Now, there are more mutual funds than stocks. Yet no one would ever suggest putting 100 percent of your money in one mutual fund, even if it is the S&P 500 index.

Conversely, it is hard to argue against putting some, or all, of your money in mutual funds for the following reasons:

- If you stay with true no-load funds, you can't find lower fees.
- The total costs are laid out in plain English and easy to compare.
- The choices and ability to diversify are unlimited.
- If your needs change, you can easily change your goals if you are in a large family of funds.
- Conflicts of interest are very limited.
- Your returns are spelled out clearly and take all costs into consideration.
- Doing a comparative analysis of your returns is a cake walk.
- Your need for involvement, research, or monitoring is limited.
- If you did not look at your account statements for months, it would probably not make a difference.

Last, remember that once you make your decisions using the three criteria of cost, performance, and conflicts, continue to use them as a monitoring tool at the end of every year.

INSURANCE AGENTS

We would hate to be accused of providing warnings and educating investors about brokerage secrets without giving insurance agents their fair share of the same, usually when insurance agents try to become financial advisors.

Let's start with the premise that no one can do all things. Chiropractors don't deliver babies. Tracy doesn't handle divorce or family law work, and Douglas doesn't give tax advice. Just as stockbrokers should not be selling life insurance, life insurance agents should not be selling stocks. You don't think that the broker and the insurance agent got into each other's other business because they thought it would be in your best interest, do you? Brokerage firms and insurance companies are selling each other's products because they figure they already have someone out there pedaling financially related products, so why not just get that someone another license and thus more ways to create fees and commissions for the firm.

Douglas sold life insurance for less than a year and learned quickly that it was a whole different science. He felt he was doing a disservice to clients to try to sell them a product that required much more knowledge than he had from merely passing a few insurance exams. On the flip side, insurance agents making stock recommendations are about as reliable as your calling a brokerage firm and being given the "broker of the day," a broker who has been in business about six months. To complicate matters, most insurance agents are given a fairly narrow line of insurance products to sell. A representative sample of products might include annuities; mutual funds, which are usually the commission-laden underperformers managed by a subsidiary of the insurance company; or some special group of investments created by the insurance company. We hope the word *conflict* is flashing before your eyes. If you find an investor who bought any of New York Life's limited partnerships and made money, have that investor call us, because that would be a first for us.

Sure, one-stop shopping is a great convenience but only when it benefits you by increasing your bottom line. Don't get too carried away with the concept. Next thing you know, you'll be writing to tell us your broker is doing your tax return. No way, José.

BANKERS

Effective March 1997, the Federal Reserve Board more than doubled the revenue that a bank's subsidiary could derive from dealing in securities. Since then, banks have been on a buying and merging binge with brokerage firms. In 1997, banks bought Piper Jaffray, Oppenheimer, and Alex Brown. In 2000, Credit Suisse bought Donaldson, Lufkin and Jenrette (DLJ); the Royal Bank of Canada bought Dain Rauscher; and Regions Bank bought Morgan Keegan.

Again we are critical of firms, and mainly individuals, stretching their expertise. Finding someone at your bank's brokerage department who can adequately explain stock option straddles will be quite a feat. Let's get real. Incredibly knowledgeable and sophisticated traders in Citibank's New York office could give Douglas a headache explaining some of the foreign currency hedging strategies they employ on a daily basis. But when you stop by your local branch or call an 800 trading number, don't expect an experienced securities veteran to be the one handling your business. Online firms can't find people experienced and knowledgeable enough to handle the phones. What makes you think that the banks, which are notorious for lower wages, are able to attract anyone better?

Now maybe banks, insurance companies, and even some online firms will change their modus operandi and severely restrict employees to advising investors only in areas in which the employees are fully trained, licensed, and knowledgeable. And maybe elephants will fly! Blame it on low unemployment or the fact that the United States rates lower than Europe and Asia in its educational system, but we find far too often the so-called experts we get on the phone at various financial institutions are, well, far from experts. Currently, Douglas has a slew of cases against online firms in which investors allege that they were given false information on option quotes. In many cases, it is discovered that the person at the firm answering questions about options has little, or no, understanding about them.

Douglas once taught tennis at a summer camp, not because he was a great tennis player or teacher, but because he knew more than the students. That may be okay for tennis, but we don't think you should be getting financial advice from someone who knows only slightly more than you do. Next time you're talking to one of these consultants, experts, or whatever, ask them, before you think seriously about taking any advice they may offer, their credentials, licenses, how long they have been at that position, and what experience in the securities industry they have.

Let us make one final point about banks. Once you move from savings, checking, and CDs to the brokerage division of the bank, forget about "insured" or "FDIC" or "safety." You have stepped into a vastly different world where you now know there are no assurances. If you don't believe us, find some investors who bought the Government Income Term Trust 2003 & 2004 mutual funds from NationsBank. You will get an ear full. The NASD fined Nations-Bank/NationsSecurities $2 million for the sale of those products.[1]

INVESTMENT NEWSLETTERS

You know the old cliché, "Those who can, do, and those who can't, teach." In the securities industry, it seems that those who can't, write market newsletters. As we are so fond of reminding you, if someone really had a black box that could tell you which stocks were going to go up and when, they would not tell you about it. But then why do Americans pay millions of dollars a year to individuals who write monthly market/investment newsletters that claim to tell investors some combination of how the stock markets, the economy, and interest rates in general are going to perform and how particular stocks are going to perform? Just like mutual funds, far too many of these letters' performances are no better than what you would obtain by putting your money in one of the broad index mutual funds. The numbers are staggering if you consider the thousands of investors who pay $200 a year for these various newsletters. It's easy to see how an author of one of these newsletters with thousands of subscribers finds it much more profitable to *tell* you how to manage your money than to actually manage it.

Here comes the heartbreaking news. These market fortune tellers are mere humans. They have no crystal ball. They make the same mistakes that you and I make. And they have many of the same conflicts of interest we have been discussing all along. Just like everyone who is giving investment advice, they want to be right and they want you to make a lot of money. But the problem is that just like everyone else, they don't really have any special magic. Douglas has collected various letters over 20 years and has found the majority to be disappointing. The worst part is that they so much remind us of all the nasty idiosyncrasies of financial stock analysts that we discussed earlier. They are bullish at the top and bearish at the bottom, just like the rest of us. They are paid a lot of money to be different, yet they are not.

If you haven't experienced this already, you will learn to hate the way these letter writers tend to gloss over their earlier—and incorrect—recommendations and predictions. You can be assured that when they are right, you will be reminded of it time and again, even years later. Yet when they fail, you may never hear about it. It is ignored, a nonevent. If it can't be ignored, then it is eloquently explained away. Losers are sold off or replaced with "better opportunities." They love to distance themselves from their losing recommendations as quickly as possible, so that you don't cancel your subscription.

Many market newsletters can be dangerous if you take them too seriously or rely on them too exclusively. The most dangerous are the specialty newsletters; those that specialize in a particular investment like gold, foreign stocks, or commodities can be doubly dangerous. What helps fuel the danger is that most investors who subscribe to a specialty market newsletter do so because they already have a special interest in that particular area. This creates a problem from the start because the investors tend to be less objective and cynical about the advice they are reading. Nothing is worse than the investor who gets goldbug fever, subscribes to a goldbug newsletter, and before long is 100 percent invested in gold stocks and gold bullion.

Speaking of goldbugs, we're reminded of some of the worst damage done by specialty market letters. Do you remember Bunky Hunt's silver crisis in the late 1970s? Silver went to $52 an ounce and gold to $800 an ounce? Goldbug and doomsday market letters were having a field day. And what do you think many of them were telling their readers when gold was approaching $800 an ounce? "Buy more gold," because they were predicting the price was going to go over a $1,000 an ounce. History tells us that the price went down very quickly and has basically stayed down for the last 20 years.

If you do subscribe to market newsletters, don't get caught up in their ether. If you catch them hiding from their bad recommendations, take them to the mat. Write them, and ask for clarifications and explanations. If they don't respond to your inquiries appropriately, cancel your subscription and demand a refund. If you take a specialty newsletter, limit your investments to a very small percentage of your assets.

This advice on newsletters can be applied to just about any financial professional on which you rely—that is, take everyone's advice with a grain of salt. Don't put all your eggs in one basket. Investing is not an exact science. No one has a black box, so if you place your money with various advisors, you better your odds of at least matching the averages. And you definitely lessen the chance that someone will sink your financial ship.

NO ONE REALLY KNOWS

The real question should be, If your broker or advisor is able to guess what the market is going to do, what is he doing wasting his time talking to you? Think about it; if you had a black box and were always right, why would you tell others? They might steal the black box. If everyone had the black box, the black box would no longer work because there would be no one on the other side of your trade. If you had this black box, you could turn a thousand dollars into a billion dollars in a short amount of time. And with leverage, options, commodities, and other investments, you could then quickly turn this billion into trillions.

So why would the person with the black box or a person who claims to know share his knowledge or secrets with you? Sure, you'll pay him $50 for his tape you saw on TV. If this person is an analyst or head technician at Salomon Brothers, maybe you'll trade your stocks there so you can have access to some of this special advice. Maybe the person with the black box is just an independent broker, and he will gain lots of commissions if you trade with him. Maybe the black box is owned by the money management team or mutual fund that has had the hot hand the last few years, and now Morningstar is giving them five stars. Of course, if you put your money with them, they will charge you 1 percent a year to manage it. And last, the guru may have started his own investment newsletter and will charge you $250 a year to subscribe to his special insights.

But all of these charges, fees, and commissions levied by the owners of the black box, while cumulatively could be very lucrative, pale in comparison to what the owners of the black box could make if they just managed their *own* money. And they wouldn't have to work very hard. They wouldn't have to cater to a boss, put on a tie, or commute to work. They would just sit at their office or home and trade their accounts to levels that would rival King Tut's for accumulation of wealth.

There are more people willing to tell you how to make money investing than there are mothers willing to tell you how to cure a cold. We all should know by now that there is no cure for the common cold, but who knows that no one knows what the stock market is going to do. People want to believe that someone knows how the stock market will move. *No one knows what the stock markets are going to do, much less what individual stocks are going to do.* Do you need proof?

If there were a person or even a group of people who really knew which stocks were going to go in which direction and when, you would know who they are because they would have all the money. Bill Gates would have to borrow money from them. They would not only be on the front of every magazine but they would also own the magazine. Even some of the greatest names in investing, such as Paul Tudor Jones, Bob Farrell, Peter Lynch, George Soros, Benjamin Graham, and Warren Buffett, are wrong some of the time. Don't misunderstand; these guys and many others have made billions. And there is no doubt that some people are better than others.

This not really knowing also reaches down to the very basic recommendation by your stockbroker or advisor. Let's assume for this example that your broker is as honest as they come, the conflicts of interest have been cut to a minimum, and he and his firm have really done their research on the stock he is recommending that you purchase. And if he really is an honest stockbroker, he has also included all of the risks and downsides to the stock he is recommending. So what is left that he has probably not told you? That he really does not know what the stock market is going to do and neither does his firm. There is no black box.

CHAPTER 13

Selecting and Evaluating a Stockbroker

What makes a broker or financial advisor good? In our opinion, it's a person who has figured out the game himself. He has sold investments that he thought were great only to lose lots of money for his clients. He has listened to the highly paid gurus only to realize they knew little more than he does. He is a veteran of up-and-down markets, an attribute hard to find considering that from 1982 to the first part of 2000 we have basically been in a bull market. The problem is that our little list always excludes the young brokers. When Douglas started out as a stockbroker for Merrill Lynch in 1980, he could brag that he had never lost money for any clients. That lasted about two days.

Choosing a broker or advisor is not like choosing a doctor; an age-old question is whether you are better off with an older doctor or a younger doctor. The younger doctor has the benefit of recent medical training, where he was exposed to the latest techniques, medicines, and instruments. We know how quickly things can change in the medical world, and so recent schooling is a perceived benefit. Yet the older doctor has years of firsthand experience dealing with real patients and performing the very operation that you are considering having. Which one to choose? We don't have the answer when it comes to doctors. But when it comes to brokers, we are full of advice.

Go for the experienced broker. It may be harder to find experienced brokers because they have all retired rich. Just kidding, but the reality is that any advisor who has really been successful should have a very good core of clients and is not aggressively looking for new business. If he is, you had better know why. An 18-year bull market should have made him and his clients lots of money. It will also be hard to find the experienced broker because there are so many inexperienced brokers to sort through. The boom years in the securities markets and the industry created a hiring craze for brokerage firms. There are thousands of young, green brokers running around these days. You should know—you usually receive a phone call from them just as you sit down to dinner.

But it's not just stockbrokers who are young and inexperienced in the securities industry these days. Such youth also extends to financial analysts and mutual fund managers. Our concern is that anyone under the age of 38 who is currently working in the securities industry has not seen a real bear market in stocks or bonds until recently. If you think the crash of 1987 was a bear market, you must be younger than 38. People in the business during the 1970s saw five years straight of negative returns on government bonds. And those who witnessed the stock market go down big and stay down during the years 1973 and 1974 and 1981 and 1983 also have a different insight.

Until the year 2000, the current generation of money managers, brokers, and advisors had known only a bull market. And how do you argue with them by dredging up the past? Their world is full of such mottos as "Buy every dip," "When in doubt, take the more aggressive route," and "Leverage whenever you can." The worst part is that in the absence of a sustained downturn, they may turn out to be right, but 2001 might prove them wrong.

You'll be better off in the long run to find a broker or advisor who can tell you stories that include big losers with the winners. Douglas's grandfather was once one of the richer men in Iowa, but he lost everything during the depression. In high school, Douglas's father made his spending money by selling golf balls at the country club that was built on land his father earlier owned. He earned college money by selling honey. And to pay for his master's degree, he mopped floors in the hospital where he met Douglas's mother. To this very day, Douglas turns off a light in a room that he leaves, even at someone else's house. Certain traits are instilled in people so deeply that time will never wear them out. Though Douglas never experienced the depression, the event had such a great effect on his father that it was passed almost by osmosis to his brothers and him. Brokers and advisors who only know how to be aggressive are dangerous.

In Chapter 3, you learned that stockbrokers are salespeople. Now, let's qualify that. Let's again assume that your broker or the one you are considering is an honest, smart, hardworking individual. And let's assume that he just started working at a major brokerage firm. As a new stockbroker, he won't be given any accounts to manage. The best he can hope for is to be the "broker of the day." He has only one choice to succeed as a new broker; he must be a salesman. The firm knows this, which is why so much of the firm's basic training is concentrated on selling as opposed to managing money.

Any broker who is really worth his salt and someone you would want as a broker should be working toward not being a salesperson. He should be working toward being a portfolio manager—your portfolio manager. He should be building his business toward having clients, not customers.

BEING A CLIENT VERSUS BEING A CUSTOMER

As an investor, you want to strive to be a *client* rather than a *customer*. A customer is someone who probably has a limited amount of funds with a firm. Brokers accordingly give customers less attention. They have only the most basic knowledge of a customer under the "know the customer" rule. They have probably never met customers personally. Customers will probably not rely solely on brokers' investment advice but will either consult with others or know enough themselves to call the shots. The communication and contact between a broker and a customer are limited. They would usually only have contact when the broker had a specific investment idea or the customer wanted to buy or sell an investment.

A customer might also be someone who would use a Registered Investment Advisor on a one-time basis. A customer may hire the RIA to simply review and evaluate his portfolio once and never again. The customer may ask the RIA to help him only in a very limited area of concern or only in evaluating a single investment.

The RIA has no ongoing obligation or commitment to this person because that is not the object of the contact.

On the other hand, being a client is advantageous for both parties. To a broker, a client is, in many ways, the opposite of a customer. In this relationship, the broker is almost always in control of managing the assets, at least the assets that are in the account at his firm. That doesn't mean the broker is managing the assets on a discretionary basis but rather that the client is relying on the broker to make the majority of recommendations and decisions. Even if there is not a lot of communication between client and broker, and hence trading, there should be a detailed and clear understanding and agreement as to how the account is to be managed.

Money managers and RIAs who run small shops tend to mostly have clients as opposed to customers. Their clients want a long-term, dependent relationship. Brokers are more likely to attract some individuals who are only looking for an occasional execution of a trade. Brokers may acquire accounts because a broker at his firm left to join another brokerage firm. Most RIAs are, and should be, financial planning oriented, not trade oriented. If they aren't, go elsewhere. The only caveat is that there are RIAs like Douglas who do a percentage of their business rendering second opinions. Some of the individuals for whom Douglas has rendered second opinions he refers to as clients and others as customers.

For clients, there is reliance, trust, commitment, and often a fiduciary relationship with the broker, which may not exist in a customer relationship. This is not to say that a broker or advisor still cannot fulfill legal and ethical requirements when dealing with a customer versus a client. From the legal standpoint, the broker that calls you from New York trying to hustle you into some hot stock he is pushing has the same legal standards to follow as your regular broker who talks to you every day.

We separate the two relationships mostly for you to better understand. You should decide early on in any relationship which type you prefer.[1] Before online firms exploded on the scene, it was common for an investor to have a discount brokerage account at Schwab or Brown & Company and always talk to a broker when entering trades. The majority of the time it didn't matter which brokers the investor talked to because they were merely order takers and were not distributing advice. You were always a customer. With online firms, you don't even have the opportunity to talk to a broker, with certain exceptions, and your status is solely that of a customer.

If you have an account at a major brokerage firm and are paying its high commissions, you had better be treated like a client. If you aren't, move your account tomorrow. There are plenty of brokers who will treat you like a client.

WHAT A CLIENT SHOULD EXPECT FROM HIS BROKER OR ADVISOR

Following is a list of responsibilities you as a client should expect your broker or advisor to undertake:

- Learn all the essential facts about you so he can make suitable recommendations[2]
- Act as an advisor, not a salesperson
- Always have your best interest at heart and not make any recommendations based on his conflicts of interest or commissions
- Thoroughly analyze every investment that he recommends to you to ensure that it fits your goals and needs
- Follow all securities regulations and internal policies of his firm
- Help and assist you in learning about his services and your accounts
- Monitor and review your portfolio and individual investments, and advise you of needed changes and developments
- Advise you against any investment or strategy you suggest that might be unsuitable for you
- Alert you to other investment products and strategies that might also be a suitable alternative or addition to your current portfolio

We have some bad news if you fall under various firms' thresholds for client service: A number of the larger wire houses are either requiring or encouraging their brokers to move their smaller, full-service accounts to call centers. Licensed individuals staff a call center, but you will no longer have a specific broker nor will you receive the detailed attention to which you may have become accustomed. At one firm, accounts with less than $100,000 are routed to call centers. We find this practice disturbing, especially from an industry that has always, at least on the surface, portrayed themselves as wanting to bring Wall Street to Main Street. Mimicking his firm's familiar TV commercial tag line, one broker said that "the firm serves one investor at a time, so long as you come in reasonably successful in the first place."[3]

MAZERATI OR CHEVROLET

We would not be so trite as to insinuate there are only two types of brokers, those in the fast lane and those parked at Kmart. But taken to the extreme, the typecasting will serve our purposes for evaluation.

A successful stockbroker (remember that the industry defines a successful stockbroker as one who generates a lot of commissions, not by how much he makes for his clients) is usually outgoing, gregarious, self-confident, driven, ambitious, and a forceful, if not fast, talker, all of which basically adds up to the definition of a great salesperson.

These great traits for salespeople are not necessarily great traits for financial advisors, at least from the clients' point of view. Don't be taken in by Mr. Mazerati stockbroker. I know that is hard for many people to swallow in this day and age. If you insist on your lawyer's having a fancy office, that's fine. If you insist that your interior decorator drive only the latest BMW, that's also fine. And if your shrink must be able to name drop at least three famous people during lunch, have at it. But when it comes to associating with someone who is going to manage your money and give you investment advice, go for Mr. Chevrolet. And we don't mean Mr. Corvette.

We know all the clichés: "Success breeds success" and "Successful people should surround themselves with successful people." Dallas, Texas, where we both lived for many years, is the epitome of this line of thinking. The Dallas motto was: "If you've got it, flaunt it. And if you don't got it, flaunt it twice as much, and they will think you've got it." We always wondered why the Range Rover dealer in Dallas had such a booming business in an area where there are no mountains, hills, dirt roads, or snow on which to drive that expensive off-road vehicle.

Now, you may think—erroneously—we are recommending that you find some broker with his pants hiked up to his chest and tape on his glasses. There is a happy medium. We listed earlier what kind of service you should expect from a competent broker or advisor. Now let us give you a list of what qualifications you should look for.

But first, we must share with you a recent war story from an arbitration in which Douglas participated, and the stockbroker epitomized Mr. Mazerati. He looked like he had just stepped off the cover of GQ magazine. He was well built with broad shoulders, meticulously cut hair, perfect teeth, a strong jaw, eyes that could pierce armor, and incredibly articulate, sharp, and bright. You know the kind of man—the one that every mother wants her daughter to bring home. He had been in the securities business for a number of years and had built up a good clientele. And he had all those great acronyms after his name on his business card. Douglas had the honor of being in the arbitration and hearing this broker pontificate on everything from modern portfolio theory to Kafka. The claim against the broker was for mutual fund churning, which you know is a securities law violation. You would wonder how Douglas's client, a professional educated abroad, had a chance against such a demigod. But as most good arbitrators are unusually perceptive, they saw through this slick salesman and awarded Douglas's client his losses.

MORE TRAITS OF A GOOD BROKER OR ADVISOR

You read earlier what the industry considers prime qualifications when new brokers are hired (remember—the ability to sell, sell, sell). Now let's consider what qualifications are important to *you* the investor:

- Preferably a business background of some kind, which can be a combination of school and work
- Work experience that preferably goes beyond the brokerage industry
- Enough business to be able to take on new clients but at the same time not starving for new business
- Your account not the largest or smallest but preferably average

- Thoroughly trained and maintains the training to be able to properly evaluate all alternative investments and strategies
- Not a novice in the securities business
- Smart or sharp but never slick
- Established with a history of seldom or never changing firms
- A good communicator (not to be confused with being a good salesperson)
- A positive track record that can be documented
- A solid list of referrals that you can and should check out
- Ability to demonstrate has taken and continues to take steps to further credentials, training, and qualifications in investments and the securities industry

Have you noticed that our list does not contain the following attributes: wears suspenders and silk suits; belongs to your country club; smokes fancy cigars; or drives a Beamer? Save those attributes for your golf buddies, not someone who is managing your assets.

The more of a high roller *you* tend to be, the more you should want your advisor to be the opposite. If you're in the fast lane, making a fortune in your job, and have some land deals working on the side, the last thing you need is a broker who likes to roll the dice. During the technology run-up of the late 1990s, many CEOs and high-ranking officers at tech firms sold large blocks of their company's stock. Bravo! Either they are just smart or someone was giving them good advice. The point is that a good advisor will help you to diversify to avoid too much risk or concentration; that is your advisor's job.

There is always an exception to our guidelines and stereotypes. But if you follow most of these basics, you're going to be better off in the long run. Sure, if you want to peel off 5 percent of your portfolio to give to a college buddy that swears to you that he can double the money overnight, go ahead. Just qualify what you are doing. Don't get carried away. You notice we said only 5 percent. We're sure you might think 10 percent is fine. So what if you lose the entire 10 percent? Keep in mind that until the last few years, 10 percent was the average return on stocks. So if in the same year you give your buddy 10 percent of your portfolio, the other 90 percent earns 10 percent, you end up losing money for the year. Doesn't sound too good, does it? Flyers and long shots hurt people's performance more than they realize.

MULTIPLE ACCOUNTS
FOR MULTIPLE REASONS

With the introduction of online trading and flat fee accounts, the client versus the customer relationship is grayed a bit. Your needs for what works for you may vary or you may have a combination of relationships. For example, it is not uncommon for an investor to have numerous accounts at different firms. You might have an account at a full-service, full-commission firm like Merrill Lynch because you want access to its research. You may also have found a broker at that firm you trust, and you want him to advise you on a certain portion of your money. It would make little sense, though many Americans do it, to run your trades through Merrill that are 100 percent your idea. As of December 1999, Merrill lets you run your trades through its online trading division at discounted commissions. If you don't trade often, this might make sense. But if you trade a lot or in large blocks (2,000 shares or more), you will save a huge amount in commissions by opening a trading account at a firm like Datek, National Discount, Ameritrade, or Brown & Company.

Though generally the more money you have in your account, the more respect you will garner from your broker, it is probably more prudent to have various accounts at various firms to meet various objectives. It's almost never wrong to be too diversified.

HOW TO GET THE SKINNY
ON YOUR BROKER

Unbeknown to many, there is a way that you can obtain information on your current stockbroker or one you're considering. And it's anonymous, online, and can be done at home in the comfort of your pajamas. First, go to <www.nasdr.com>, which is the NASD Regulation Web site, where you will see on the front page, "About Your Broker." Click the Go button to the right of it and you'll be taken to a page that describes the various ways that you can obtain information about your broker. Click on Perform an Online Search. You'll see a page of Terms and Conditions that you must agree with by clicking the Agree button at the bottom of the page. Next, click on the drop-down arrow for Select Requester Type and choose General Public/Individual Investor or whatever group best describes you and then click on either Broker or Firm, depending on what you want to search.

If you want to search for a broker, you need to input limited information on the next page, such as the broker's first and last name and the firm where the broker is currently employed or was previously employed. You don't need to fill in all of the requested information here. Then click Begin Search for Broker. You should get a match, assuming your spelling is correct, as long as this individual is currently licensed with the NASD or was so licensed within the last two years.

The first page of results identifies the broker and lists the states and entities with which he or she is currently licensed. You might want to run this check if you are doing business with an out-of-state broker. Your state's abbreviation should show up in this box. If it doesn't, then you should notify your state regulator, your broker's branch manager, and fire your broker. This page also lists the name of the broker's current employer and the city in which the broker is employed. A drop-down box identifies the names of any previous employers.

You can dig deeper by clicking on the name of the broker (it should be highlighted). Four choices are on the left side of the next page: Current Employment, Previous Employment, Registrations, and Disclosure Events. If you click on Current Employment, you'll see the name of the current employer, the office where the broker works, and the date the broker began employment at the firm. Previous employment discloses the same information, including start and end dates, for all previous employments in the securities industry. The registration section provides the jurisdictions with which the broker is currently registered or licensed to do business, the category of each registration, and the date on which the registration approval was granted.

If on the left side of the screen next to Disclosure Events, you see "No," you can be fairly sure that the broker has a clean record. If you see "Maybe," then you are being told that the broker has something to disclose, such as:

- Criminal event(s) (for example, felony convictions, certain misdemeanor charges and convictions such as theft of money, bribery, etc.)
- Financial disclosure events (for example, bankruptcies, unsatisfied judgments, and liens)

- Regulatory actions (for example, suspensions, bars)
- Customer complaints
- Civil judicial events (for example, injunctions)

If you want more details about these events, click at the top of the page on Deliver Report. You will then be directed to a page where you are asked to fill out contact information about yourself. The NASD will e-mail you the report usually within 72 hours. Note that neither the broker nor the firms that you review online or on which you request reports have any knowledge about your investigation; that is solely between you and the NASD's Web site.

The report that you receive by e-mail is known as a CRD (Central Registration Depository) and may be chock full of juicy information. It contains not only all the information you could view online but much more. There will be a succinct summary chart that shows statistics for various disclosure events. For example, a broker's chart may reflect the following:

Criminal Actions:	1
Regulatory Actions:	0
Civil Judicial Actions:	0
Terminations:	1
Customer Complaints:	3
Investigations:	0
Bonds:	0
Bankruptcies:	1
Judgment/Liens:	2

The report then gives additional details about each event. For customer complaints, the information reported is as follows (the detail is hypothetical):

******** CUSTOMER COMPLAINT (2 of 3) ********

Reporting Source: Broker (Form U-4) [This means that the broker reported it. There may be several sources for the same complaint, such as the broker and his employer.]

Date Reported: 08/26/1997 [Brokers and firms are required to report complaints within 30 days of their receipt.]

Date Received:	07/26/1997
Employing Firm:	ABC Brokerage Firm [This is where the broker was employed when the events giving rise to the complaint arose.]
Allegations:	Speculative and unsuitable investments [This report could be triggered by a simple complaint letter containing these claims.]
Alleged Damages:	$100,000
Action Pending?:	No
Resolution:	Arbitration/Reparation
Resolution Date:	07/17/1998
Arbitration/Reparation Details:	NASD # 97-00000
Service Date:	07/17/1997
Pending?:	No
Disposition:	Settled
Monetary Compensation:	$50,000
Individual Contribution:	$25,000
Disposition Details:	A total settlement was agreed to in the amount of $50,000, which was split evenly between ABC BROKERAGE COMPANY and myself.

To research a brokerage firm, you run through the same steps above, although you click on Firm instead of Broker. Also, note that you can go directly to any of the firms listed as a broker's employer as those names are highlighted. Choices on the Firm page include address information, the types of business the firm is engaged in, the legal status of the firm, the firm's registrations, and disclosure events.

You should also be aware of what is *not* included in disclosure events. Not included, for example, is information that was never reported, that is not required to be reported, or is no longer required to be reported, such as the following:

- Misdemeanors unrelated to investments and originally reported in error
- Judgments and liens originally reported as pending that subsequently have been satisfied
- Bankruptcy proceedings filed more than ten years before
- Consumer-initiated complaints that were settled for less than $10,000 or have not resulted in arbitration claims or civil litigation, unless these have occurred within the last two years
- Information ordered expunged by a court or required by law to be expunged

For the full and complete record of your broker's disciplinary record, it is best to contact your state securities regulator and ask for a copy. You need only provide your broker's CRD number, which is displayed when you find a match online. We have found that the regulators' records are more complete than the NASDR's Web site records or the toll-free NASD hotline at 800/289-9999.

We hope that you will use this chapter for checking on your current broker or in the near future if you are selecting a new or additional broker. If you are a stockbroker yourself, we hope you will use this chapter and others in this book to help you improve your relationship with your clients.

THE SMALL BROKERAGE FIRM— IS BIGGER BETTER?

We have previously cautioned you about investing at small brokerage firms. Resources are often slimmer there. Small and dubious brokerages come and go relatively quickly. If you have a problem, you may find yourself with a monetary judgment but no entity from which to collect. As we mentioned, Tracy represented almost 100 investors in arbitration claims against Dickinson & Company. Dickinson had offices and brokers all over the country, but within a year or so of filing her cases, Dickinson closed its doors and ceased doing business in the securities industry. So even if their claims had prevailed, there wouldn't have been enough money left to go around.

Many people are surprised to learn that brokerage firms don't have insurance. If they do, it kicks in at such high levels that for all practical purposes, the firm is self-insured. We like to say that it is because the brokerage industry is like a roller coaster—insurance companies know that the smallest problem can lead to big monetary claims, so they refuse to insure them. In that sense, small brokerage firms are no different from bigger firms. However, the larger firms are able to pay investors' claims and stay in business. Keep that in mind, too, when dealing with a small brokerage firm.

With the hopscotch game being played so often in the securities industry, we generally prefer a seasoned broker and one who has tended to stay at one firm or a very small number of firms. You will find many brokers leaving the larger firms to go to small boutiques where the payout to the broker will double from 40 percent to 90 percent, which is usually of no advantage to you. You end up at a smaller firm with fewer resources. Fewer resources is not a problem with such midsize firms as Raymond James, Legg Mason, or Janey Montgomery Scott, but when you go down one more tier, the advantages to the customer may often dwindle.

Reputation plays into it a bit. We find it incredible that even some of the better firms say things in their advertising that totally contradict the way they treat their customers. Politicians perfected this art of saying one thing to get elected and then doing the opposite. We hope you learned early in life that advertising has little to do with reality. But with that said, bigger firms like Merrill Lynch and A.G. Edwards will do more than other firms to protect their reputation. This shows up in their hiring practices, training, supervision, and even in how they approach and settle customer complaints. A firm that has a history of run-ins with the regulators is not that concerned. You are just one more complaint in a long list.

Bigger is generally better, but there are many, many exceptions. You may have a wonderful relationship with a small regional firm in your town, a relationship that may be just perfect for you because of its many other ancillary benefits. When it comes down to it, you must make your choice of a brokerage firm based on myriad factors, not the least of which is your broker. And the nice thing is that whatever your choice, you can simply switch firms if it turns out to be wrong, if you have any money left.

CHAPTER 14

What You Need to Know about Specific Investment Products and Strategies

Consider this chapter a broad overview of the majority of investments with which you'll come into contact during your investing experience. Our purpose is not to provide you with all of the details about each type of investment but rather to alert you to some of the hidden nuances and conflicts related to each type. Nor do we seek to discourage you from purchasing any of these investments (well, maybe a couple). If you decide to purchase any of the following investments, you will do so as a more informed and knowledgeable investor.

Keep in mind that there exist only so many investment vehicles: stocks, bonds, commodities, real estate, and collectibles. Even options, which are considered by most to be a separate investment, are merely a way to invest in an underlying security. Mutual funds are just a collection of stocks or bonds. We commend the brokerage industry for creating so many different ways for investors to invest, speculate, and hedge their investments. With the numerous products that are available in today's market, however, you must proceed with caution. It's easy to be fooled by all the smoke and mirrors.

Even professional money managers can be fooled. In the 1980s a new product emerged: *collateralized mortgage obligations*, or CMOs. At first, CMOs were relatively simple investments, but the securities industry began to fiddle with the underlying investment, creating things called *derivatives* and *traunches*, making them much more complicated and difficult to price. Many professional investors lost millions of dollars on CMOs. You may recall news stories about Orange County, California, suing Merrill Lynch for $2 billion in connection with the county's purchase of CMOs. What made the case unusual was that the county officials who managed the $20 billion investment fund were professional money managers. But they had little, or no, experience in investing in these advanced debt instruments and strategies. Orange County was forced to file for bankruptcy and Merrill Lynch made a monetary settlement with the county. What emerged from the whole CMO debacle was that there were but a few people from both sides of the fence who truly understood how CMOs were priced.

Whether you are a professional money manager or an average investor, following a few general guidelines, like the ones listed below, will serve you well regardless of the investments you choose:

- If it sounds complicated, it probably is. Don't invest in something unless you have a fairly good understanding of it.
- If it's a new fangled investment, let someone else try it first.
- If the minimum investment is high, pass.
- If it sounds too good to be true, it probably is. If it sounds like the investment of a lifetime, why is it being offered to you?
- If the fees, costs, and commissions are high, say, "No thanks."

INSURANCE—A BASIC NECESSITY BUT . . .

Because we may have some in the securities industry cursing our names for writing this book, we once again might as well pick on the insurance industry so no one feels left out. Douglas's first job in the securities industry was working for IDS, a mutual fund and life insurance company. Though Douglas sold his last life insurance policy and annuity in the 1980s, a month never passes that we are not confronted by a problem with insurance products.

We believe that any person in the securities industry who is managing another person's money should have a broad knowledge of all investment products, but that isn't to say that she should attempt to be all things to all people. The abuses we see in these products often come in the area of insurance and taxes. Stockbrokers should leave insurance sales to insurance specialists, and insurance agents should leave stocks to stockbrokers. But ever since Prudential bought Bache, it has been hard to pull the two apart. Getting a second opinion and having more than one financial advisor is always a good idea. And keeping your insurance needs separate from your investment needs is another good idea.

Your state insurance board regulates most types of insurance, such as life, medical, disability, and home/auto. Like commodities, these products are not considered securities, but in the 1970s, two insurance products that became very popular are securities and are still being sold today: whole life insurance and variable annuities. The insurance industry, with its strong lobbies, convinced Congress to give favorable tax treatment to life insurance and annuities, and benefits flowed to these two products. The insurance industry might have been relegated to the status of a fledgling fast-food chain if not for these kindly acts of Congress.

We warn you about variable annuities later in this chapter. Its counterpart—whole life insurance—requires its own set of warnings. One type of whole life insurance is variable life insurance. Like a variable annuity, variable life insurance has stocks as part of its makeup and thus is regulated by the securities industry. A broker must have two licenses—an NASD Series 7 license and a state insurance license—to sell these products.

You've seen the ads by insurance companies that portray smiling young families saving for the children's college education and their own retirement by buying whole life insurance. You can fill a bookshelf with treatises on insurance, but we have a few tips and concepts we hope you'll keep in mind.

Compared with most other investments, whole life insurance has been one of the worst-performing investments you could have made for basically two reasons. The first is that the fees and commissions are among the highest you'll pay on any investment. If you don't believe us, just ask your insurance agent the next time he whips out a new whole life policy for you to buy what you'll pay in fees and commissions for the first three years of your premiums. Get it in both dollars and a percentage versus the premiums. After 30 minutes of trying to avoid your question, the agent will need the question asked again. If you really want to have some fun, ask him what he will collect over the life of the policy if you make your premium payments for the full 30 years. He's probably figured that one out beforehand.

The second reason that whole life insurance rates poorly when compared with other investments is because it is not just an investment. It is also life insurance. And life insurance is a unique purchase because to win you have to not only die but die before the life insurance company thinks you are going to die. Like brokerage firms, life insurance companies are not in the gambling business. They have two items that keep their risks to a bare minimum. First, they have millions of policyholders, so the risks related to any one insured are minuscule. Second, they have life expectancy tables. You know, tables that based on a few scant facts tell you how long you are supposed to live.

You pay premiums of $20,000 a year. On top of that, a large chunk of your investment goes to your agent in commissions. Another sizeable piece goes to the insurance company to cover the basic insurance. Other chunks go for fees and costs. And, of course, the insurance company is in the business of making a profit. What is left is what goes toward any investment aspect of the policy, and hence the reason for low returns.

Those who truly need insurance—for example, anyone with young children or a nonworking spouse—should consider buying term instead of whole life insurance. Realize though that insurance salespeople don't favor term insurance because the commissions are small in comparison with whole life. Their favorite pitch to sway you to whole life is that whole life is insurance with a forced savings plan attached. That is effective bait. Because most folks have trouble saving, they like to be forced into it. When whole life owners realize the mistake they've made, they typically decide against canceling their policy because they realize they are in too deep. If you don't believe us, take a look at your cash value on a whole life insurance policy the first few years. Compare this with the premiums you paid, and you may turn blue.

Ever notice how insurance salespeople almost refuse to meet with you unless both spouses are present? We find the scare tactics used by these salespeople much like those used by burglar alarm salespeople. You know, they spend the first 30 minutes showing you newspaper clippings of all the houses in your city that have been burglarized. Insurance salespeople harp on the catastrophic ramifications of your dying without life insurance and, conversely, the benefits of dying with the insurance, regardless of your life situation.

Don't let insurance agents wear you down, and be sure to keep your checkbook in a separate state. We totally agree with the agents who preach that you should do anything you can to avoid excessive probate and estate taxes. But at the same time, before you buy millions of dollars of a commission-laden, poorly performing whole life insurance product that someone will receive long after you're dead, keep in mind that you have to pay for that million-dollar policy with today's dollars. The odds are very high that you will be much wealthier in the long run if you buy term insurance and invest the savings elsewhere.

Also keep in mind that as you grow older, your need for life insurance lessens. Your debts should be paid down; you should have acquired some savings and assets; your children are out of college; and your spending needs are not as great. The insurance industry can't afford to let that happen; now that your years of hard work have finally made you financially comfortable, it's only fair that you share this wealth with the industry. Keep that motivation in mind.

Be wary if an insurance agent tries to get you to switch insurance policies. Churning stocks is wrong; churning mutual funds is criminal; but churning life insurance should be a hangable offense. Appreciate, however, the insurance agent's dilemma. She has already invested all of your disposable income and savings in life insurance and annuities. She may be collecting some residuals from each year's premiums (you wondered why insurance agents are such great golfers), but she also has her eye on the latest speedboat.

What you will hear are purportedly sound reasons for canceling your current life insurance and moving to the new company. The reasons range from the contention that this firm has a better A.M. Best rating, a better track record on returns, or some other bells and whistles your current policy doesn't have. What you will *not* hear is that an insurance agent gets the bulk of her commissions in the first year or couple of years in the insurance product. Therefore, after a few years, the pressure is on to flip you to a new insurance company or product. You can imagine what damage this flipping can do to your attempt to build up cash value, much less any decent rate of return.

A recent insurance product is a *viatical*, an investment that allows you to buy the rights to a terminally ill person's life insurance policy. At this point, these investments are not fully regulated and many stories of their fraudulent sale abound. Viaticals fit nicely into our advice that you should stay away from newfangled and complicated investments.

ANNUITIES—ALL ABOUT TAXES AND FEES

An annuity is an insurance product that can be sold by brokerage firms and insurance companies as well as by a slew of other money managers so long as they have the proper insurance licenses. However, an annuity is the opposite of traditional life insurance. When you buy life insurance, you are betting the insurance company that you will die sooner than the insurance company expects. When you buy an annuity, you are betting the insurance company that you will live longer than the insurance company expects.

An annuity is usually considered a long-term investment mainly because of its tax benefits and tax penalties. The money you put into an annuity is not tax deductible as is the money you put in an IRA. But like an IRA or qualified pension plan, the annuity grows tax-free on your dividends, income, and capital gains each year. These earnings in your annuity are tax deferred until your required age of $70\frac{1}{2}$ (unless exceptions apply), when you must begin withdrawing the money and are taxed. In theory, your money should grow faster each year because you don't incur the tax drain for those years. No wonder there are billions of dollars of annuities sold to investors each year.

There are fixed annuities and variable annuities. A *fixed annuity* means that your yearly rate of return is fixed from the date you make the investment. A *variable annuity* is usually invested in stocks and bonds and thus the rate of return you receive each year varies with the markets. Life insurance and fixed annuities are not securities; they are insurance products that are regulated by each state's insurance regulators. However, variable life insurance policies and variable annuities are regulated by the securities industry because they are invested in stocks. Today, with insurance agents selling stocks and stockbrokers selling annuities, the distinction between the two has really blurred. Throw in the myriad options available in all types of annuities, and you have one confusing product for the average investor.

Carefully study the laundry list of payout options when considering annuities. Get advice from several sources. Keep in mind that if you choose a payout option that depends on your life expectancy, the insurance company knows the odds better than you do.

With such incredible tax advantages, you may wonder why you shouldn't put all of your money into annuities. Before we offer our criticism, we'll quote from a February 19, 2001, article entitled "Annuity Gratuity": "We said it three years ago in a cover story (February 9, 1998) and we'll say it again at the outset here: Most variable annuities are very bad investments."[1] The main reason is that, like most insurance products, annuities are laden with high commissions and fees. The same old conflict rears its ugly head: the better the commissions and fees for the seller, the worse the product for the purchaser. The commission on annuities is one of the highest of all investments—usually 4 percent and as much as 8 percent. This compensation is the reason that insurance agents, brokers, and now bankers love to sell annuities. Thankfully, Vanguard, the pioneer of lower fees in mutual funds, has entered the annuity business with fees that are far below the average. Annuity owners also pay yearly fund and insurance expenses to boot, all of which serves to hamper investment performance.

Another drawback to annuities is that once in, you tend to be locked in—locked into the huge up-front commissions that are not refundable. You are locked into the investment because the government will levy a penalty on you if you withdraw your funds before the required age. You are locked into the investment because a 1035 tax-free exchange isn't always financially advantageous. A 1035 exchange is a shift from your current annuity company to another; problem is, you'll get hit with another high front-end commission in the shift. Paul Roye, director of the SEC's division of investor management, said: "The motivation for some 1035 exchanges is principally to line the broker's pocket, and not in the best interest of the investor."[2] As of this writing, the SEC is sweeping through selected brokerage firms, looking for high levels of exchange activity.[3] Therefore, when it dawns on you that your annuity has been underperforming for years and years, it also dawns on you that you cannot easily switch or get out. You're stuck.

When Douglas is hired to evaluate someone's portfolio and he sees annuities in an IRA or qualified retirement plan, he knows that the investor has been scammed. Now that you have read the preceding paragraphs, you too should come to the same conclusion. There is little justification for putting an annuity into an account that already has the same tax advantages, although some will make such an argument. You can almost always accomplish the same goals by buying a mutual fund for your IRA, and you can do it for a lot less in fees and costs. In addition, you lose one of the major benefits of an annuity when you purchase it for an IRA, as many annuities don't have to be cashed in until you reach your mid- to late 80s. But with an IRA, you must start withdrawing monies much earlier. You should see brokers and insurance agents explain their rationale on the witness stand. They may try to argue that their client absolutely wanted and needed the life insurance benefit and was willing to pay for it. But the reality usually is that the salesperson made a 4 percent commission.

The SEC and the NASD have been critical of annuity sales, particularly variable annuities. The SEC published a brochure about variable annuities that can be found on the SEC's Web site at <www.sec.gov/consumer/varannty.htm>. Among other things, it suggests heeding the following warnings regarding variable annuities:

- Most investors should make the maximum allowable contributions to IRAs and 401(k) plans before investing in a variable annuity.
- Because you'll pay for each benefit provided by the variable annuity, carefully consider whether you need the benefit. If you do, consider whether you can buy the benefit more cheaply separately (e.g., through a long-term care insurance policy).
- Be very careful when exchanging an annuity, whether a 1035 exchange or not. Consult with a tax professional. You may be better off keeping the old annuity.
- Bonus annuities may sound appealing, but they have higher costs than nonbonus annuities, costs that may outweigh the benefit of the bonus. The annual fees and costs are higher when compared with similar investments and will eat into your rate of return over the long term.

At about the same time the SEC raised concerns about variable annuities, the NASD cautioned all stockbrokers and brokerage firms to adhere to the following guidelines when selling variable annuities:[4]

- A registered representative should discuss all relevant facts with a customer, including such liquidity issues as potential surrender charges and the Internal Revenue Service (IRS) penalty; fees, including mortality and expense charges, administrative charges, and investment advisory fees; any applicable state and local government premium taxes; and market risk.
- Lack of liquidity, which may be caused by surrender charges or penalties for early withdrawal under the Internal Revenue Code, may make a variable annuity an unsuitable investment for customers who have short-term investment objectives.
- A variable annuity investment may be unsuitable for some customers of advanced age.

What the foregoing establishes is that annuities can be complex investment vehicles. Before agreeing to an annuity purchase, make sure you understand all of the pros and cons. Consider getting a second opinion from a third party who doesn't stand to gain financially if you agree to the transaction.

BONDS—BORING BUT A GREAT ALTERNATIVE

For most investors, bonds are boring. Although you often hear the phrase *stocks and bonds* bantered about, bonds have always been perceived as much less risky than stocks. For one, if a company goes bankrupt, the bondholders are the first in line to get paid, followed by preferred shareholders and then nonpreferred shareholders. This payoff order can be very advantageous when the company is a lesser-known one with a scanty track record and a likelihood of bankruptcy.

Second, bonds have a fixed interest rate, called the *coupon*, which usually provides the investor with semiannual interest payments. These fixed payments tend to buffer bonds from as wide a value fluctuation as stocks. They still fluctuate, though, depending on the movement of interest rates.

The main thing you need to watch out for is the spread on bonds. Wider spreads occur primarily on tax-free municipal bonds, corporate bonds, and, to a lesser extent, long-term government bonds. Some bonds trade on the open market, but the majority of retail investors purchase these types of bonds from brokerage firms' inventory. Brokers review their firm's bond inventory and make a recommendation based on what their firm has on hand. Bonds are also sold in a new offering by the firm. Both situations allow the firm to mark up the price to you and pocket the spread.

There is hope and some talk that the system will change and that, in the future, investors will be able to trade bonds like stocks on more of an auction basis. One factor working against such an event is that the number of bonds in the public's hands for any given company is much more limited as compared with the company's stock. On any given day, a company may have millions of outstanding stock shares traded by thousands of buyers and sellers. Not so with the majority of bonds.

As an investor, you will almost never see the commission or markup on the bonds you purchase. You only see a net price, and it includes the markup the firm levied when it sold it to you out of inventory as well as the commission. Nor will the firm disclose the kickers it offered its brokers to move certain bonds out of its inventory. Brokers steer toward the bonds on which they make the most commission as opposed to the bonds that are the best for you.

To make matters worse, it is almost impossible to price "shop" bonds. On any given day, it would be almost blind luck for you to find another brokerage firm that had the same bonds in its inventory. You are at the mercy of the firm. It is not surprising then that many bond investors prefer to buy bonds as new issues. At least that way they know they are paying the same as everybody else and the markups are not excessive.

When buying bonds, be wary not only of the spread but also of the negative spread. The negative spread occurs when you let your broker talk you into buying bonds on margin. Brokerage firms love for you to buy bonds on margin, just like stocks, because you can buy twice as many and the firm can make twice as much. When you are buying bonds as an investment, buying them on margin is just plain stupid. The difference between the margin interest cost and the bond interest coupon is a negative spread (save for high-yield junk bonds). If this were not the case, then everyone and their grandmother would borrow on margin to buy bonds. When you consider that you buy bonds for an interest return, how can it make any sense to buy them on margin if you are losing money each year?

When Douglas evaluates an account and sees bonds purchased on margin, he knows that some broker has not played fair. And don't let your broker fool you by saying, "Buy the stocks on margin and pay cash for the bonds." You still have a negative spread! It would be like having money in a savings account earning 6 percent while you have a 12 percent debit balance on your credit card. You should use your savings to pay down the credit card and save yourself 6 percent a year. The same is true for your brokerage account. Don't pay 10 percent on your margin balance when your bonds are earning 5 percent. The negative spread is 5 percent. That's how much you are losing each year.

Even worse is when a broker persuades a customer to buy tax-free municipal bonds on margin. You cannot consider the interest on the bonds tax free and, at the same time, attempt to write off the margin interest. Any accountant will tell you that the IRS will disallow one or the other. The only sane person who would ever consider buying bonds on margin is a short-term bond trader.

A number of companies, like Moody's and Standard & Poor's, issue bond ratings; you probably have seen the ratings, such as AAA or Baa. Historically, these ratings have been very reliable. If, over the long haul, you stick with higher-rated bonds, whether corporate or municipal, you'll probably not have to worry about defaults, especially if you diversify your bond portfolio adequately. We mention diversification because Douglas remembers in the early 1980s when a huge scandal erupted involving bonds of the Washington Public Power Supply System Nuclear Plants, which ultimately resulted in the bonds defaulting. The acronym for these bonds was Whoops. Many portfolios were overloaded in these bonds, in part because the rating companies had given the bonds top ratings.

Don't let the ratings give you a false sense of security. Also, watch your bond concentration. Many advisors recommend not concentrating in one particular state's municipal bonds despite tax advantages in doing so. Finally, we recommend you stay away from unrated bonds. It is probably better in the long run to buy a lower-rated bond than to buy an unrated bond.

COMMODITIES—BEND OVER

"You can make a fortune trading commodities futures!" You may have seen one of these ads on the radio or television. The ads are famous more for what they *don't* tell you than for what they *do*.

Commodities trading is trading a given commodity such as gold, sugar, wheat, cotton, or cattle for delivery by a future date. Commodities futures are unique animals and are not considered securities, which means they are not regulated by the NASD or the SEC. Rather, commodities are regulated by the Commodities Futures Trading Commission (CFTC) and a self-regulatory body—the National Futures Association (NFA).

Commodities trading is one of the oldest types of contracts, dating back to the time when silk traders traveled to the Orient. Because of the long trip by sail, the merchants would forward contract (sell) their silk, thus assuring themselves a profit when they returned months later with the goods. Today, this forward hedging of commodities is still an important aspect of commodities futures trading. One of the more recent uses involves a portfolio manager employing investment contracts (S&P futures) to hedge portfolios. But the ads and the brokers aren't soliciting you for hedging purposes; they are enticing you to speculate.

And speculate is the proper word, because in commodities trading, you can make and lose fortunes overnight. Commodities are one of the few types of investments in which you can lose more money than you invest (naked stock options is another type, and it can also happen while employing margin). In a large firm's arbitration, it was disclosed that when a client opened a commodities account, he indicated on the firm's own commodities form that he was willing to lose a maximum of $50,000 in trading. Yet in a matter of months, he lost $83,000. At the arbitration, the broker, the manager, and the compliance officer concurred that there is no trading limit for commodities, even though such a limit was requested on the form! No one can control or limit the losses in commodities. Incidentally, that client won his arbitration.

A number of factors make commodities riskier than other investments. For one, commodities can fluctuate in value depending, for example, on whether it rains on the other side of the country. If you think it's hard predicting the stock market, try predicting the weather in Brazil.

Another reason commodities are so risky is that the leverage (similar to margin) is much greater than it is with stocks. You can control as much as $100,000 in commodities with only a few thousand dollars of investment. Therefore, a small price change in the underlying commodity can exaggerate either the profit or loss on the investment.

Commodities have limit moves, the maximum daily amount a commodity can move in price within a given day. On its face, this might sound conservative; stocks don't have similar movement restrictions, as evidenced by the huge price drops suffered by many stocks in recent years. One of the reasons for a limit on commodities is that they are heavily margined. It is possible to lose great sums in a matter of days despite the daily limit move, because there's an excellent chance that you can't make a trade to cut your losses if the commodity moves the limit. If the commodity goes "lock limit" for three days or more, you may see yourself losing vast sums with no way to get out.

If you open a commodities futures trading account, you'll need to do it with someone who is licensed in this area. A typical stockbroker cannot trade commodities for you without an NASD Series 3 license. In a commodities account, anticipate roughly three times the number of documents required for you to review and sign in contrast with a regular brokerage account. You'll see a host of warnings proclaiming that commodity trading is very risky and you can lose all of your investment and then some. These disclosures make it tougher to sue even if you invested and lost your child's college education or the broker outright lied to you. If you try to sue your broker, the brokerage firm will wave these signed documents in your face. We know most investors don't spend the time they should on these dry documents in small typeface, so if you're not going to read them, then read this:

YOU CAN LOSE YOUR ASS TRADING COMMODITIES!

When Douglas traded commodities at Bear Stearns, he was aware of a photograph on the wall of a gentleman wearing nothing but a whiskey barrel with this caption: " Ex-commodities trader."

If you have a hunch and are determined to trade commodities, one way you can do it and potentially limit your losses is to trade options on commodities. As in stock options, the maximum amount you can lose is the amount of the options you purchase. But even with this strategy, keep two things in mind. One, make sure that you only purchase options and don't sell any, because selling a naked option is no less risky than owning the underlying futures contract. Second, if you think it's hard to make money trading futures, it's even harder trading commodity options; not only do you need to guess right but timing is more crucial than with futures.

As with stocks, the commissions on commodity trading are variable. You can find commission rates ranging from $20 a contract to $150 a contract. Don't hesitate to shop around or ask for a serious discount from the standard commission.

As with options, if you ever hear a broker insinuate that commodities trading is conservative or a sure thing or that the broker has an incredible track record or can control the risks, you would be well advised to cash in your chips and go elsewhere.

We have said elsewhere that if an investment sounds too good to be true, then you should ask why it is being offered to you. This is truer in commodities than in any other investment because there is no other investment where you can turn $10,000 into a $1 million in a matter of months. Next time you hear one of these incredible pitches on how you can make a fortune trading commodities, ask yourself why the one pushing the strategy doesn't just trade his own account and make the millions for himself? By now you know the answer: there's no foolproof system.

IPOs—THE ROLLER COASTERS OF THE INDUSTRY

An initial public offering (IPO) is exactly what it says it is: a firm that previously had no publicly traded stock commences an offering of stock to the public. Don't confuse IPOs with secondary offerings. A *secondary offering* refers to an offer of a certain amount of new stock by a company that already has stock trading publicly. Prior to the secondary offering, the additional stock was not publicly traded.

A question many investors fail to ask is, Why is the IPO taking place? Many large, fine, profitable companies in this country never go public. The objective of most IPOs is to raise capital, which begs the questions of why the company needs capital, particularly if it is so profitable and doing so well, and what it is going to do with the capital. Find out the answers to these questions. Owners may take their company public in an IPO to break up ownership of the company; shares of a publicly traded company are much easier to transfer and sell than privately owned stock.

Another reason companies go public is just old-fashioned American capitalism. After all those years of toiling, it is the American dream to eventually cash out by taking your company public. Typically, owners of private companies pocket a lot of money by going public. They may personally own hundreds of thousands of shares of the stock for which they paid little to nothing. An old saying is that there are three ways in this country to become very rich. You can marry it. You can inherit it. And you can take your company public.

What makes going public so attractive is that the price of the shares that will be offered to the public is usually a multiple of the company's book value and what the company could be liquidated for. Otherwise, the owners would just sell the company in a private transaction. It is the multiple that's the catch. The owners of the company and the investment banking firm they hire to take the company public usually decide the multiple. And a tug of war often ensues.

The owners want a higher IPO price so they can pocket more money, and the investment banking firm wants a lower IPO price so more people will buy. Most brokerages, even the smallest of regional firms, have an investment banking department. It is only a matter of time before Schwab, E*Trade and other online brokerages will too. Investment banking is one of the most profitable departments of any brokerage firm.

Many factors determine the share price at which an IPO will be set—a very important decision. One of the determining factors is the share price of other publicly traded companies in the same business. To compare apples with apples, companies evaluate these companies' PEs (price-earnings ratios), price-to-debt ratios, and book value, among other things. Also, the current market trends are a factor. IPOs tend to perform better when the markets are bullish and on the upswing. Conversely, you will see a rash of IPO cancellations when there is a pullback in the market. Remember that after the IPO, the share price will be determined by the markets and not by some artificial price.

No matter what price you pay for a security, someone with less sense will come along and pay a higher price for it. This is called the "greater fool theory," and it is not necessarily limited to stocks. It happened with Beanie Babies and will probably happen with whatever this year's Christmas craze is. IPOs of dot.com companies could arguably be considered part of the greater fool theory. What else could explain why so many would buy shares in a company that has never showed a profit and whose stock is being offered at multiples that are off the charts, not only in the IPO but also later in the open market? In 1998 and 1999, any company that added ".com" to its name was considered a hot offering. But missing are the years of hard work and toiling by the owners. Also missing are the earnings. How are you supposed to come up with a PE for a company with negative earnings? You can't.

The sad reality is that those who feel like fools are not the ones who bought and held such stocks as Yahoo!, eBay, and Amazon.com but those who missed buying them early on. That, of course, is hindsight. As long as a stock is going up and as long as there is a new buyer to take the stock off the hands of the earlier buyer, it all works out. Remember that every time someone buys a stock, someone is selling it (unless it has come from a firm's inventory). You should always think about what is going through the mind of the person on the other end of your transaction.

Recently, concerns have been raised about brokerage firms allocating IPOs to their favored clients. In return, clients pay higher-than-normal commissions on subsequent trades. In May 2001, the SEC and the NASD began investigating whether Wall Street securities firms charged oversized commissions to investors in exchange for hot IPO shares and whether those commissions were illegal kickbacks.[5]

Finally, although you may know individuals who profited handsomely from IPO investing in 1999 or 2000, realize that for every IPO winner, there were at least two losers.[6] That means your odds of winning would be better if you laid your investment dollars on black at the roulette table.

LIMITED PARTNERSHIPS— HIDE UNDER THE BED

A limited partnership (LP) is a business term that describes the legal form of a business. The brokerage industry uses the term with an additional twist. Some brokers have told investors that the word *limited* referred to the investor's financial exposure in the investment, which in many cases is false.

Prior to the Tax Reform Act of 1986, the brokerage industry made handsome profits selling tax shelters. Typical tax shelters involved cattle feeding, railroad boxcars, barges, and large comput-ers, investments designed to shift taxes from one year to the next and, hence, shelter your income. They also generated handsome commissions and fees for the broker, the brokerage firm, and the general partner of the tax shelter. The problem was that unless an investor's taxes were going to be significantly less in ensuing years, the investor only deferred the inevitable. Remember there are only two certainties in life: death and taxes. Most tax shelters were so poorly structured that investors lost their entire investment. Even if you are in a 100 percent tax bracket, losing all of your investment to save taxes is not a sound practice.

As tax shelters dried up as a result of the Tax Reform Act, the brokerage industry began to focus its attention on other investments that might garner them as much in fees and commissions. Hence, the limited partnership and the private placement were born. Pru-dential Securities sold over a billion dollars worth of limited part-nerships and private placements from 1980 through 1992. In 1994, the SEC levied the then biggest fine ever levied against a securities firm when it sanctioned Prudential for its deceptive sales of these distinctive investments.[7]

The most critical aspect of limited partnerships and private placements is the multitude of costs associated with them. Remem-ber that the same exorbitant costs that are so bad for the investor are what make the investments so attractive for the industry to sell.

In the oil and gas days, "money in the ground" was used to de-scribe the amount of money that actually went into the investment. Taken quite literally, it was used to pay for the actual costs of get-ting oil out of the ground. Limited partnerships and private place-ments have their own version of money in the ground. In securities vernacular, all the money that initially does not go directly toward, or in, your investment are called front-end loads. Here are some of the typical front-end loads for a limited partnership:

8%	Commission for your broker
1.5%	Underwriting fee
4%	General administration fees
3%	Commission for the agent selling certain property
1.5%	Insurance costs
18%	Total front-end load

Naturally, when limited partnerships and private placements are marketed, the costs are not highlighted. The securities industry knows that it has a much better chance of selling you an investment with the sales pitch of "The price for the investment is X," as opposed to "The price of the investment is Y and there are also up-front costs of Z." Yeah, right. Unless an investor scours the prospectus or the private placement memorandum, the investor will be in the dark about what the up-front costs are. And you can bet your broker isn't going to tell you. He is under enough pressure from his firm to peddle these investments. Plus, telling you the costs might spoil the sale and his chances of buying that Harley he has his eye on.

Sometimes the front-end load figure is as much as 25 percent of your money. In our example above, 18 percent of the money you paid for that limited partnership went to places other than the investment itself, meaning that only 82 percent of your money went toward the investment—that is, in the ground. Or did it? There's a good chance that the general partners, the ones who have orchestrated the sale of the partnership, originally owned it themselves. You don't think they're going to sell this investment without a nice built-in profit for themselves, do you?

The other kicker to limited partnerships and private placements is the ongoing fees paid to the people who manage the investment. How convenient that the very people who sold you the deal are also going to manage the deal. Usually, management is through a subsidiary or an affiliate so as to minimize the glare of the conflict. Management fees range from 5 percent to 10 percent. Off the top, that is, calculated on either gross revenues or a percentage of assets. And that's just the start; other ongoing fees like consulting and appraisal fees are tacked on as well.

So how are you, the investor, supposed to make money? You have only about 80 percent of your money working for you, and each year someone is raking 10 percent off the top. Now you understand why very few investors made any money in the billions of dollars of limited partnerships that were sold in the 1980s and early 1990s. Except for the brokerage firms. They made fortunes.

A breakeven analysis can be performed to determine just how much damage the front-end load and the ongoing fees in a limited partnership inflict. This is done by picking a competitive investment and comparing the results after taking into consideration those up-front costs. Let's compare a $100,000 investment in Fly-by-Night Limited Partnership, including its front-end fees, costs, and commissions of 20 percent, with a ten-year government bond with negligible costs. The question is, What rate of return will the partnership have to earn until it breaks even with the bond alternative? Or you can alter the equation to ask how many years it will take the partnership to be equivalent to the bond, based on a certain rate of return.

Start by taking a rate of return for the partnership of 15 percent a year, because that is what the broker told you it would earn. Take 80 percent of the $100,000 investment, because that is all that is working for you (20 percent went to up-front costs) and that equals $80,000. Take $80,000 times 15 percent a year, no compounding. After four years, your limited partnership would return $48,000, or $128,000 net.

Now let's look at your government bond. It's earning 6 percent on the entire $100,000. After four years, it will return $24,000 or a total net of $124,000. This establishes that it will take approximately four years for the partnership to catch up with the bond, which proves just how bad the partnership is. You ask, why? Because the limited partnership is four times riskier than the government bond, and yet your investment is only slightly better after four years with a 15 percent rate of return. Of course, the broker may not have told you that his 15 percent per year projections were before the general partner and his affiliates took their 10 percent off the top, which in turn would lower your return. The majority of limited partnerships we have seen rarely returned 15 percent a year. With estimates that the majority of limited partnerships that were sold in the 1980s returned a total of less than 25 cents per dollar invested, a projected return of 15 percent per year is a far cry from reality.

Breakeven Analysis

Fly-by-Night Limited Partnership

Initial investment	$100,000
Up-front commissions, fees, loads	20,000
Total money working in partnership	80,000
Earnings per year at 15% ($80,000 × 15%)	12,000
Total earnings after four years	48,000
Total of earnings and principal after four years ($80,000 plus $48,000)	$128,000

U.S. Government Bond

Initial investment	$100,000
Up-front commissions, fees, loads[8]	0
Total money working in Partnership	100,000
Earnings per year at 6% ($100,000 times 6%)	6,000
Total earnings after four years	24,000
Total of earnings and principal after four years ($100,000 plus $24,000)	$124,000

To aggravate the deception, the brokerage industry had a practice of not putting the limited partnerships' value on customers' statements. Instead, the statements reflected the cost, which was always much higher than the partnerships' value. Many investors believed that the figure shown was the value, not the cost. Even though this practice was highly criticized by the regulators, some in the brokerage industry continue to do it. A lot of brokerage firms would love to tell you that the stocks they recommended to you are worth more than their real value. They don't do it, however, because they know you can double-check the stocks' prices in the *Wall Street Journal*. Such checking yourself is not possible with limited partnerships; their true values are not publicly available. For years, many investors believed that their principal was intact, when, in fact, it had deteriorated dramatically.

PRIVATE PLACEMENTS—UNDER THE BED IS NOT A GOOD-ENOUGH HIDING PLACE

Let's distinguish between private placements and private investments. If you are a private businessperson or entrepreneur, one of the best investments you can make is in your own company. You know the company. You control the company. And your ability to understand and control the risk is something you cannot find so readily in any other investment. A friend or business associate may approach you with a business idea and ask you to invest. Many times this can be an investment of a lifetime, especially if you know and trust the person and the investment is in an area or field that is related to your own business or in something with which you are familiar.

Personally, we think the types of private investments just described are some of the best investments you can make. We love investments in which little, or no, conflicts of interest exist. It's a step in the right direction if someone approaches you with an investment deal but receives no compensation for bringing the deal to your attention or for the ongoing operation of the business. Even better is if the person who approaches you (or any of his affiliates or associates) will be paid only when you start to receive profits yourself. These factors virtually eliminate the negative conflicts attendant on most investments.

Think of private placements as having qualities opposite to those just described and as essentially in the same category as limited partnerships. Most conflicts and problems are common to both. You can spot private placements because they usually require much larger dollars to invest and are usually limited to investors with a high net worth and who make more than $200,000 a year. Private placements are almost always among the highest-risk investments you can make. We recommend you stay completely away from them. If you must invest in private placements, be sure to do the following:

- Read the Private Placement Memorandum (PPM) completely.
- Heed the warnings in the PPM.
- Have your CPA review the material for the various tax ramifications.
- Get a second, unbiased opinion.
- Invest only money that you can afford to entirely lose.

MUTUAL FUNDS—THE GREAT EQUALIZERS

Before addressing some of the problems of mutual funds, we think you should have an understanding of how profitable the mutual fund business can be. The General Accounting Office (GAO), a department of the U.S. government, issued a report in July 2000 showing that profit margins for 18 publicly held mutual funds grew from 33 percent in 1995 to 36 percent in 1999. The GAO also said that return on equity for 9 of the firms ranged from 23 percent to 26 percent over the period versus an average of 22 percent for companies in the S&P 500. Now you need no longer wonder why there are more mutual funds than stocks.

Mutual funds can suffer from some of the same pitfalls as limited partnerships and private placements. Many of them charge a front-end load when you purchase them, a separate fee when you sell them (known as a redemption fee or back-end load), and ongoing management fees. Get a grasp of what each of these fees is before you buy, both on a dollar and a percentage basis. The same mutual fund company that offers no-load funds may also have funds that, in fact, do charge loads.

Be alert for hidden or not-so-obvious fees, such as service, account, or administrative fees. Some funds, whether from banks or brokerage firms, may charge a fixed or yearly assessed fee (a level-load) as long as you own the fund. It's a given that all funds have to pay their managers a handsome salary as well as pay such overhead costs as advertising, research, long-distance phone calls, personnel, computer equipment and maintenance, and software development. You will, and should in all fairness, end up sharing these expenses. Marketing fees that are passed on to purchasers are listed as 12(b)-1 fees in a fund prospectus. These fees vary among companies and their funds. Again, keep in mind that any fees or loads that you are charged can significantly reduce the profits earned by your investments.

One of the biggest rubs about mutual funds involves in-house mutual funds—mutual funds put together and offered by the brokerage firm that's selling them. In 1999, these funds made up about 10 percent of all mutual fund assets, down significantly from a decade ago. Yet in 1999, the majority of the top-ten-selling new mutual funds were in-house funds because many of the new mutual funds offered by the brokerage industry were in hot areas. In addition, the brokerage firms were doing an excellent job of marketing their in-house funds. The problem is that the term *most successful* doesn't mean these funds made the most money for investors. It means, rather, that these new funds raised the most money.

We know of one firm that had one fund that raised over $2 billion in 1999 alone. Brokerage firms used to pay their brokers a higher percentage of commissions if the broker would sell in-house mutual funds as opposed to selling independent mutual funds. When the regulators finally woke up, they frowned on this practice, and now most firms no longer use a different pay scale. However, brokerage firms have other ways of encouraging their brokers to sell in-house funds. In 1999, brokers at another firm were asked to sign a document stating that they would sell a certain amount of one of the firm's in-house proprietary mutual funds. Make sure your broker is not getting a special incentive or any pressure from her firm for selling the fund that she is suggesting.

But brokerage firms don't need to offer a higher percentage payout on their mutual funds to encourage brokers to sell them. The commissions of 4.50 percent to 5.75 percent creates plenty of incentive for the brokers to push these products. In-house brokerage mutual funds have some of the highest commission structures, whether the funds charge front-end or back-end loads. Second, management fees and 12(b)-1 fees are also some of the highest. And your broker often gets a piece of them. What's worse is that you typically get no benefit for all of these higher-than-average fees. You get just the opposite. Historically and comparatively, in-house funds have underperformed their competitors. Higher fees are a drag on performance. The more talented money managers are drawn to independent mutual funds not connected to the industry and where they may be paid higher salaries.

One of the most misunderstood and debated aspects of mutual funds is how load funds charge differently depending on whether you have bought Class A, B, or C shares. The letters A, B, and C represent different types of loads or charges, that is, commissions and fees that you are going to pay as a result of purchasing and holding a fund over time.

We can't get into every nuance, but you need to know the basics and the conflicts so you can ask intelligent questions when your broker confronts you with the choice. Of course, very few brokers will offer you the option of buying true no-load mutual funds.

Class A shares are basically front-end load funds. You're going to pay a hefty front-end commission right off the top to buy into the fund. Depending on the fund, you may also pay yearly 12(b)-1 fees.

Class B shares have a contingent deferred sales charge, also called rear-end load funds, because rather than paying the commission charge up front, you are charged the commission when you sell the fund. Your broker is paid up front, and the fund collects this money from you when you sell or through the 12(b)-1 fees. The commission usually starts out high if you sell in the first year but tapers off each year by 1 percent. The advantage B shares have over A shares is that you have all of your money going to work from the start. But many times B shares have higher 12(b)-1 fees. Don't forget that if you own Class B shares, you can usually convert them to

Class A after so many years, which you should do because you'll save on annual fees.

Class C shares are a hybrid, so the manner in which charges are assessed is all over the place. Typically, they are in funds designed to be sold through brokerage firms. They typically have no front-end load or rear-end charge but levy a flat annual (typically 1 percent or higher) management fee or 12(b)-1 fee. They may also have a small back-end fee but usually not. If you are going to own the fund for a long time, Class C shares can be the worst to own because you will continually pay a high annual fee.

A, B, and C shares are the vast majority of classes of mutual funds, but you may also see D shares. Class D shares usually have no front-end or back-end charges. Typically, they are funds designed to be sold through brokerage firms. D shares would usually be a no-load fund that tacks on a 12(b)-1 annual fee so that the mutual fund can pay a wholesaler, like Schwab, to sell the fund but get paid for offering the fund to the wholesaler's account holders. Because buying D shares defeats the whole benefit of a true no-load fund, D shares are on the wane.

If you are buying load mutual funds, always ask your broker where the breakpoints are. All load funds lower their loads, no matter which class of shares you are buying if you buy a higher dollar amount of the fund. Because the load encompasses your broker's commission, your broker may not want you to be familiar with these breakpoints. He may recommend you buy $24,000 of a fund and not tell you that if you bought $25,000, you would have paid a lower commission to him and lower fees in general. This is a violation of NASD Rule IM-2830-1. Along this same line, a lot of load funds waive the entire commission if you buy a certain dollar amount, usually around $1 million. This is a good reason to consider buying all of your funds in one family, because the discount applies to all of your related accounts as well as to the entire family of funds.

Switching mutual funds—your broker's recommendation that you move from one family of funds to a different family of funds— is a securities violation.[9] It is a violation because mutual funds are considered long-term investments, and when the switch takes place, you'll incur new load charges on the front end, the back end, or both.

Of course, it is better to buy no-load funds. You eliminate the conflict and the drag on your return. If that's not an option, be careful. Calculate all of the options and the total costs on both a yearly and cumulative basis. Do this in percentages and in dollars. If your broker tells you a fund is a no-load, make sure there is no load on the front end, the back end, and during the period you hold the fund; 12(b)-1 charges are a load. Sometimes brokers use the term *no load* to describe no load only on the front end, but unknown to you, you'll get socked with ongoing and back-end fees when you sell. And be very suspicious if your broker recommends that you switch load funds every several years. Now you know why.

OPTIONS—VEGAS NEVER OFFERED SO MUCH

You may have seen advertisements on the financial news networks about options. Each segment starts with a "Fact," followed by language that encourages viewers to buy options software that enables investors to trade options and become a profitable options trader. Not only are some of the so-called facts misleading, but many are simply missing. We were surprised by the lack of warnings that typically accompany any advertising or marketing that encourages folks to trade options. Option advertisers better watch out. They may get fined $90,000 by the NASD, which should be quite a disincentive but unfortunately does not appear to be. Options, since their entrée into the markets in the early 1970s, have always been high risk and thus one of the more highly regulated investment products. In some forms, they can be even riskier than commodities.

If you're interested in trading options, we encourage you to get the numerous pamphlets and books written on the subject. Even then you are likely to learn just enough that's dangerous. An option is the right to buy or sell property (shares of stock, for example) in exchange for an agreed-on price. Options consist of puts and calls; you can either buy or sell puts and calls. You can trade options if you are bullish or bearish and with or without owning the underlying security. How you trade options determines how risky a position you take.

Stockbrokers love clients who trade options because they are so commission intensive. Options are relatively short-term investments because they have a time limit within which they expire. If you buy or sell an option, you close out your position usually within a matter of weeks or months (as opposed to a stock or mutual fund that you might buy and hold for a couple of years). Trading options causes your account to turn over more often, which means that on each transaction your broker collects a commission. Also, on a percentage basis the commissions tend to be much higher on options than on stock. With people now commonly trading stocks at a commission of ten cents a share or less, you'll find that commissions on options are a much more profitable venture for your broker, even if you have an online trading account. Don't be fooled if you see that the dollar amount you pay for an options trade is less than the amount you are used to when you purchase shares of stock. If you are trading stocks with a reputable, full-service brokerage, you'll find your commission as a percentage of your investment to be less than 1 percent. Yet with the same firm, the commission on your options transaction will be anywhere from 2 to 5 percent. Now consider this increased commission with the likelihood of increased trading activity and you can see why options trading is so costly for the investor and so profitable for the broker.

In addition, any time you make a lot of short-term options trades, you also have the cost of the spread between the bid and the ask on the security. Options trading subjects you to the constant dilemma of overcoming these spreads and commissions to make money.

The term *conservative*, in our view, does not properly describe *any* kind of options transaction. Though some argue that a covered-call option contract is conservative, it's not necessarily conservative or a particularly bright investment concept. Let's see why by looking at the following covered call. If you own 100 shares of XYZ.com and sell a call on that 100 shares, whoever buys the call pays you a certain amount of money, called a "premium," to buy those 100 shares of XYZ.com at a set price. Those who claim that covered-call writing is conservative contend that if XYZ.com goes up, the stock is called away from you at a higher price and, in addition, you get to keep the premium. You might say, "What a wonderful transaction; I made money and on a relatively short-term basis."

What is misleading is that as a result of such a transaction, you own XYZ.com, and XYZ.com can go down. Sure, you collected a small premium by selling the call, but XYZ.com can go down a whole lot more than the small premium you collected. You have only reduced your risk through owning the underlying security by the amount of the premium you obtained for the option contract. Thus, on its face, covered-call writing can be one of the most stupid investment strategies there is. It's an investment with a very limited upside and totally unlimited risk on the downside. Doesn't that sound stupid? Brokers and brokerage firms love it, because not only does it create a lot of options trading but your broker has reaped another commission if the stock is called away.

Another argument you'll hear from the profiteers of options is that if you want to control the risk of options, only be a buyer of puts and calls. The theory is that if you buy only puts and calls, you can lose only the amount of money you pay for them. No argument there. The problem is that your chances of making money are extremely slim. If you buy a call (bullish) or buy a put (bearish), you're making a bet that the stock will move in a certain direction. But the big difference is that to make money, you not only have to guess right on which way the stock is going to move, but you now have a time limit on when it has to happen. If one or the other doesn't happen, the option expires, and you lose all your money.

Also watch out for the trading strategy of selling naked options—that is, selling an option contract without owning the underlying security. This is one of the riskiest transactions you can make in the investment markets. Let's say that XYZ.com has been trading between $100 and $200 all year, and you feel there's no way it is going to trade below $100 a share. You sell ten XYZ.com October 100 puts for $5 each. Each option is for 100 shares, so by selling ten you have sold the right for somebody to make you buy (put) 1,000 shares at $100 between now and October. For this, you collect $5,000 and get to keep the $5,000. But if you're wrong and XYZ.com goes below $100 before October, you may be forced to buy 1,000 shares at $100. That's a $100,000 cost to you. Sure, you got $5,000 so you can say your real cost is only $95,000, but what if the stock goes to $70? At $70, you are staring at a $25,000 loss. Compare this with your total upside in this transaction, a measley $5,000.

You can conduct the same strategy but at the opposite end where you sell calls and bet that the stock doesn't go over a certain price. You can be lulled with this strategy for months on end, thinking it's like taking candy from a baby. That's because you are guessing right and the market is going in your direction. But when the market turns (and it will), it can wipe out your entire life savings. In today's volatile market, you are probably better off going to Vegas than trading naked options.

If you mention this section of our book to your broker, and she responds, "They don't know what they're talking about," ask your broker the following questions:

- If options aren't so risky, then why are there special sections in the NASD and the NYSE manuals specifically devoted to options?
- If options aren't so risky, then why must I fill out a special form before I can trade in them?
- If options aren't so risky, then why is it the only investment for which you are required to give me a special book describing the risks before I can invest?

We have talked about how the October 1987 crash hit margined investors hard because they were sold out at low prices and couldn't participate in the market recovery that occurred over the ensuing months. However, another group of people suffered greatly. Can you guess who this group was? It was those investors who were short puts; that is, those individuals who sold naked puts. When the market crashed, these investors were forced to purchase the stocks on which they had shorted puts. Because most of these investors didn't realize or understand the magnitude of being put so many large blocks of stock, their cash position or margin-buying power was not sufficient to purchase all the stocks. Yet the purchases were made and then the brokerage firms immediately sold the securities at huge losses for the investors because there wasn't enough money to meet the margin calls. Keep this story in mind when a broker tells you what a great strategy shorting puts is.

It is our opinion that for the majority of investors, options are not investing. Rather, they are nothing more than rank speculation or, better put, gambling. If you must speculate in options, do so with very limited amounts of capital and don't throw good money after bad. If you must trade short term, we recommend doing so in stocks, where there is no expiration. Options are dwindling assets and if your timing is wrong, you could lose everything.

SELLING SHORT—PLAYING BOTH SIDES OF THE SAME GAME

Okay. It's not really a product. It's a strategy. Selling short means you sell a stock or bond that you don't currently own. You do this by actually borrowing the shares. That's right—it's a margin transaction and you pay interest on that margin. Your hope is that the stock price goes down; then you can buy back the shares and thus close the position at a lower price than you paid. It's the opposite of the buy low–sell high strategy. A short seller sells high and then hopes to buy low.

It was rare 20 years ago to find retail investors selling short, and short selling was typically confined to institutional and professional traders. However, as more and more investors make trading decisions for themselves, more and more short sales occur on the retail side.

Shorting stock has always been considered much riskier than simply owning the stock. Because the short position is always a margin position, you can be forced out at the worst possible time. Compare shorting with owning a stock outright—your downside is that the stock goes to zero. In a short position, because the stock's upside is unlimited, the amount you can lose is unlimited. If you have ever shorted a stock that becomes a merger or takeover candidate, you know what we mean; the stock price can shoot up dramatically. Generally, even the worst shorts go up only so high, but think how much you would have lost if you were short Dell Computer during the 1990s when Dell went up more than tenfold? Also, we all know that reading brokerage statements can be very difficult. If you have a short position in your account, plan on your brokerage statement being even harder to read.

Brokerage firms are not fond of recommending short positions in stock. First, there is no additional incentive in terms of commissions, fees, or expenses. In fact, firms actually have a disincentive to recommend shorting stock; doing so may alienate their investment banking clients. A firm like Morgan Stanley has lots of analysts covering lots of industries. Within these industries are quite a few companies, each of which provides Morgan Stanley's analysts with information on a regular basis. For Morgan to recommend shorting the stock of one of these companies . . . well, that would a death knell. It would be like Morgan's analyst recommending that it be sold. And we know that rarely happens.

Shorting makes sense conceptually: why should you be limited to playing only one side of the market? However, just remember that, indeed, you are "playing" when you short stocks, and the U.S. stock markets have trended up, not down.

CHAPTER 15

♪ It's Your Money, Do What You Want to Do, We Can't Tell You Who to Sock It To ♪

The title is a slightly updated version of the Isley brothers song "It's Your Thing." We won't tell you who to sock it to, but we can tell you that it's your money, you've earned it, and you should protect it. Here are some ways to do just that.

THE INITIAL INTERVIEW— HAVE YOU HAD YOURS?

Whether it's a phone call or an in-person meeting, the initial conversation with a prospective broker or financial advisor is key. You learned in Chapter 4 that the broker is required by regulations to know you, her customer, which can only be accomplished by a detailed interview with you. Though you now know what the broker is required to learn about you, you need to learn to be the judge of how well this process goes. You may have some very particular goals or special needs. Does the broker/advisor really take the time to conduct the interview in a manner that shows she is learning what you are all about or is she just going through the motions to fill out a form and get on with the selling?

One would expect the broker to spend some time bragging about herself and her company, but this boasting should be in the early part of the contact. During the actual interview process, the broker or advisor should be doing very little talking other than asking probing questions. She should not cut you off but should encourage you to provide as much information as possible. She should document the conversation by taking notes. If you find later that the broker keeps forgetting key information that you have given her, you should begin to suspect that she may have never really had an interest in what you were saying.

If you have not gone through this interview process with your current broker or advisor, do it now. Arrange a time to meet in person, if possible, and, if not, have a lengthy phone conference. If the conference is not a rewarding experience for you, think of changing brokers.

You can use as a guide the obligatory questions that we listed in Chapter 4 in our discussion of suitability and the new account form. But neither you nor your broker should be limited by these basic requirements. Your broker is required to know the essential facts about you. You know what they are. Make sure that your broker knows and remembers them too.

YOUR INVESTMENT OBJECTIVES— THE UNDERLYING ESSENTIALS

In one of Tracy's arbitration cases, the broker testified that he asked his client what his investment objectives were and the client replied, "To make money!" Without further clarification, this cavalier response sent a message that the client was willing to take big risks to get big gains. The broker noted "speculation" as the client's investment objective, yet the client testified in a subsequent arbitration that what he meant was that he wanted his money to grow, but not at the expense of his principal. The broker failed in his duties to inquire how much risk the client was willing to take and instead used the client's response to enable him to engage in more speculative and hence more profitable trading—for the broker.

Investment objective is a term of art in the securities industry. It doesn't mean that you know what specific investments you want to make. Nor does it require some abstract or philosophical response. Several standard investment objectives and their meanings are shown in the following table.

Objective	Meaning
Safety of Principal	You don't want to lose any of the money you're investing. You generally are more comfortable with conservative, stable investments and are not willing to take any risk of principal (the only risk you might be willing to assume is the amount and certainty of the income or appreciation).
Income	You want or need to generate income from the money you are investing and are not willing to take much risk to receive increased income.
Growth & Income	You want diversification to achieve a combination of both income and some capital appreciation. You are comfortable with moderate to low risk.
Growth	You have more of a long-term investment horizon. You may be saving for a future goal and are willing to take some risk (approximately 10 percent of your portfolio) in order to increase your growth potential.
Aggressive Growth	You are willing to assume more fluctuation in your portfolio value to obtain above-average returns. Somewhere around 20 percent of your principal is the maximum you are willing to risk.
Speculation	You are investing to maximize your returns and are willing and able to lose a substantial portion of your principal to obtain high rates of return, usually on a short-term basis.

The brokerage industry tried to introduce a different term several years ago that was confusing to many people: *businessman's risk*. If you see this objective on your new account form, we suggest you cross it out. We'd love to define it for you, but there is really no acceptable definition—which is exactly why the brokerage firms like it. They get to define it to fit how they handle your account, and they'll use it to defend riskier investments and strategies.

Most customer-brokerage disputes center on the customer's investment objectives, and, unlike an order error, the arguments are rarely black and white. First, the great majority of investors don't have a clear understanding of what their financial objectives are. And for many who do, they don't clearly express those objectives. Second, brokerage firms usually require their brokers to check a few preprinted boxes of investment objectives (such as those above) on the new account form. These categories may prove to be either too limiting or too susceptible to interpretation.

A third problem reared its ugly head in one recent arbitration case of Tracy's. The broker had checked *all* of the boxes for the client's investment objectives, reasoning that the client said she wanted to do a little of everything. This defeats the purpose of the information—how can the manager supervise the broker to ensure that suitable investments are being made? Arguably, if every box is checked, everything is suitable and the broker has carte blanche to recommend anything and everything under the sun to you.

Make sure that your investment objectives reflect the overall guideline for how you want your investments handled. Don't focus solely on what specific types of investments you anticipate purchasing over the years. You could, for example, buy a couple of options for one reason or another, but even though options are speculative investments, the fact that you purchased a couple of them should have little bearing on your overall objectives. Your investment objectives should reflect the bigger picture for the majority of your money.

Don't let terminology get in the way; use your own terms to describe what you think you want. Say things like "I'd like an annual return of X percent, but I don't want to risk more than X percent of the money I invest." Percentages are the great equalizer; no matter what amount of money you are dealing with, the rule is the same. Use percentages with your advisor on both the upside and downside, and write them down.

Your broker or advisor should assist you in determining your investment objectives. You would be well advised to send your broker a letter apprising her of your objectives in your words lest your broker neglects to write everything down, much less remember it.

Clearly spelling out your investment objectives is like the oil in a high-performance piece of machinery. It makes everything run smoother. Clear objectives allow *you* to monitor your brokerage account; allow *your broker* to determine what investments are suitable for you; and allow *your brokerage firm* to properly supervise your account. It is very important that the correct investment objectives are on these forms.

SETTING A GAME PLAN—GETTING SERIOUS

One of the first important pieces of advice we gave you in this book was to always find out what the conflicts of interest might be with any investment you purchase. We are now going to give you the second most important piece of advice relating to your investments: *Have a game plan!*

You may be confused as we just finished advising you about setting your investment objectives, so you may be wondering how a game plan differs from investment objectives. Actually, there are three components of the investment procedure, best illustrated by the following:

Game Plan
Investment Objectives
Investment Strategies

It is important to start from the top of this chart and work your way down, because otherwise, you may not know what you are working toward. A game plan may be something like, "I want to send my children to expensive colleges" or "I want to retire early in five years." In and of themselves, they may not appear investment related, but they are necessary prerequisites in formulating investment objectives and investment strategies.

Everything that you do with your broker or advisor pales in comparison with the importance of establishing and then communicating your game plan to your broker. In the combined 30 years that we have been in the business and the thousands of investors and advisors with whom we have come in contact, you would be amazed how many of them not only don't have a specific game plan but don't even grasp the importance of a game plan or how to put one together.

We particularly like game plans because the less worthy stockbrokers don't want you to have one. In our experience, it appears that the securities industry certainly doesn't facilitate the process; even the better brokerage firms' new account forms have no place to describe what your game plan is.

If you bought this book in a bookstore, you probably noticed numerous books about retiring rich or saving for your children's college education. Investing books generally can be broken into two groups: those that try to teach you how to trade the markets and those that talk about investment goals, saving strategies, and financial planning. Game plans typically are discussed in detail in the latter group.

When Douglas worked at Procter & Gamble, he was taught the difference between "features" and "benefits" to enable him to become a good salesman. A feature is what a product can do for a buyer/user. A benefit is what a buyer/user obtains from using the product. For example, a feature of Joy dishwashing liquid is the way it cuts grease better and faster than the competition. The benefits are that by using Joy people spend less time in the kitchen and more time with their families.

Specific actions that you take, or specific investments that you make, are neither objectives nor a game plan; they are investment strategies. For example, day trading is not an investment objective; it is merely a means to an end, an investment strategy. Buying 1,000 shares of General Motors is also merely an implementation of objectives and plans, not the plan itself.

If your investment objective is speculation, you and your advisor may determine a strategy, which could include day trading stocks and purchasing options. If your investment objective is income, your investment strategy might be creating a ladder of municipal bonds with various maturities. But without a game plan, you allow your advisor to create a number of problems such as the following:

- It is almost impossible to measure the success or lack of success of your investment strategies or objectives without a game plan.
- It is hard to monitor the activities of your advisor if you haven't agreed on a game plan.
- Not having a game plan is an open invitation to a commission-based advisor. She can shift strategies and investments to achieve the greatest amount of commissions.
- If you have no game plan, then you cannot change your game plan when things go awry.
- If you seek advice or a second opinion from another advisor, it will be difficult for that advisor to do a proper comparative analysis when no game plan is in place.

Make sure when you are setting up a game plan that you have both a short-term game plan and a long-term game plan, which are sometimes referred to as short-term or long-term goals. Let us give you one example of what not having a game plan can do to your investment performance. Not that we would recommend it, but many investors have concentrated their investments over the last few years in the more speculative high-flying, high-tech securities. As the Nasdaq stock market made quantum leaps in the late 1990s, these investors reaped millions of dollars in paper profits from their stock holdings. It very well may have been their investment strategy to concentrate their investments in these types of securities. Problems began to surface after these folks had doubled and tripled their money and had no exit strategy. Instead of taking some or all of the profits and diversifying, they just watched their investments tank. They were immobilized while holding onto the thin hope that they would see a reoccurrence of such dramatic upward swings. Their high-tech, high-flying investments tanked, leaving them with no game plan, just watching and wondering as their profits vanished.

Another recent example was an arbitration that Douglas was involved in, where a broker who held himself out as a financial planner and advisor had taken his client from mutual funds to stocks back to mutual funds and back to stocks within a year's time. You know, as we discussed earlier, that this is usually a better game plan for the broker than for the investor. The arbitration panel apparently agreed that this game plan was not in Douglas's client's best interest, so the panel ordered the broker pay back money to the investor.

If you want to test what your investment advisor or broker is really made of, ask her the following series of questions. If you can get her to put the responses in writing, you are really ahead of the game and probably have not only an excellent broker but what also appears to be an excellent relationship:

- Are there different investment objectives for different parts of my portfolio? If so, what are they?
- What is the strategy and game plan for each portion of my investment portfolio?
- What specific types of investments will we be using for my portfolio to meet my objectives?

- What types of investment strategies will we be using to meet my objectives, such as short-term trading, buy and hold, and so on?
- What can I expect to make in both dollars and percentages on an annualized basis based on the foregoing strategies and investments?
- What risks am I assuming based on the investments and the types of strategies that you plan on employing?
- What could I lose on an immediate basis and an annualized basis in both dollars and percentages if your investment strategy doesn't work?
- If our game plan is met (in either dollars or percentage gains), what changes will we need to make and when?
- What is our ultimate goal and game plan one year, five years, and ten years out?

If only every investor knew the answers to the above questions, the world would be a much better place. Seriously, it's amazing to think of the benefits that can accrue from asking a few simple questions, like those above. You send a message to your broker that you are serious and concerned about your money and the game plan. If your broker knows that you are writing down the answers, the exercise will serve as a restraint on your broker. She will be less likely to take actions against your best interest. If you really want to pull in the reins, send a copy of the questions and answers to your broker with a note that says, "Let me know if I wrote down any of your answers incorrectly." And date it. Last, the exercise will provide you with a wonderful framework to compare your portfolio and monitor your broker over time.

COMMINGLING YOUR MONEY— JUST DON'T DO IT

If you have decided on opening a new brokerage account or moving your existing account, you obviously must now go through the paperwork process. We suggest that you adhere to the following advice:

DO NOT COMMINGLE YOUR INVESTMENT AC-COUNTS WITH YOUR PERSONAL CHECKING

AND SAVINGS ACCOUNTS, AND CREDIT CARD ACCOUNTS!

In case you're having a cocktail while you're reading this section, which we don't discourage, we'll repeat this advice another way: Do not open a brokerage account and mix investments with check writing and credit card privileges!

Merrill Lynch was one of the original developers—with its CMA account—of putting all of a client's assets along with his checking, banking, and credit card services in a single convenient account. There are probably more assets in Merrill's CMA accounts than in all but the largest banks in the country. All kinds of benefits accrue to the brokerage firm when you consolidate your finances within one firm:

- The firm knows where all your money is.
- The firm knows your spending habits (and believe us, they will use this against you if you ever get in a legal battle with them. Tracy had a client who was extremely embarrassed when his brokerage credit card records were produced in an arbitration hearing and revealed, well, let's just say a sizeable number of payments to Fredericks of Hollywood).
- The firm knows if you are sending money to competitors.
- The firm picks up extra revenue from credit card charges, bank charges, and spreads on certain deposits.
- The firm knows it is hard for you to change firms when you are so tied to it with your banking, checking, and credit card accounts all in one place.
- The firm loves this arrangement because it so easily encourages investors to borrow on their stocks (margin) by writing checks or spending on their credit card.

If the above list is not enough reason to avoid commingling, here are more. Your brokerage firm knows that if you make numerous withdrawals from your brokerage account or your checking account and use your credit card often, it will be almost impossible for you to figure out how your portfolio is performing. Even if you're lucky enough to be receiving one of the fancy monthly statements that breaks down and compares realized and unrealized losses and gains, and changes in net asset value, it will still be confusing. If you're as busy as most people these days, you don't have the time to review your monthly statement every month. But if you know that on February 1, 1998, you put $300,000 in you're A. G. Edwards account and you have added $50,000 since then, it will be easy for you to take a quick look to see how your investments are performing. Not so if you have lots of withdrawals and deposits each month.

We have found over the years that our attitude about commingling funds can apply to a number of areas of investing. When Douglas purchases a new group of funds, for example, he may do it with a set amount of dollars that are easy to remember. A couple of years ago, Douglas was looking at a number of closed-end funds that specialize in China. After doing extensive research, he could not differentiate them enough to decide which one to invest in, so he bought $50,000 of each. It was then very easy for Douglas to determine which funds were outperforming the others without having to go to annual reports and prospectuses. He just looked at the current value and subtracted $50,000 from each. A similar practice may be helpful for you.

The other problem with mixing your banking with your investment accounts is that it creates mass confusion for any basic game plan you've established for your investments. Basically, you should have a certain amount of money set aside for investing. You may also decide to add to this amount each year or if you receive certain bonuses. You should stick by this game plan and adjust it no more often than yearly and then only after careful consideration. Money for living expenses and yearly needs should have no relation to your investments. How are you going to keep this straight if you have your money mixed up in one account?

If you still insist on having a checking account and/or a credit card account at your brokerage firm, then make sure you open a totally separate account and don't defeat this separation by transferring money back and forth a lot.

Your CPA will love you for keeping them separate. And if you have to hire someone like Douglas to review your portfolio, do a comparative analysis, or ascertain if you are being screwed, the job can be done more quickly and more cheaply without all this irrelevant banking business mixed in.

Conclusion

We wish we could finish this book with some incredible news about how the brokerage industry is going to change dramatically for the better in the near future. But this book is about realities. Even as we prepare to go to press, news stories appear every day about how one firm or another has just been fined or sued for defrauding the investing public.

We are hopeful that the NASD and the SEC will be even more aggressive in protecting the public's interest. Linda D. Fienberg has made some excellent advancements as president of NASD Dispute Resolution. We are hopeful that the newly appointed SEC chairman will continue to follow in the footsteps of Arthur Levitt, who made such great strides in investor protection.

There is, in fact, a very positive ending to this book. Our purpose was to heighten your awareness to the conflicts and secrets of the securities and brokerage industry. Only with this knowledge do you have the wherewithal to protect your hard-earned money.

You now have that knowledge—in other words, most of the tools to do battle as shown in the following:

- You can find and evaluate hidden costs, fees, and commissions.
- Knowing many of the conflicts, you can now properly evaluate recommendations.

- You know the key rules and regulations, so you can monitor your account for violations.
- You now know not only what hype is but the reasons for it, which provides you with insight into sales pitches and marketing campaigns.
- You will be able to recognize some of the key tricks that brokers employ in a variety of situations, enabling you to question their best interests.
- You know the basics of setting goals and guidelines for how you want your money to be managed.
- You have some clear guidelines as to what type of firm you should use to help you.
- You know how to evaluate your current or future broker or advisor.
- It is hoped it will never happen, but if you are ever defrauded and suffer losses, you know how and where to get help.

As we said in the beginning of the book, there are thousands of hardworking, honest, and talented people in the investment industry. Using our advice, insights, and lists, you are now equipped to find those people and build the kind of relationships that should be a rewarding experience for you for years to come.

Endnotes

Chapter 1. The Brokerage Industry: More Secretive Than You Know

1. Securities Industry Association, "Securities Industry Trends," 17 April 2001, <www.sia.com/reference_materials/pdf/April01Trends.pdf >.

2. The brokerage industry will sleep well knowing that *Webster's* defined a "screwer" as "one who or that which screws" and made no reference to brokers or brokerage firms.

3. That reminds us that Douglas's Web site address is <www.securitiesexpert.com>; he was initially refused entry into several search engines because the word *sex* is in his domain name!

4. *Shearson/American Express Inc. v. McMahon*, 482 U.S. 220 (1987).

5. Order Instituting Public Proceedings, Making Findings and Imposing Sanctions in *Prudential Securities Inc.*, Release No. 33082, 21 October 1993.

6. "SEC Ends Some Probes at Prudential Due to Expiry of Statute of Limitations," *Wall Street Journal*, 29 May 1997.

7. "Swindler Milken to Serve Rest of His Term at Home," *Chicago Tribune*, 5 February 1993.

8. *In re Olde Discount Corp.*, Securities Exchange Act Release No. 40423 (10 September 1998). Olde Discount is now H&R Block Financial Advisors.

9. Greg Cresci, "E*Trade Slapped with Fine for False Advertising," Reuters, 9 July 2001; and "E*Trade Agrees to Buy Online Broker Web Street for $45 Million in Stock," Dow Jones Business News, 21 May 2001.

10. <www.gao.gov>, GAO Report, No. GAO-01-653.

11. <www.nasdr.com/sipc_protection.htm>.

Chapter 2. Conflicts of Interest: Which Side Are Firms Really On?

1. Robert Lacey, *Little Man: Meyer Lansky and the Gangster Life* (London: Century, 1991).

2. SEC Chairman Levitt's final speech, Philadelphia, January 2001.

3. *In re Olde Discount Corp.*, Securities Exchange Act Release No. 40423 (10 September 10 1998).

4. Remember that the firm's commission schedule will not necessarily disclose all compensation flowing to your broker or your firm.

5. The Street.com at <www.thestreet.com/pf/stocks/brokerages/943746.html>.

6. Penny Stock Disclosure, Exchange Act Release No. 30608 (20 April 1992), Fed. Sec. L. Rep. ¶84,938 at p. 82,656.

7. "Sharp Drop-Off in Margin Loans Could Squeeze Online Brokers," *Wall Street Journal*, 21 April 2001.

8. Testimony of Barry R. Goldsmith, Executive Vice President for Enforcement, NASD Regulation, Inc., before the Permanent Subcommittee on Investigations, Senate Committee on Governmental Affairs on the Securities Day-Trading Industry, February 25, 2000.

9. Tony Chapelle, "2001 Compensation Survey," *On Wall Street*, March 2001.

10. Tracy Herman, "Dollar Signs," *Registered Representative*, February 2001.

11. <www.sec.gov/investor/pubs/analysts/htm>.

12. Remarks by Arthur Levitt before the Securities Industry Association's Legal and Compliance Seminar, 13 April 1999, Boca Raton, Florida.

13. Aaron Elstein and Nick Wingfield, "Prudential Bucks Tradition by Issuing 'Sell' Ratings," *Wall Street Journal*, 16 February 2001. Gerard Klauer Mattison has sell on 1 percent of the stocks it follows. Wall Street powerhouses Goldman Sachs and Merrill Lynch both rate

fewer than 0.8 percent of the stocks they rate a sell, and at Morgan Stanley Dean Witter less than 0.6 percent.

14. *White, Lombardi v. Bear Stearns*, NASD # 99-02960; claimants represented by Dennis Taylor and Tracy Stoneman.

15. Despite the negative connotation, the term *squawk box* is used today for such things as the preopening segment on CNBC.

16. Ken Brown, "Analysts' Top Picks Get Failing Grade on Risk Meter," *Wall Street Journal*, 15 August 2001.

17. Ibid.

18. Ibid.

19. Speech by Arthur Levitt, "The Future for America's Investors—Their Rights and Obligations," Investors Town Hall Meeting, Philadelphia, Pennsylvania, 16 January 2001.

20. Remarks by Robert R. Glauber at NASD Regulation Fall Securities Conference, San Francisco, California, 17 November 2000.

Chapter 3. Stockbrokers Are Salespeople

1. Dan Jamieson, "Fees versus Commissions," *Registered Representative*, March 2001.

2. NASD, Article II, Section 4 "Definition of Disqualification."

3. "Prudential Securities Halts Training Program for Firm's New Brokers," *Wall Street Journal*, 10 July 2001.

4. Relax. Hibbard Brown is out of business and no longer exists.

5. *NASD Regulation, Inc. v. Steven D. Goodman*, Complaint No. C9B960013 (9 November 1999).

6. Ibid.

7. Ibid.

8. Ibid.

9. *In re Olde Discount Corp.*, Securities Exchange Act Release No. 40423 (10 September 1998). Olde Discount is now H&R Block Financial Advisors.

10. Tom Nelson, "Prudential Securities Opens Checkbook," *Registered Representative*, August 2000.

11. Gregory Zuckerman, "CSFB Offers Perks to Stem Defections by Senior Talent," *Wall Street Journal*, 20 March 2001.

Chapter 4. Suitability: The Number One Abuse in the Industry

1. NASD Notice to Members 96-32.

2. *Scherk v. Alberto - Culver Co.*, 417 U.S. 506, 526 (1974) (Douglas, J., dissenting).

3. Arizona Securities Act, R144-130.

Chapter 5. Tricks of the Trade: What Wall Street Doesn't Want You to Know

1. *Hudak v. Economic Research Analysts, Inc.*, 499 F.2d 996, 1002 (5th Cir. 1974).

2. *Morgan v. Schipa*, 585 F. Supp. 245, 250 (S.D.N.Y. 1984).

3. *Strand v. Griffith*, 97 F.2d 854, 856 (8th Cir. 1899).

4. *Brown v. E.F. Hutton Group, Inc.*, 735 F. Supp. 1196, 1202 (S.D.N.Y. 1990), *aff'd.*, 991 F.2d 1020 (2d Cir. 1993).

5. *In re Prudential Securities Inc. Limited Partnerhsips Litigation*, WL 308527 (S.D.N.Y. June 10, 1996).

6. *In re MGSI Securities, Inc.*, SEC Administrative Proceeding, File No. 3-9702 (January 12, 2000).

7. *Tottenham Corp. v. Bear Stearns, et al.*, NASD #90-02700 (May 21, 1992).

8. Douglas has long been an advocate of including spreads in this umbrella of a cost number, on the basis that . . . well, it is a cost that the investor pays, just like margin interest and just like commissions.

9. If you are shorting stocks or writing option contracts, you should use the opening position as the purchase.

10. Winslow and Anderson, "A Model for Determining the Excessive Trading Element in Churning Claims," 68 N.C.L. Rev. 327 (1990).

11. This would not include the large number of investment advisors that have a Series 7 and are affiliated with a brokerage firm. Though these advisors may appear to be independent, as far as the law is concerned the brokerage firm the RIA is affiliated with is required to supervise all products the RIA markets.

Chapter 6. The Regulators: Whose Side Are They Really On?

1. Remarks of Robert R. Glauber, president of the NASD at NASD Regulation Fall Securities Conference, San Francisco, California, November 17, 2000.

2. <www.nyse.com/regulation/regulation.html>.

3. <www.sec.gov>.

4. Nicole Coulter, "Disappearing Regulators," *Registered Representative*, January 1999.

5. There is talk of the NYSE going public.

6. <www.nasd.com/corpinfo/co_ove_histr.html>.

7. Remarks of Robert R. Glauber, president of the NASD at the NASD Regulation Fall Securities Conference, San Francisco, California, November 17, 2000; Glauber and the NASD, however, are making headway in this area by developing more high-tech inspection tools to monitor market and brokerage firm activities. Remarks of Robert R. Glauber, president of NASD at the Annual Conference of the Securities Industry Association Compliance & Legal Division, March 19, 2001.

8. *In re National Association of Securities Dealers*, SEC Administrative Proceeding File No. 3-9056, August 8, 1996, viewable at <www.sec.gov/enforce/adminact/3437538.txt>.

9. "Closing the Book on Research That Actually Made a Difference," *Barron's*, 18 January 1999.

10. "SEC Staff Report on Order Execution Quality," January 8, 2001.

11. Coulter, "Disappearing Regulators."

12. AP Newswire, "Feds Charge 20 in Stock Plot," March 9, 2001.

13. Jay Mathews, "Stratton Oakmont Expelled from Securities Industry," *Washington Post*, 6 December 1996, quoting Mary L. Schapiro, president of NASD Regulation.

14. Ibid., quoting Barry R. Goldsmith, NASD Regulation's executive vice president for enforcement.

15. Remarks of Robert R. Glauber, president of NASD, at NASD Regulation Fall Securities Conference, San Francisco, California, November 17, 2000.

16. Order Instituting Consolidated Proceedings and Findings, Opinion and Order in *Prudential-Bache Securities, Inc.* 48 SEC 372 (1986).

17. Order Instituting Public Proceedings, Making Findings and Imposing Sanctions in *Prudential Securities Inc.*, Release No. 33082, October 21, 1993

18. "SEC Chairman Levitt Calls for Pay Raises to Retain Employees," *Wall Street Journal*, 28 February 2000.

Chapter 8. Online Trading: Are You on Your Own?

1. NASD Notice to Members 01-23, March 19, 2001.

2. Ibid.

3. North American Securities Administrators Association (NASAA) statement on NASD online suitability guidelines (NTM-01/23).

4. Douglas J. Schulz, "Unauthorized Trading, Mismarked Tickets, and the Abuse of Time and Price Discretion," Practicing Law Institute, Securities Arbitration 2001, New York City.

5. Matthew Goldstein, "A Most Unsuitable Rule," SmartMoney.com, 17 April 2001.

6. 66 Fed. Reg. 20,697 (April 24, 2001).

7. Report of the Division of Securities and Retail Franchising of the Virginia State Corporation Commission on the Statutory and Regulatory Requirements Concerning Broker-Dealers Who Provide Discount Brokerage Services, December 2000.

8. Ibid.

9. Renee Barnett, "Online Trading and the National Association of Securities Dealers' Suitability Rule: Are Online Investors Adequately Protected?" *American University Law Review*, June 2000, citing to Douglas Schulz.

Chapter 9. Online Trading—Step into My Web Site, Said the Spider to the Fly

1. Stacy Forster, "Web Brokers Ads Are Strong Despite the Sour Market," Wall Street Journal.com, 11 January 2001.

2. "TD Waterhouse Earnings Double, Amid Increases in Trading Volume," Dow Jones Newswire, 15 November 2000.

3. Forster, "Web Brokers Ads."

4. Ibid.

5. Thomas Kostigen, "Informed Dissent: Gripes against Online Brokers Are on the Rise," CBS MarketWatch.com, 1 March 2001.

6. Ruth Simon, "TD Waterhouse Is Fined for Outages That Hampered Online Trading," *Wall Street Journal*, 1 March 2001.

7. SEC, "Examinations of Broker-Dealers Offering Online Trading: Summary of Findings and Recommendations," 25 January 2001.

8. Gretchen Morgenson, "Market Watch: A Request for the Boss-to-Be at the S.E.C.," *New York Times*, 13 May 2001.

9. Aaron Elstein, "AOL-Time Warner Deal Gives Early-Bird Investors Rude Lesson," *Wall Street Journal* Interactive Edition, 11 January 2000.

Chapter 10. Bucket Shops and Boiler Rooms

1. David L. Scott, *Wall Street Words* (Boston: Houghton Mifflin, 1997).

2. "Movie 'Boiler Room' Wins 'Thumbs Up' from Top State Securities Cop NASAA President Skolnik, Commends Film's Realism, Cautionary Message," PR Newswire, 1 Febuary 2000.

3. Steven H. Gifis, *Dictionary of Legal Terms* (1983).

4. All firms that are no longer with us today.

5. *NASD Regulation, Inc. v. Monitor Investment Group, Inc.*, Disciplinary Proceeding No. C10970145, December 1999.

6. *NASD Regulation, Inc. v. Steven D. Goodman*, Complaint No. C9B960013 (9 November 1999).

7. "A high school dropout . . . could sound like the chairman of the Fed with these scripts," New York State Attorney General Dennis C. Vacco in the Bureau of Investor Protection and Securities Report on Micro Cap Stock Fraud, December 1997.

8. Some scripts directed brokers to advise their prospects that they were not mail carriers and didn't have time to send out paperwork to every client. Ibid.

9. Ibid.

10. John Aidan Byrne, editor, *Traders*, citing an official at the National Securities Clearing Corporation, a subsidiary of the Depository Trust & Clearing Corporation.

11. Henry F. Minnerop, "The Role and Regulation of Clearing Brokers," *The Business Lawyer* 48 (May 1993): 841–68.

12. Gretchen Morgenson, "Sleazy Doings on Wall Street," *Forbes*, February 24, 1997. This is the issue of *Forbes* referenced above with a rusty bucket on the cover. The article focuses on Bear Stearns's clearing for numerous bucket shops.

13. Ibid.

14. "Ten Ex-Brokers from Defunct Firm Fined Total $837,500," Dow Jones Newswire, 23 March 1999.

15. "A. R. Baron Ex-Broker Sentenced to 3-to-9 Yrs In Prison," Dow Jones Newswire, 7 July 1999.

16. *Dow Jones Business News*, 5 August 1999.

17. Morgenson, "Sleazy Doings," quoting Bear Stearns's spokesperson Hannah Burns.

18. SEC Order Making Findings *In re Richard Harriton*, SEC Administrative Proceeding File No. 3-9963 (April 20, 2000) (Finding that Harriton willfully aided and abetted and caused Baron's violations).

19. "Fraud at Bear Stearns? Two Views," *Wall Street Journal*, 1 September 1999.

20. SEC Order Making Findings *In re Richard Harriton*, SEC Administrative Proceeding File No. 3-9963 (April 20, 2000).

21. "Bear Stearns to Pay $38 Million in Clearing-Case Settlements," *Dow Jones Business News*, 5 August 1999.

22. Ibid.

23. Charles Gasparino, "Settlement Is Among Most Stringent for Wall Street Executive," *Wall Street Journal*, Europe, 25 April 2000.

24. "FBI Agents Raid JB Oxford's Offices in California," *Wall Street Journal*, 20 August 20, 1997.

25. Administrative and Cease-and-Desist Proceedings Instituted against Greenway Capital Corporation and Joseph M. Guccione, SEC Administrative Proceeding, File No. 3-9014, May 30, 1996; SEC Order Making Findings *In re Cortland Capital Corp., Mayor Amsel, and Joseph M. Guccione*, SEC Administrative Proceeding, File No. 3-9444 (June 19, 1998).

26. NASD Press Release, September 23, 1998. "NASD regulation continues micro cap market focus; complaints name brokers at Greenway Capital and Kensington Wells."

27. *Koruga v Hanifen Imhoff*, NASD No. 98-04276 (October 5, 2000).

28. Quote by Mark Griffin, president of the North American Securities Administrators Association, August 1997.

Chapter 11. What to Do When Things Go Awry

1. NYSE Rule 351(d) requires the reporting of verbal complaints; however, this rule arguably applies only to NYSE member firms.

2. *Circuit City Stores v. Adams*, 2001 U.S. LEXIS 2459 (March 21, 2001).

3. Agreement to arbitrate provision in Citibank's Credit Card Agreement and Disclosure Statement, effective June 1, 2001.

4. Linda Stern, "The Claim Game," *Newsweek*, 7 May 2001.

5. SEC Web site at <www.sec.gov/news/data.htm>.

6. These statistics are now reported at the National Association of Securities Dealers Dispute Resolution Web site at <www.nasdadr.com>.

7. Susan Scherreik, "Wall Street's Stingiest Judges," *Money*, November 1996, 110.

Chapter 12. Inundated with Choices: Distinguishing the Players

1. NASD Disciplinary Actions for June 1998 <www.nasdr.com/pdf-text/9806dis.txt>.

Chapter 13. Selecting and Evaluating a Stockbroker

1. Harry Pappas Jr., "Fire Customers, Keep Clients," *Registered Representative*, May 2001, 111. Pappas advises brokers that unlike customers, clients rely on brokers for advice, don't constantly call their broker, focus more on their own life than on the markets, and attempt to develop a friendship with the broker.

2. Legally and ethically, brokers and even online brokerage firms are re-quired to learn all of the essential facts about you, which is the basis of the NYSE's Know Your Customer rule, even if they want to treat you as a customer.

3. Tom Nelson, "MSDW to Move Small Accounts to Call Centers," *Registered Representative*, March 2001.

Chapter 14. What You Need to Know about Specific Investment Products and Strategies

1. Carrie Coolidge, "Annuity Gratuity," *Forbes*, 19 February 2001.

2. Jeff D. Opdyke, "Shifting Annuities May Help Brokers More Than Investors," *Wall Street Journal*, 16 February 2001.

3. Ibid.

4. NASD Notice to Members 99-35.

5. Randall Smith and Susan Pullman, "Credit Suisse Says Two Employ-ees Violated Firm's Policies on IPOs," *Wall Street Journal*, 15 May 2001.

6. "For Every IPO Winner, Now There Are at Least Two Losers," Dow Jones Newswire, 4 December 2000.

7. Order Instituting Public Proceedings, Making Findings and Imposing Sanctions in *Prudential Securities Inc.*, Release No. 33082, October 21, 1993.

8. If you purchase a U.S. government bond through a bank or other fi-nancial institution at an initial new offering, the fees and costs are negligible.

9. NASD IM-2310-2, "Fair Dealing with Customers."

Index

BROKERAGE FRAUD

For special discounts on 20 or more copies of *Brokerage Fraud: What Wall Street Doesn't Want You to Know*, please call Dearborn Trade Special Sales at 800-621-9621, extension 4364.

Dearborn™
Trade Publishing
A **Kaplan Professional** Company